WILD
guide

Greece

Hidden Places, Great Adventures
and the Good Life

Sam Firman & Nick Hooton

Martsalo Beach, Central Crete p285

WILD
guide

Vathi Beach Mani pi88

Contents

Regional
Overview

Kátar Beach, Central Crete p285

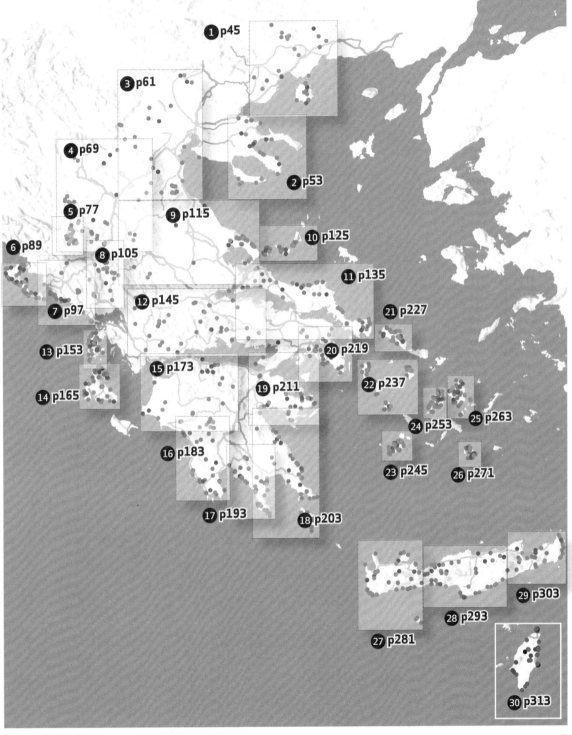

1 p45
3 p61
4 p69
5 p77
6 p89
8 p105
9 p115
2 p53
10 p125
11 p135
7 p97
12 p145
21 p227
13 p153
20 p219
15 p173
19 p211
14 p165
22 p237
16 p183
24 p253
25 p263
23 p245
26 p271
17 p193
18 p203
29 p303
28 p293
27 p281
30 p313

Kafar Beach, Central Crete p285

Introduction

Snorkel above ruins submerged in an azure cove. Trek up astonishing river gorges and towering peaks. Dive into the turquoise embrace of a giant sea crater, or the dark depths of a sinkhole abyss. Explore pitch-black caverns alive with bats and myths. Roam ancient settlements and ridgeline castles, or contemplate in mountain monasteries and cliff-top churches. Seek secret waterfalls in old-growth forests and along twisting canyons. Savour morning-fresh fish, farm-to-table cooking and artisanal *raki*. And, when it's time to rest, watch golden eagles from an alpine refuge or shooting stars from beside a driftwood fire.

Travelling in Greece can feel like being placed into a postcard, only to discover that the scene in fact extends to the horizon in all directions. The signature sugar cube houses perched above deep-blue island bays aren't cherry-picked snapshots, but reasonable representations of much of Greece's celebrated coastline – and just the maritime tip of a magnificent iceberg.

The country unfolds from the virgin forests of southern Bulgaria to the sparkling Libyan Sea, and is bordered by Turkish islets to the east and Albanian peaks to the west. The diversity is a delight, and sailing the archipelagos is only one possibility.

Places and people forged by fire

Three tectonic plates – the Eurasian, Aegean Sea and African – meet beneath Greece. Over geological epochs, slow but formidable activity at this boundary has created a northwestern arc of mountainous scars, from the mighty Pindus range (the 'spine of Greece') to vertiginous Crete. Within this embrace, the volcanic islands of Santorini and Milos are the most famous members of the South Aegean Volcanic Arc, which continues to forge, and violently shake,

Polylimnio Gorge, Messenia p179

a landscape of relentless peaks, plunging gorges, mysterious caves and crashing waterfalls.

This natural splendour is overlaid with myth, faith and history (oh, and goat droppings). A shrine or a story means you are never truly alone in Greece's wild places; every nook provides a portal into millennia of rich human tapestry. The absence of wildness, or wildness in another form?

Between these wild places, it seems impossible to find a Greek village without a tree-canopied square and a fabulous taverna serving local ingredients and family recipes. Even the cosmopolitan hubs, often charmingly overgrown, possess a relaxed radicalism of good-life slowness playing out before polemical, psychedelic street art. As guests, we quickly learned that Greeks know how hard life can be, and how to live well anyway.

Wild places

The waypoints in this book inevitably tell only tiny fragments of a big story. But with that caveat laid, what can you expect?

Beaches Europe's longest coastline is an epic poem of peninsulas and emerald islands. From coves beneath colossal cliffs to fishing-village inlets, perhaps the biggest challenge in writing this book was finding new superlatives to describe beaches. Please forgive any repetitions.

Mountains & Gorges Greece is an alpine array of peaks and ridgelines above river gorges and dusty canyons, a deep-time mountain landscape that hides many of this book's best wild places. To behold it and delve into it is a privilege.

Rivers, Lakes & Waterfalls Mountains mean mighty catchment areas, resulting in rivers replete with rushing rapids, secret waterfalls, lazy meanders and lakes both lofty and lowland. Wild swimming abounds far beyond the beaches.

Caves Complex geology makes Greece a speleological wonderland. Limestone mountainscapes create karstic underworlds riddled with legendary caves, while colourful volcanic coasts harbour glistening sea caves and gaping sinkholes.

Spilia Beach, Skopelos, Sporades p119

Forest & Trees Greece is carpeted with forest, some of it truly ancient, partly because the towering landscapes above its arable plains are too sheer to deforest. Greek adventure plays out against backdrops of aromatic pines, wizened olives and old-growth Norwegian spruce. And venerable planes provide convivial canopies in village squares and shelter for jewel-box churches.

Ruins From its golden shores to its white zeniths, this land is a historical and mythological canvas. From 40,000-year-old Paleolithic digs to Second World War hideouts, via Bronze Age temples and Roman baths, swathes of European history have been written here.

Sacred Sites Greece is a deeply, widely and wildly religious country, with Eastern Orthodox shrines, churches and monasteries scattered across its landscapes, often in places of solitude and spiritual significance.

Many places recorded in this book lie far from the usual path, and some sit squarely on it, too splendid to omit. Countless others aren't represented – a book can only be so big, after all. Do let us know about more gems for next time!

Wild spirit

This book is a collection of wild waypoints, but a journey is made of more. The 'places in between' often feel guidebook-worthy themselves, given so much of the country is woven together with spectacular, inaccessible terrain. On countless occasions we have found ourselves threading between mountain villages in the golden hour, the low light lingering in the canyons below, wondering whether to simply revise our destination. A few rules of thumb may help you travel widely and wildly.

The local people are your friends, typically happy to chat (or gesticulate) with curious, respectful visitors. And though Greek isn't the easiest for those accustomed to the Roman alphabet, a few choice terms – a *Kalimera* here, a *Yamas* there – will bring warm smiles, helping hands and maybe even shared escapades.

Given today's bonanza of travel books and blogs, it's surprising how places can still feel wild if approached with open-

Cape Fourni, Rhodes p310

mindedness and a few resources, even on the islands. If you can, pack a tent, a hammock or some local delicacies to allow for deeper, longer stays. Similarly, the ability to drive, bike, paddle or hike will broaden the map.

Remain attentive to Greece's landscape. Even its arid southern hills are alive with aromas and wild herbs ready to bewitch, or brew around the campfire. Its skies swoop with birds of prey; its northern forests harbour bears, wolves and deer aplenty; and its seas swim with fish, loggerhead turtles and Greece's national animal, the dolphin.

So too with the cultural landscape. Flicking through a compendium of Greek myth or history on the ferries will enrich your journey, as will looking up the undercurrents of the places you go. And remember that village squares and unexpected diversions can contain more adventure than the wildest peaks. Offering fire and a blanket to lost hikers, missing ferries from the ice-cream queue, impromptu skinny dips beneath the hunter's moon: the memorable moments will only loosely align with the waypoints you meant to meet.

Whether you scribble in it, gift it, accidentally drown it or leave it on the coffee table, we hope you enjoy this humble book and the magnificent country that made it possible. And please, let us know how you go!

Sam and Nick

adventure@wildthingspublishing.com

Finding your way

Each wild place can be located using the overview map provided at the end of each chapter, along with the detailed direction, but to be sure of finding your way you will need to use the latitude and longitude provided. This is given in decimal degrees (WGS84) correct to 10m and can be entered straight into any web-based mapping program, such as Google Maps. Approximate walk-in times are given at around 20 mins per km, typically for one way only, and abbreviations in the directions refer to left and right (L, R) and north, east, south and west (N, E, S, W).

Greek words and place names are typically translated into the Roman alphabet with much inconsistency, creating multiple spellings. We've prioritised usefulness over consistency and gone with the spellings most likely to help you find your way. We hope you agree with our approach.

Wild camping is, in practice, perfectly acceptable in Greece, providing you always leave no trace, use common sense when it comes to impacting people and wildlife, and avoid private land (or respectfully vacate in the event of a mistake).

Acheron Springs, Western Epirus p95

Wild & responsible

1. Private land isn't always clearly marked in Greece, but always heed signs and other requests to leave an area.

2. Take your litter home – and why not collect rubbish left by other people while you're at it.

3. Keep your dogs under close control, especially around livestock and in nature reserves.

4. If you wash in streams or rivers, only use biodegradable soap, or none at all.

5. Park considerately and don't block passing places on single-track roads. Many unsurfaced rural roads are rough, or can become so after heavy weather; you may be fine driving very slowly, but hiring a 4x4 gives you the most options.

6. Take a map, compass, whistle, water and appropriate clothing into remote areas. In the Greek summer, water and a hat are sensible even on shorter adventures.

7. Always tell someone where you are going, and do not rely on your mobile phone.

Best for
Beaches

Greece is Europe's treasure chest of beaches. Its coastline is the continent's longest, and includes thousands of mostly uninhabited islands. Canyon-mouth coves and endless strands, pretty village ports and pine-dappled dunes, volcanic virtuosos and historic curios: from friendly family hangouts to remote amphitheatres of coastal wonder, the riches are preposterous.

World's-best-list stalwarts, funky beach bars and popular boating circuits abound, and are often splendid despite their popularity. But Greece's coastline is so abundant, and often so wild, that even astonishing beaches often remain empty year-round. And an afternoon of boat exploration, with curiosity and a good crew, can help escape the crowds and turn even nameless bays into wonderlands.

Wild camping is generally welcome on Greek beaches, providing you're respectful, so always chuck some camping gear into the car. Nudity is also popular in many places; we've noted where this is the case. Some wilder beaches can be tricky to access, and most lack facilities and shade, so go prepared. As well as swimsuits, a towel, snorkelling gear and wet shoes, bring good footwear and sun protection – a parasol won't go amiss. And remember that beaches are also havens for wildlife, from spiky sea urchins to vulnerable loggerhead turtles; always take care for your sake and theirs.

Best for
Wild swimming

The joys of wild swimming in Greece extend beyond its beaches. Many of the most striking coastal swims are sinkholes, lagoons, shipwrecks and cliff-jumping inlets. Inland, towering peaks cradle spectacular alpine lakes said to be made by dragons, and feed mountain rivers that rush through gorges, pause in pools and meander beneath elegant arching bridges.

These waterworlds offer moments from the slow and lazy to the fast and visceral. Either way, swimming them often assumes the atmosphere of that landscape: bobbing beneath ornate bridges brings whimsy, stroking out into alpine lakes inspires awe and snorkelling above shipwrecks entices shivers of excited dread. These are wonderfully enlivening experiences, and Greece is a fine place to feel them.

Swimming in these places means immersing yourself in everything from bath-like shallows to piercing ice melt, so take care to dip your toe in first. Always depth-check if jumping, and consider water shoes for leaping from height, walking slightly less gingerly over pebbles and scrambling up muddy banks.

Be safe ⊽

1 Never swim alone, and keep a constant watch on weaker swimmers.

2 Cold water can dramatically decrease swimming ability, create cold shock and cause drowning through panic. Know your limits, enter slowly and stay close to the shoreline.

3 Never jump into water until you have thoroughly checked for depth and obstructions.

4 Avoid strong currents that can drag you under, such as those directly under large waterfalls or weirs, or in river rapids during floods.

5 Always make sure you know how you will get out before you get in.

6 Wear footwear if you can.

7 Avoid direct contact with blue-green algae, and be wary of water quality in lowland areas during droughts and heavy rain. Cover cuts with plasters if worried, and if you develop flu-like symptoms tell your doctor you have been in a river.

Best for
Waterfalls

Waterfalls are poetic, powerful phenomena: forging their path with force, but dancing and shimmering with impossible beauty as they go. Greece's forested foothills are replete with these wondrous descents from mountain to sea. Some play out year-round, even freezing apparently in motion with the winter snows; others run fleetingly, drying up in the summer sun. Always check the listing, and try to double-check with locals.

Many of Greece's falls are reached along pretty woodland trails tracing the river and rapids on either side; others require long, sweaty gorge hikes. Some are melodic sequences of cascades, others single-cataract crescendos of power and noise. Whatever the waterfall, the magic and refreshment of a gladed freshwater pool – sometimes with a rope swing – is incomparable, especially when they offer shelter from the mid-summer scorch.

Hearing a waterfall's roar, or better still glimpsing it between the trees, is an exhilarating jolt, often followed by a quickening of step. But always proceed with caution: mountain rivers are cold, the surrounding rocks will be slippery, and waterfalls create powerful suction and rapids.

Best for
Caves

Greece's complex mountainous geology is abundant in limestone, which groundwater dissolves to create karstic labyrinths of tunnels, caverns and sinkholes, often adorned with ornate stalagmites and stalactites. Exploring these underworlds can be spellbinding.

Some caves burrow for hundreds of metres, even kilometres, the pitch-black descending with shocking immediacy. Others yawn enormously, enticing but ominous like geological Venus fly traps. Friendlier caves are shallower, lighter places of refuge or spiritual reflection, and fruitful caves come in the form of those cut for marble and mineral quarrying. And Greece's most famous caves swallow the sea, their chambers glimmering mesmerically, at least for the first few metres. Almost all hold stories, historical or mythical – sometimes both.

Caves promise exhilaration but also risk, so approach them with proper awe and respect. Always bring a powerful light per person, plus one extra and spare batteries, as well as sturdy shoes and appropriate clothing. Never navigate or descend beyond your ability to confidently retrace your steps, or beyond the recommended limits without professional guidance. Ah, and be prepared for bugs, bats and jumping cave crickets!

Best for
Ancient wonders

Is there any other European country so synonymous with ancient ruins? For millennia Greece has been a seafaring civilisational crossroads of migration, conquest and cultural evolution. Every street, cove and ridgeline seems to bear a settlement, an acropolis, a castle or a tower – a mark recording the unfolding of one of humanity's most significant historical spheres.

Greek remains stretch right back to the Paleolithic, but its major ruins begin with three Bronze Age civilisations: Cycladic culture in the Aegean (c.3200–1050 BC); Minoan civilisation in Crete (c.3500–1100 BC), possibly ended by a giant Thera (Santorini) eruption; and Mycenaean Greece (1750–1050 BC), the time of many Greek myths such as the wanderings of Odysseus. The Greek Dark Ages followed these, but from darkness came the light of Ancient Greece: democracy, philosophy, the Parthenon and the vast Hellenistic empire under Alexander the Great.

After this zenith came long subjugation: first by the Romans (146 BC–324 AD) and then eight centuries under the Byzantine Empire (the Eastern Roman Empire, following the fall of Rome). This ended in 1204 only to be followed by 300 years of Frankish (French and Italian, especially Venetian) influence known as the Frankokratia, and eventually 300 years of Ottoman rule. From the spectacular to the overlooked, the ruins in this book originated in one of these eras, and many were altered during subsequent occupations.

Best for
Sacred sites

The Greek Orthodox Church has deep cultural roots, and has scattered its seeds across every nook and cranny of the Greek landscape. Any journey through Greece travels both natural and spiritual terrain. Shrines, chapels, churches and monasteries are ubiquitous, often hunkered along wild coastline, hewn into cliffs, perched on soaring peaks or hidden in dark caves.

The solitude and asceticism of remote natural outposts partly explains this correlation. Protection was also a factor; Meteora's remarkable monastic community, for example, assumed its precipitous position atop geological columns to evade Ottoman raiders. Many churches also cover old pagan places of worship once dedicated to the ancient Greek gods, so are often on mountains and in other wild places associated with these mythical figures. Indeed, Greece's sacred spots are often threaded with pagan myth as much as Christian faith.

Specific Greek Orthodox saints also help explain the wildness of so many Greek sacred sites. Agios Nikolaos (St Nikolaos) is the patron saint of sailors and travellers, so seamen praying for safe passage often erected coastal churches bearing his name, especially on the islands. Likewise, many Greek peaks are adorned with chapels dedicated to Profiti Ilias (Prophet Elias), who was associated with natural elements, and thought to have nearly drowned so many times as a sailor that he eventually sought refuge as far from the sea as he could.

Best for
Local food

Fabulous food awaits around every Greek corner – usually disarmingly simple, sometimes fine and fancy. Home cooking with organic produce, either local or homegrown, is the default in many Greek tavernas. Many produce their own olive oil, wine, honey and other ingredients, and all follow dinner with a complementary raki or dessert. Seafood and meat are often the mainstay, but even the meatiest tavernas typically serve a delicious range of classic vegetarian dishes.

Some Greek dining experiences stand apart, though. All regions contain a handful of exceptional traditional tavernas, often with tiny unwritten menus and scant online presence. And immersive foodie experiences abound: market tours, fishing tours, foraging tours and olive tours; or permaculture workshops, cooking classes and farm stays. Tuck in, we say.

Also look out for regional specialities, of which there are many. Some of our favourites include Egklouvi's famous lentils, in Lefkada; Milos' classic *karpouzopita*, a baked watermelon pie; the Pomak cuisine of Greece's Bulgarian-speaking Muslims; and goat *stifado* (stew), cooked overnight in a bread-sealed clay pot and smashed open at the table in Rhodes. Drink-wise, try to sample Naxian *kitron* liqueur, Volos' signature pomace brandy, *tsipouro*, and the volcanic wines of Milos and Santorini.

Best for
Wild stays

All great adventures should end with magical nights, and the accommodation collected in this book – both the official listings and the wild camping recommendations – are chosen to help you fulfil this ideal. From chic havens to rustic retreats and beachside campsites, all options feature at least a wild twist, whether a fabulous view, a sprawling vegetable garden or a private swimming dock. Many are wild through and through.

Stays vary in character from region to region. In the mountainous north, there is a fantastic network of refuges, often stationed on long, dramatic walking routes, with bunk dorms and hearty food. Down in the Cycladic islands, on the other hand, the whitewashed villas and cave houses of postcards abound. Everything from wooden cabins to stone windmills awaits in between.

Where the accommodation listed is only available to book via Airbnb, the web address is provided. In these cases, the coordinates listed are not always exact, but communicating directly with your host will confirm the precise location.

Whilst wild camping is officially illegal in Greece, it is widely practised and accepted. Campfire circles mark many beaches, sometimes with makeshift driftwood furniture. Camp away from touristic areas, set up camp late, leave early and leave no trace, and you will likely have no issues.

Tymfi Dragon Lake, Zagori p73

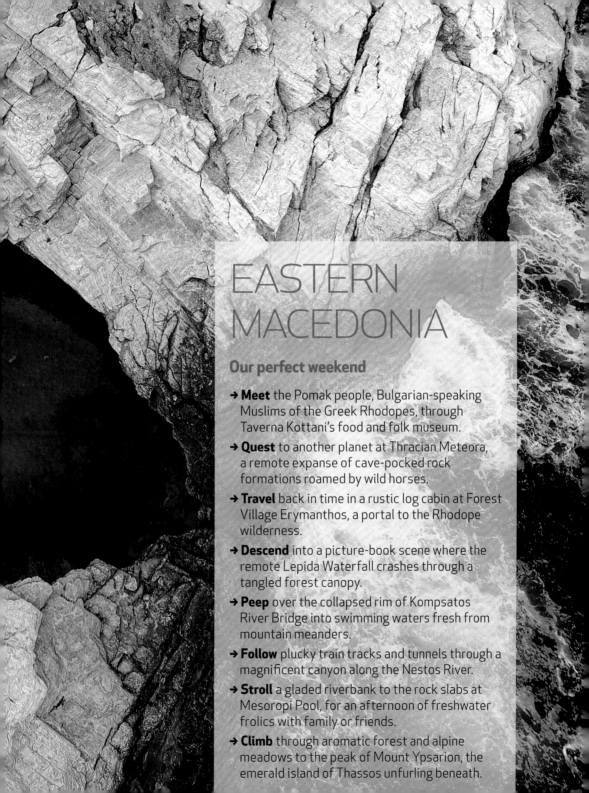

EASTERN MACEDONIA

Our perfect weekend

→ **Meet** the Pomak people, Bulgarian-speaking Muslims of the Greek Rhodopes, through Taverna Kottani's food and folk museum.

→ **Quest** to another planet at Thracian Meteora, a remote expanse of cave-pocked rock formations roamed by wild horses.

→ **Travel** back in time in a rustic log cabin at Forest Village Erymanthos, a portal to the Rhodope wilderness.

→ **Descend** into a picture-book scene where the remote Lepida Waterfall crashes through a tangled forest canopy.

→ **Peep** over the collapsed rim of Kompsatos River Bridge into swimming waters fresh from mountain meanders.

→ **Follow** plucky train tracks and tunnels through a magnificent canyon along the Nestos River.

→ **Stroll** a gladed riverbank to the rock slabs at Mesoropi Pool, for an afternoon of freshwater frolics with family or friends.

→ **Climb** through aromatic forest and alpine meadows to the peak of Mount Ypsarion, the emerald island of Thassos unfurling beneath.

Tucked in the northeastern corner between Bulgaria and Turkey, seemingly a million miles from any brochure, Eastern Macedonia & Thrace guards Greece's deepest nature. The forested Rhodope Mountains in the north are almost unfathomably wild, a folkloric jungle into which Greece simply vanishes. The mountains here feed roaring waterfalls along rivers that surge south to cross a fertile plain looking to emerald Thassos, the most northerly Aegean island.

The wilderness of the Rodopi Mountain Range National Park is an ecological paradise – a land of bears, wolves and red deer roaming wizened old growth punctured by craggy karstic vantages. To go really deep, gather supplies and journey far north to Frakto Forest, considered Greece's only true virgin woodland. Alternatively, join other outdoor folk at Xanthis Livaditis Refuge to forest bask, and venture to spectacular cascades like towering Livaditis and thundering Lepida, both plunging into fantastical misty forests. The Rhodopes are also home to most of Greece's Muslims, including the Bulgarian-speaking Pomaks. Sample their cuisine and culture at Taverna Kottani and its folk museum.

The Nestos River rules the Rhodope waterways. This natural border between Greek Macedonia and Thrace flows from Bulgaria's Rila Mountains to a secluded delta across from Thassos, passing through remote ravines and flood plain forest. Walk the river's wilder side north from Galani, where a trail follows its magnificent meander through a stupendous canyon, at times a cacophony of rare birdsong. You can trek for up to 23km, via train tracks and tunnels, if you wish. Further south, the brackish Nestos Delta unfurls between curving sandbanks and life-giving forest that shelters flamingos, pelicans, turtles and more. You won't regret the tricky journey.

The arable corridor crossing the Nestos here is dotted with more accessible delights. Aggitis Canyon and the magnificent Alistrati cave system nearby make a memorable trip, and ruined Vranokastro affords splendid views across the nearby plains. Mesoropi Pool is a fantastic place to cool off with the family, and fallen Kompsatos River Bridge, further east, marks a swim spot both beautiful and melancholy. Stop at To Araliki between the two to plot further adventures over a banquet of tasty sharing dishes.

Even after all this splendour, the luscious circle of Thassos might be the crescendo. Walking to the ancient Thasos Acropolis via the old city-state's *agora*, theatre and temples is a wonderful way to arrive. Retire to adjacent Limenas House, with its sumptuous sea-view terrace and a garden enlivened by peacocks. From here work clockwise around the island. Pair a woodland wander to ivy-covered Dragon Cave with a valley-vista feast at Utopia Restaurant. Continue via Giola Lagoon – a place so improbably perfect that you'll need to arrive around sunrise to avoid the circus – then retreat into the island's mountainous interior for a menu of secluded adventures.

BEACHES, BAYS & LAGOONS

1 THASSOS FISHERMAN'S HUT

This storybook hut, nestled in a hidden cove, is home to friendly fisherman Mr. Angelo. He may sing you a song if he's home.

➜ Boat access is easiest. Tours from Thassos may pass, and in Chrysi Ammoudia to the S you can rent a boat from Golden Beach Watersports (+30 69 4528 8732). Difficult foot access is possible: follow directions for Ancient Thasos Acropolis (see entry), but continue past the parking area and take a track R, downhill, on a L hairpin. Follow it to the end, where a path continues and curves left, then scramble down through the steep trees to the R (40.7768, 24.7274).

2 mins, 40.7775, 24.7266 🏊🏖️🏊🛶🚶

2 FARI BEACH, THASSOS

A gently curving double bay of orange sand and rock ledges beneath small cliffs. Head to the eastern end for solitude.

➜ Heading E on the coastal road, turn sharply R on a L bend just past Skala Marion, signed Beach Atspas. Take the first L track and park before the gate. Skirt to the R of it down to Emerald Beach, then

duck L through the trees to Fari. There is a beachside parking area, but locals tend to block access.

10 mins, 40.6363, 24.5239 🏊🏖️

3 GIOLA LAGOON, THASSOS

This ovular micro-lagoon provides a picture-perfect plunge pool, ringed by rock ledges for lounging and leaping in. It gets busy, so visit for an early morning swim as the sun rises across the sea.

➜ Heading E on the coastal road, turn R 2.5km after Astrida (40.5916, 24.6764) and park for free down the hill. The comically plentiful signage makes it impossible to get lost.

10 mins, 40.5863, 24.6787 🍴🏖️🅱️

4 LIVADI BEACH, THASSOS

A large valley-mouth beach between looming coastal hills, with pleasant rocky nooks at either end and an expansive bay for swimming.

➜ Head E from Astrida, pass the turning for Giola Lagoon (see entry) and turn R after 5km on a sweeping R hairpin after seeing the beach below to your R. The track leads to the beach.

1 min, 40.5980, 24.6919 🏊🏖️

RIVERS

5 AGGITIS CANYON

A deep, verdant river canyon lined with delightful trails. You can tour the breathtaking limestone complex that is Alistrati Cave above, and walk west to a smaller cave with ancient petroglyphs.

➜ To park on the S rim, turn L off the road heading NE from Nea Mpafra, by four silos, and continue 3km N to a car park. On the N side follow the road 7km SE from Alistrati to park at Alistrati Cave. Either way, it's a short trail down to the canyon bottom.

5 mins, 41.0248, 24.0172 🚶🏃

6 NESTOS RIVER

Follow the magnificent meanders of the Nestos River through a stupendous canyon, alive with the echoing cries of eagles and vultures. From beautiful Galani Beach in the southern canyon – a worthy stop in its own right – the trail follows the river's eastern bank, traversing train tracks and tunnels, for 23km to Stavroupoli. Choose your own adventure.

➜ Head W from Galani for 1.4km to the long parking area, then continue on foot to the

beach, adventure park and a trail, paved for 800m but still good thereafter.
15 mins, 41.0970, 24.7567

7 NESTOR RIVER DELTA

The Nestor River joins the Thracian Sea here, meandering between curling sandbanks flanked by endless beach and rich vegetation and bird life. A poignant, isolated meeting place.

→ The tracks giving direct access have faded, so getting there is tricky. Drive S from the SW corner of Dasochori. Turn R at the T junction, take the second L, then the next second L again into the trees after 850m. Continue 1.2km until an obvious L bend leads to the beach (40.8671, 24.8222). Turn R and continue as far as you can. Without a 4x4 you'll have at least a 1.5km beach walk to finish.
40 mins, 40.8463, 24.8038

8 KOMPSATOS RIVER BRIDGE

A magnificent three-arch stone bridge, built in the 17th or 18th century, crossing a picturesque bend in the Kompsatos River as it leaves the mountains for the plains. The western arch has fallen, adding an air of melancholy. Walk to its precipice before entering the water from the sandbanks below.

→ Heading E of Iasmos, turn L after 2.5km as you meet the river. Follow the road over a bridge and park on the L at its far end (41.1391, 25.2129). Continue on foot, forking R to the bridge or L down to the river.
5 mins, 41.1411, 25.2107

WATERFALLS

9 MESOROPI POOL

A crystal pool in a shaded glade, fed by a gentle waterfall scurrying between rock slabs that double as sun loungers. The easy riverside trail is delightful, and great for kids.

→ Park in Mesoropi, take the main trail leaving the village to the NE, fork R and walk around 800m to the pool.
15 mins, 40.8734, 24 0888

10 PALEA KAVALA WATERFALLS

Twin waterfalls feed a turquoise pool, shaded by diagonal trees. Take a picnic and cool off using the makeshift rope swing. The path continues uphill to a pleasant wooded stream.

→ Leave Prosfyges to the NE. Take the first big R after 1km, then bear R onto a track after 300m. Continue 800m, bending R past a building, and park at the junction under a large tree (40.9977, 24.3956). Take the L fork and

walk 800m past a quarry to the falls.
15 mins, 41.0027, 24.4011

11 ST BARBARA WATERFALL

A considerable cascade roaring over an angular rockface into a broad swimming pool buried deep in virgin forest. Picnic benches and campfire remnants complete the heavenly scene.

→ Enjoy a wonderfully winding 7.5km drive E from Vounoplagia, via one R turn after 2km, and park in the picnic area on the R. Follow the trail over the bridge into the forest. Branch L near the pool to explore the pools above the fall.
10 mins, 41.3439, 24.5908

12 LEPIDA WATERFALL

One of Greece's finest waterfalls, thundering as if from heaven into a tumbling forestscape of rock pools, tangled canopy and rushing rapids. Come prepared to savour this place of wild solitude.

→ Continue N from St Barbara Waterfall (see entry) through Dipotama hamlet, where the road becomes a track. Follow 5km to a gazebo, park here and descend the signed trail via steep switchbacks for 500m to the falls.
20 mins, 41.3874, 24.6200

13 LIVADITIS WATERFALL

A stunning 60m torrent plunging through thick beech forest, with an icy pool beneath. A fantastic outing year round, including in winter, when the water freezes in fantastical shapes until the first spring warmth.

→ Take the road heading NE out of Livaditis (41.3062, 24.6706). After 4.5km turn L onto a dirt track (bad in the winter) and continue 2.2km to a signed trailhead on the L. It's a 2km walk down, steep at the end. You can also hike directly N from Livaditis.

40 mins, 41.3270, 24.6718 🏕🏔🚶🏊

14 APOSTOLUS WATERFALL, THASSOS

Crystal waters falling over a rocky lip framed by thick mossy boughs in the Ypsarion foothills.

→ From the NE corner of Kastro village follow a dirt track roughly 3.5km. A lovely hike, though also drivable with a 4x4.

90 mins, 40.6908, 24.6626 🏊🚶🏊

15 KEFALOGOURNA WATERFALLS, THASSOS

Two waterfall plunge pools ensconced between cave-like rock walls and overhanging trees, a short amble from pretty Theologos. A popular summer spot.

→ Park in the small area just NE of the folklore museum in Theologos (40.6608, 24.6958). Walk the road E, turn R into an alley after 50m and trend left and downhill for 200m into the trees.

10 mins, 40.6603, 24.6989 🍴🏊🐟 B

CAVES & RUINS

16 VRANOKASTRO

Originally a Macedonian castle built to protect nearby gold mines, and declining when they were depleted, it was reactivated by the Byzantines in the 12th century before being laid waste in 1383. It sits on the zenith of a forested ridgeline with massive views over the crescent of surrounding villages and the plains beyond.

→ Weave to the SE edge of Palaiochori (40.9411, 24.1816), take the R track into the trees and park before the impassable sharp L after 500m. Continue for almost 1km on foot, bending L and climbing stairs at the end.

30 mins, 40.9454, 24.1899 📷🏔

17 ANCIENT THASOS ACROPOLIS, THASSOS

The acropolis of ancient Thasos stands on a hill surveying the temples, theatre, agora and city walls that once comprised

a powerful city-state. Its remnants offer a transporting walk with splendid sea views.

→ On the road from Limenas E to Makriammos, turn L 650m after the football club and park on the first R hairpin. A short trail leads up to the acropolis. You can also walk a lovely trail up from the NE end of Limenas, looping R via the theatre.

10 mins, 40.7783, 24.7200

18 DRAGON CAVE, THASSOS

Named because some of its wall formations supposedly look like dragons, this ivy-draped cave lies in a thick forest humming with life. Note that the ivy attracts lots of bees in the summer.

→ Park in Panagia and walk a lane NE, passing the school on your L and bending L downhill. In 400m, after a R hairpin, a short trail enters the forest R. Follow it to the cave.

15 mins, 40.7320, 24.7320

19 ANASTASIOPOLIS-PERITHEORION

Ivy-clad ruins hidden in a thick copse home to wild boars. Originating as a staging post, the site was fortified in the 6th century and later became an important Byzantine stronghold in this strategic fertile corridor. A secret picnic spot.

→ From Amaxades drive S under the E90. Turn L at the T junction to follow the farm track E, take the first major R and head S for 1km. Turn L and continue around 800m to park at the edge of the trees (41.1035, 25.0893). The trail leads through an obvious gate to the ruins.

5 mins, 41.1024, 25.0908

WILD WONDERLANDS

20 FRAKTO FOREST

Considered Greece's only true virgin forest – a protected wilderness of 500-year-old trees and vertiginous crags roamed by bears and wildcats – Frakto may be the country's wildest place. Access the trails and jagged viewpoints from this forest village (+30 2521 057841), but bring camping gear in case.

→ The asphalt road N from Paranesti becomes a dirt track after 45km in Thermia, a collection of tin-roof huts. The route from here is 17km and complex, so download a map to your phone in advance. Bring plenty of fuel and supplies, because you won't find any.

15 mins, 41.5061, 24.5052

21 MOUNT YPSARION, THASSOS

The island's highest peak at 1204m, rewarding hikers with vistas that encompass the mountain's sheer, stratified ridgelines, the entire island and the mainland beyond.

→ The well-signed 12km hike (6km each way) starts on the W edge of Potamia (40.7171, 24.7271). You can also walk or drive up with a 4x4 around 11km from Maries.

4 hrs, 40.7031, 24.7055

22 THRACIAN METEORA

This faraway landscape of otherworldly geological formations is pocked with caves and alcoves interspersed with beech trees and wild horses. A remote paradise for ramblers, scramblers and wild campers, with the E6 hiking trail passing nearby, akin to the famous Meteora in Thessaly (see entry).

→ Heading W from Iasmos, bear R 300m after the leaving-town sign onto a dirt road. Turn L at the T junction and continue 8km to an intersection (41.1664, 25.1623). Fork L and follow 13km. The last 3km beyond Poliarno are rough, so a 4x4 is advisable. Park in the parking area and follow a track R, round the farm, towards the formations.

15 mins, 41.2184, 25.1244

LOCAL FOOD & DRINK

23 TO ARALIKI

Warm, buzzing neighbourhood dining with consistently delicious fish, meat and vegetarian dishes, plus homemade wine – all in the shadow of the castle walls.

→ Kavala 652 01, +30 6984 718521
40.9331, 24.4141 🅱️

24 SALONIKIOS BEACH CANTINA, THASSOS

A simple cantina playing chill music and serving drinks and snacks, including a tasty saganaki. Beautifully sited on a golden beach with wooden shade structures on a secluded, shrubby peninsula.

→ Heading W on the main road skirting S of Astrida to the coast, turn L onto a track just after the petrol station (40.5819, 24.6471). Bend R after 400m, go straight over the first crossroads and R at the second to a sandy parking area. Reachable in a normal car, but walk the final part if nervous.

40.5715, 24.6435 🅻

25 UTOPIA RESTAURANT, THASSOS

Upscale dishes, fabulous views, excellent music and a brilliant wine, beer and cocktail selection. Reserve to ensure a balcony table.

26 TAVERNA KOTTANI

A taverna with a folk museum upstairs celebrating the Pomak culture of the region's Bulgarian-speaking Muslims. Order a fresh salad or meat special and enjoy the remote river-valley scenery.

→ Kottani 673 00, +30 6945 009855
41.3150, 25.0923 🅻

STAY

27 XANTHIS LIVADITIS REFUGE

Managed by mountain lovers, this cosy refuge is in a tiny, bucolic village ensconced by southern Rhodope forest. It has rudimentary dorm beds for 36, a crackling fire and endless forest trails starting right outside.

→ Livaditis Xanthis 670 62, +30 2541 068023
41.3042, 24.6712 🅰️🅻

28 FOREST VILLAGE ERYMANTHOS

A hamlet of rustic log cabins deep in the Rhodope forest; a little worn around the edges, but an excellent retreat for hikers, families and mushroom foragers. The on-site taverna serves tasty food.

→ Stavroupoli 670 62, +30 2542 021008
41.3323, 24.7125 🏔️🎿

29 HOTEL NEMESIS

A curious collection of eight faux medieval castle towers, each with a couple of homely suites, all set in grounds featuring a pool, a small zoo and kids' play facilities.

→ Komnina 670 62, +30 2542 021005
41.1743, 24.7247 🎿

30 LIMENAS HOUSE, THASSOS

The terrace of this charming guesthouse has a stone barbecue, a hammock and splendid sea views beyond the balustrades. The sprawling garden is alive with fresh fruit and vegetables and free-roaming peacocks. Sleeps six, with four in bunk beds, so ideal for a family.

→ Limenas Thasos, 640 04, airbnb.com/rooms/6085151
40.7759, 24.7256 🎿

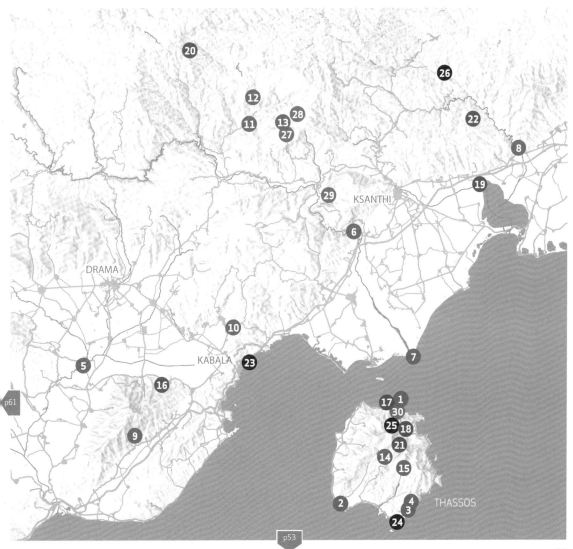

CHALKIDIKI

Our perfect weekend

→ **Journey** south to the end-of-the-track beach and headland of Sithonia Cape, one of Chalkidiki's wildest places.

→ **Voyage** across the alluring shallows surrounding Diaporos Island, pausing in the tranquil embrace of Kryfto Bay.

→ **Order** a selection of delicious recommendations at For Friends - Kafe Mezedopoleio, in pretty port village Pirgadikia.

→ **Plot** your path to the secret sea stacks and swimming waters of Trimi Beach, on the Mount Athos border.

→ **Creak** across your personal footbridge to Agramada Treehouse's terrace, and enjoy a breakfast of homemade bread and local delicacies.

→ **Quest** far from other holidaymakers to the outer reaches of Brostomnitsa wildlife refuge, and the hidden cove of Katafigio Beach.

→ **Grow** wiser (possibly) as you stroll the remnants of Ancient Stageira, birthplace of Aristotle.

→ **Retreat** from Chalkidiki's celebrated sands to the refreshing woodland pools of Varvara Waterfalls.

Chalkidiki, often spelled Halkidiki, is a trident-shaped region of three peninsulas – Kassandra, Sithonia, and Mount Athos – separated by the Toronean and Singitic gulfs. These prongs are famed above all for two things: the secluded monastic community of Mount Athos, and the beaches that attract Thessaloniki weekenders and a growing number of international visitors. If you'll be in the north and love the sea and sand, read on.

As Chalkidiki's westernmost prong, Kassandra is closest to Thessaloniki and the most developed with beach resorts. But wilder pockets await beyond its northeastern seaboard of holiday towns. Agios Nikolaos Bay is a deliciously private curve below a steep track and the quiet gaze of a church, and the jagged inlets surrounding Osta Sofia Sea Caves provide a fun afternoon in calm weather. Charming stays also offer refuge from the hubbub: two wooden hideaways – Pinetree Cabin in an almond garden, and iCamp Rentals' tented cabins in a beachside glade – are tranquil choices.

Though still popular, Sithonia peninsula has fewer resorts and more wilder, quieter spaces. The double-sided beach at Sithonia Cape, in the far south, is a remote and reflective outpost. Taking a boat from Vourvourou around Diaporos Island, via popular Blue Lagoon and the quieter turquoise of Kryfto Bay, is one of Chalkidiki's quintessential days out, if you can avoid high-season weekends. And Mirsinio Beach hides from most of those travelling the coastal crook leading to Mount Athos above. When it's time to eat, head inland for the region's best tavernas; succulent lamb and live music beneath a trellis of flowering vines at Klimataria Tavern is a fine option.

Most of Mount Athos belongs to the autonomous community of twenty Eastern Orthodox monasteries known as Agio Oros ('Holy Mountain') – Greece's most important monastic community, finding spiritual sanctuary amidst the plunging coastal crags around the eponymous mountain. Unfortunately visiting requires a permit available only to men, but you can get close. The sea stacks of nearby Trimi Beach make it arguably Chalkidiki's finest, partly because you'll need to wade, scramble or rent a boat to get there. Alternatively, spend a night or two in tastefully hand-built Agramada Treehouse en route to the region's northeastern coastline. The well-preserved remnants of Aristotle's birthplace, ancient Stageira, await here, flanked naturally by two delightful beaches. And the cold pools of Varvara Waterfalls punctuate a pretty woodland river in the forested foothills above, if you fancy a change from the gold and blue below.

BEACHES

1 AGIOS NIKOLAOS BAY

A narrow strip of sand curving away from a little church beneath overhanging pine boughs and a sole villa peeping through the canopy. The hill down is steep enough to keep this place quiet.

→ Follow the coast road S for 2.3km from the main junction for Siviri and turn sharply R onto a sandy track 850m S of a big L bend (40.0256, 23.3652). Turn L and continue down the very steep but good track to parking by the church (park at the top if nervous).

2 mins, 40.0238, 23.3638 🏖️🏊🚶✝️⛱️

2 POSSIDI CAPE

A long sandy cape with a distinctive hooked end. The southern shoreline tends to be calmer; there is no shade.

→ Head 2km SW from Possidi along the coast and park in the free parking area. It's roughly 800m to the tip of the cape.

5 mins, 39.9564, 23.3569 🏖️🏊🅿️B

3 SITHONIA CAPE

This double-sided beach, open and wild, is an isthmus to a gorse-covered islet, extending from the end of a wobbly peninsula like the prow of a ship.

→ At the SE edge of Porto Koufo Beach, fork R onto a track opposite a small shrine (39.9621, 23.9296). Continue straight along the main track, turn L at 1.3km, fork R then L, and continue carefully for 2km, ignoring turns, to park behind a beach. Continue 500m on foot.

10 mins, 39.9385, 23.9317 🏖️🏊🏕️⛰️🔺🚶

4 HEART-SHAPED BAY

A very small, unheralded beach in a deep swimming bay with no facilities. A good place to be alone with the morning rays; a second, rocky cove to the left makes the heart shape.

→ Head 2km N from the N edge of Sarti on the coastal road and fork R onto the second track - the one after, not opposite, the L fork. Immediately fork L and park, then walk the R fork around 600m to the bay.

10 mins, 40.1096, 23.9909 🏖️🏊🚶

5 FAVA BEACH

This long stretch of sand below villas at the northern end, is broken into semi-private sections and pools by smooth rock bookends and boulders. Explore to find your spot.

→ From the crossroads in S Karidi, head E, take the first R and park near the end (40.1849, 23.8177). A 100m track leads from the end to the beach.

2 mins, 40.1848, 23.8194 🍴🏖️🏊🐾🅿️B

6 KARYDI BEACH

Wonderful twin crescents separated by an attractive rocky peninsula dotted with pines and rock pools, with a more secluded peninsula to the west. A fine accompaniment to a boat trip over to Diaporos (see Kryfto Bay).

→ Take the N from the main road between Karidi and Vourvourou (40.1883, 23.8060), signed 'Karidi Beach Apartments'. Bear R on a L bend after 350m to park behind the beach.

2 mins, 40.193, 23.8083 🏖️🏊🐾B

7 KRYFTO BAY

This shallow turquoise bay, in a deep northern inlet on uninhabited Diaporos Island, is quieter but similar in beauty to the more popular Blue Lagoon and White Beach (see image) nearby. Explore all three, and other island nooks, with a boat, a snorkel and food for the day.

→ There is no public ferry to Diaporos, so you'll need to explore by boat. Queen Boat (+30 69 4695 3442) and Get Wet (+30 2375 091250) are both great options, side by side in Vourvourou just W of Karydi Beach (see entry). Blue Lagoon is at 40.2218, 23.7885; White Beach is at 40.2114, 23.7858.

2 mins, 40.2233, 23.7788 🏖️🏊🐾B

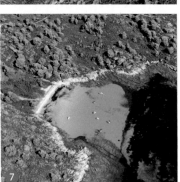

8 MIRSINIO BEACH

This secret strip of coarse golden sand, in a wide, shallow bay cradled by green craggy hillside, is one of the region's finest beaches, but escapes the attention of many visitors.

→ Park in a dirt layby on the coastal road around 1.8km S of Agii Theodori. Take the track opposite and turn immediately L onto a smaller path, which leads, in places steeply, to the beach. Thieves operate here, so don't leave valuables.

5 mins, 40.3201, 23.6988

9 MARI KOURI BEACH

A tiny, delightfully private sand-and-pebble beach hidden beneath steep coastal cliffs, with an even smaller beach round the corner to the south for inquisitive swimmers.

→ Entering Pyrgadikia from Agii Theodori, bend L past the little marina, go straight over the crossroads and take the first R. Fork immediately L, fork L again and park on a wide paved section just around the bend at 40.3396, 23.7270. Walk on and turn R down to the beach.

5 mins, 40.3396, 23.7284

10 ASSA BEACH

This unheralded beach, at the end of a track beneath a sloping garden of olive trees that provide shade, is a fine place to escape the Chalkidiki crowds.

→ Head NE along the coast from Assa, behind Ladhario Beach. Keep R just after the beach, then continue 2.1km to a hairpin R down to the beach just before another hairpin R. The track is a little rough but drivable.

1 min, 40.3503, 23.7486

11 TRIMI BEACH

This divine beach of golden sand, scattered boulders, pretty sea stacks and translucent swimming waters, all bordering the monastic community of Mount Athos, is very tricky to access. If you can make it, you'll likely enjoy Chalkidiki's most paradisal beach alone.

→ Easiest access is by boat: hire from Rent a Boat Lampou (+30 69 4811 9960) in Ouranoupoli. Alternatively, park at the Monastery of Zygos, head R to the beach and walk, wade or possibly swim 200m R along the coast to the beach. Trickier is to walk a track R (40.3195, 23.9958) 700m before the monastery and skirt/scramble precariously around the R edge of the field down to the beach.

2-20 mins, 40.3175, 23.9965

9

12 KATAFIGIO BEACH

One of three fabulously secluded coves at the far end of Brostomnitsa wildlife refuge. A fine place to camp, but open fires are prohibited.

➜ Head 5.3km N from the viewpoint at the N end of Stratoni and take the signed track R to 'Zepko' (40.5547, 23.8252). Follow the complex track system around 12km SE; map and 4x4 strongly advised.

3 mins, 40.5257, 23.9085 🏊🛶⛺🎣🐚

13 KEPHALAS BEACH

A charming sandy cove guarded by lush headlands, creating a bay ripe for snorkelling in the shadow of ancient Stageira (see entry), Aristotle's birthplace.

➜ Follow either road E from Olimpiada to the layby 280m SE after they join together and park on the L (40.5883, 23.7929). Follow the obvious track around the bend, and turn R to the beach before a fence.

3 mins, 40.5883, 23.7947 🏊🛶

14 SIKIA BEACH

Along with Kephalas Beach (see entry), this sweep of sand makes a fine place to swim after a visit to ancient Stageira (see entry). It stays surprisingly quiet, but watch out for sea urchins.

➜ Take the NE exit from the roundabout near Olimpiada port on the E edge of town and continue 400m to a parking area R, passing stairs down to the beach on your L.

2 mins, 40.5912, 23.7913 🏊🛶🐟🔭💧▽

SEA CAVES & WATERFALLS

15 VARVARA WATERFALLS

Two waterfalls with accompanying pools along a pretty woodland river and walk, with flowing water and visitors until late summer. An enchanting alternative to the region's ubiquitous beach swims.

➜ Head W from the main crossroads NW of Olimpiada. Turn R at 950m, fork immediately L and climb 4.8km to a sharp R onto a dirt track. Follow it 3.3km, with one L turn at 2.3km, to the parking area. Head R for the lower falls or L for the upper (more accessible) falls.

5 mins, 40.5964, 23.7215 🏊🛶🔭🚶🚶

16 OSTA SOFIA SEA CAVES

A series of rock fissures hiding micro-beaches and tiny caves, some swimmable in calm conditions.

➜ Heading SE from Loutra, turn R onto the sweeping L bend just after the parking area (39.9233, 23.5928) and park where a track

10

17

heads R after 100m. Follow it to the beach and walk, scramble or swim R to explore.

5 mins, 39.9213, 23.5937 🍴🏊🐟🚫👣🚲🐾

CASTLES & ANCIENT RUINS

17 RENTINA CASTLE

A castle and fortified settlement dating back to the 4th century, but embellished during the Byzantine and Frankish periods, hidden on a forested, overgrown hillock above Rentina.

→ Turn off the 2 onto a track 200m SW of the main Rentina junction (40.6553, 23.6135) and park after 700m in an open area. A clear path leads up.

3 mins, 40.6561, 23.6228 ⛰️🚲

18 ANCIENT STAGEIRA

The well-preserved remains of the birthplace of Aristotle, scattered delightfully across a meandering headland of conifers and golden coves, protected by the walls of a Byzantine castle. Free entry, with Kephalas or Sikia beaches (see entries) to visit after.

→ Follow either road E from Olimpiada to an obvious parking area where they merge. You can't miss the ruins 50m beyond on the L.

2 mins, 40.5896, 23.7923 ⛰️🚲🚶

LOCAL FOOD & DRINK

19 O PLATANOS

This friendly village-square taverna makes a fine place to tuck into succulent Greek classics against the backdrop of Arnaia's gentle comings and goings.

→ Arnaia 630 74, +30 69 4000 3818
40.4863, 23.5952 🅱️

20 FOR FRIENDS - KAFE MEZEDOPOLEIO

A cosy family taverna serving consistently tasty dishes, on a corner that's a satisfying stroll from Pirgadikia's pretty port. Not to be confused with Kouros cafe over the road (though that's also excellent).

→ Pirgadikia 630 78, +30 2375 093045
40.3366, 23.7209 🔼

21 KLIMATARIA TAVERN

A pretty taverna festooned in flowers, specialising in divine lamb dishes – especially the chops or lamb on a spit. There's often relaxed live music too.

→ Metagkitsi 630 78, +30 2375 092365
40.3240, 23.6563 🅱️

22 BONGO BEACH BAR

Chilled island vibes set back from the beach in a garden of palms and shaded wooden furniture, serving delicious cocktails and varied music.

➜ Ammouliani 630 75, +30 69 8451 7773
40.3354, 23.9173

23 5 STEPS IN THE SAND

One of the best beachside tourist tavernas in Chalkidiki, serving fresh seafood from a charming patio terrace above a small, organised cove.

➜ Sithonia 630 72, +30 2375 041207
40.0347, 23.9960 🅱

STAY

24 AGRAMADA TREEHOUSE

A handcrafted treehouse for two, with delectable design touches, a rain-drip shower and a homemade breakfast combining local ingredients with homemade jams and bread. The property also has B&B rooms and a communal fire pit.

➜ Paleochori 630 74, +30 2372 032151
40.4596, 23.6546 ▣

25 PINETREE CABIN

This wooden cabin is set in a luscious green garden of almond trees, with room for two plus a little one. The covered dining area looks out to a hammock and an open-air shower.

➜ Kalandra 630 77, airbnb.com/
rooms/12832756
39.9709, 23.3960 ▣

26 ICAMP RENTALS

Luxurious wooden cabins (sleeping four) and tent-cum-studios (sleeping two or four) sitting in a tranquil beachfront glade, with easy access to a beach bar down the sand.

➜ Paliouri 630 85, +30 69 4242 2639, ihouse.
com.gr/rentals
39.9412, 23.6860 ▣

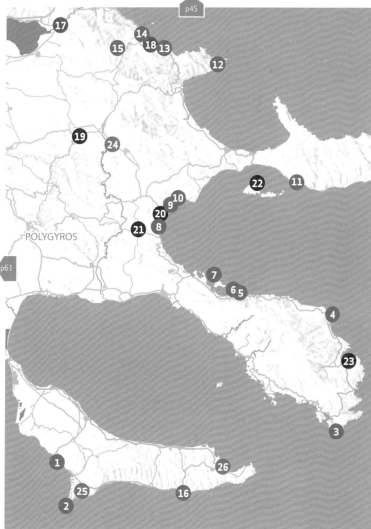

CENTRAL MACEDONIA

Our perfect weekend

→ **Sample** wild buffalo and other Turkish-influenced Pontic Greek cuisine at Evora taverna.

→ **Swing** into the aqua waters of the stunning pool fed by Skra Waterfalls.

→ **Leap** into the crisp, crystal Pozar River as it rushes through a forested valley.

→ **Cross** the rickety wooden bridge over the spring-fed pond at Edessa River Springs, picnic in hand.

→ **Snorkel** along the submerged hull of the Epanomi Shipwreck off a long, sandy peninsula south of Thessaloniki.

→ **Bathe** in sludgy but soothing mud baths in the vast Pydna Salt Pan.

→ **Hike** the famous E4 trail in the forested Mount Olympus foothills to a tiny whitewashed church hiding in St Dionysios Cave.

→ **Wake** to astonishing mountain vistas after a night on Mount Olympus in Giosos Apostolidis Refuge on Muses Plateau.

The homeland of the Olympian gods and Alexander the Great, the middle third of Greek Macedonia arcs around a huge developed plain west of Thessaloniki, Greece's second city. It meets the neighbouring nations of North Macedonia and Bulgaria in the north and follows the Aegean to Mount Olympus further south. The aura of this legendary mountain, combined with Thessaloniki's cosmopolitan allure and the unheralded wildness of the borderlands, mean there is plenty more than farming towns to explore here.

Mount Olympus is Greece's highest and most revered mountain – a 2917m mammoth and mythical home to the 12 Olympian gods who, led by Zeus, defeated the Titans in the Battle of the Gods. More than a mountain, Olympus is a metaphorical higher place, and there is nowhere better to feel this than Muses Plateau, spread beneath the peak as if in reverence. Hike to Giosos Apostolidis Refuge and beyond for a memorable, epic adventure. Then, down in the foothills, follow the E4 trail via the string of snow-fed icy pools and waterfalls at Enipeas to the tiny church hiding in St Dionysios Cave downstream.

Buzzing Thessaloniki is considered Greece's cultural capital, its bustling waterside promenade giving way to lively hillside neighbourhoods that ascend to Ano Poli, the Old Town. Welcome the chance to pass through, and seek out the wilder pockets in the hinterlands. Axios Delta is a vast wetland of flamingos, wild horses and water buffalo, all within view of downtown. The Haliacmon River also enters the Aegean here, ending the longest river journey entirely in Greece; enjoy it, and then swim in its broad valley meanders further upstream if you can. And why not slather yourself in healing mud at the Pydna Salt Pan further south, keeping an eye out for interesting bird life? You can always wash off at nearby Alkyona Houseboat.

Slingshotting north then west from Thessaloniki is one of Greece's more underrated road trips, with no end of life-giving locations en route to the wonders of Western Macedonia and Zagori. Evora, dead north, is a fantastic place to sample Pontic cuisine; many of the Pontic Greeks settled for millennia in the region of Pontus came to Central Macedonia in the 1920s, when expelled from Turkey. Further west, Skra Waterfalls features a watercolour waterfall cave and a classic of the rope-swinged-pool genre. Kounoupista Waterfall, upstream from indulgent Pozar Thermal Baths, is the crescendo of a rousing riverside ramble. And it's hard to imagine, as you stand at Greece's biggest waterfall in Edessa, that just ten short kilometres away the river rises at Edessa River Springs, a tranquil countryside pond of reeds, swans and lowing cows.

BEACHES & MUD BATHS

1 PYDNA SALT PAN

Smelly but therapeutic mud baths in the vast Pydna salt pan. Lather yourself in mud, float in the salty water and spot flamingos overhead.

→ Park at Alikes Kitros beach, just SE of Alyki marina, and cross the track behind the beach.

3 mins, 40.3758, 22.6309 🏖🐚

2 EPANOMI SHIPWRECK

The rusted, vibrantly coloured top of this wreck is easily visible from the vast sandy point that proved its undoing in the 1970s. Bring your snorkel to explore what lies beneath. A fun day out from Thessaloniki.

→ Follow lanes due S from Epanomi and turn R when you hit the coast - about 4.5km from the S edge of town. Follow the sandy road that runs parallel to the shore and park near the wreck, which is about 800m back from the point and a 20m wade out to sea.

3 mins, 40.3759, 22.8970 🚗🏖🐚

WATERFALLS

3 SKRA WATERFALLS

A double whammy of sublime water features, not to be missed. The first waterfall spills over a scenic mossy overhang, with space for you to venture behind the cascade. A stone's throw away, upstream, a second fall and a vivid turquoise pool with a rope swing await.

→ Drive S from Skra 4.5km, taking two obvious L forks around 800m and 2.6km from the edge of the village, and park at the end of the tarmac road. Follow the short, clearly marked trail downhill. The large pool and second set of falls are 100m after the first.

10 mins, 41.0642, 22.3923 🍴🏖⊙

4 KOUNOUPISTA WATERFALL

This picture-perfect woodland cataract creates an inviting, if cold, plunge pool deep in the forest. Magical.

→ The marked 2.5km trail descends the NE side of the valley from the viewpoint in abandoned Ano Loutraki village (40.9811, 21.9003). It's also possible to follow the river up about 5km from Pozar Thermal Baths (see entry), via the viewpoint, crossing the river at multiple points.

60 mins, 40.9844, 21.8870 🏖🚶🔦🪂

5 EDESSA WATERFALL

Powerful, crushing waterfalls in an organised garden with viewing platforms and a walkway leading to a spot behind the falling water. This is a popular place on the edge of town, so visit early to avoid crowds.

→ Park anywhere in NE Edessa, including the dedicated car park, and walk E. There are plenty of signs.

3 mins, 40.8039, 22.0556 🏔B

6 AGIA KORI WATERFALLS

A series of chute-like waterfalls cascading through the forest towards a hidden valleyside church, with a pleasant dipping pool beneath the first fall accessible via a wooden walkway.

→ Take a signed fork L around 3.6km SW of the edge of Vrontou (40.1676, 22.3977) and continue 1km to park in the open area by Agia Kori Church. A footpath leads down many steps to the church, then 300m S to the falls. A trail also leads directly between the falls and parking area (8 mins) to make a loop.

15 mins, 40.1612, 22.4062 🏖⊙

7 OURLIAS WATERFALLS

Three idyllic waterfalls – two easily accessible, the third requiring a long hike – with accompanying pools deep enough for swimming and jumping, all in the jaws of a forested gorge. They are busy in high season.

→ Park on a big L hairpin 5km SW of Dion (40.1511, 22.4391). The right path leads to the first two falls; the stairs on the left lead to the third, more distant fall.

3–45 mins, 40.1501, 22.4377 🍴🏊🚶🅱

8 ENIPEAS WATERFALL

A string of mountain-cold waterfalls, rivulets and pools connected by wooden bridges along the famous E4 trail. A fine cooling spot for hikers.

→ Follow the road from NW Litochoro for around 18km, twisting through the mountains W then SW, keeping L at a fork around 14km. Park at the end, by Prionia restaurant. Continue uphill and R for the small falls; take the E4 route 1km N (doubling back) from the parking for the large falls, which can also be reached by turning R at the bottom of the steps for St Dionysios Cave (see entry).

5–15 mins, 40.0832, 22.4057 🏊🚶

RIVERS

9 POZAR RIVER POOL

A crystal-clear, fast-running plunge pool in a frigid forest river, with a rock for jumping and gorge views on the walk in.

→ From Pozar Thermal Baths (see entry), continue upstream along the initially paved path with the river on your L, ascending to a viewpoint and continuing for 250m or so to the pool on the L. Explore upstream for your own secret spot.

10 mins, 40.9728, 21.9069 🍴🏊🚶▽🐾

10 POZAR THERMAL BATHS

Natural thermal baths at the start of a lush valley beside an ice-cold river. The setup is somewhat sprawling, with 48 individual baths, six indoor pools, hammams and a jacuzzi and spa. Head upstream to the Pozar River Pool or Kounoupitsa Waterfall (see entries) if you'd rather escape the crowds.

→ Follow the road around 2km W from Loutraki Pellas to the car park just before the baths.

5 mins, 40.9711, 21.9146 🏊🅱ℹ

11 AXIOS DELTA

A unique expanse of protected wetland with abundant wildlife – including wild horses, water buffalo and over 300 bird species – a watchtower and working fishing huts. Mount Olympus looms in the distance.

→ The highway SW out of Thessaloniki runs 20km across the delta, and multiple tracks

14

run S to criss-cross it. Be sure to close the gates behind you.

1 min, 40.5362, 22.7274 🏕️👣♨️

12 RIVER HALIACMON

This is one of the longest rivers in Greece, important once as a protective border and now as a wetland habitat and hydroelectric resource. This is a fine spot for a shaded swim and a picnic. Be respectful of anglers.

➜ Head NW from Sfikia for 5km, dogleg L then quickly R at a staggered junction (you could also detour down a 2km dead-end L to see the dam), and follow the track 1km to the shore.

1 min, 40.4161, 22.1979 🏊🏕️♨️

LAKES

13 LAKE KERKINI

The grassy shore of this broad lake, surrounded by arable plains and verdant foothills, makes for a lovely picnic and fruitful place to see birds – particularly flamingos and pelicans.

➜ There is good access via tracks on all sides for exploration. A tarmac road runs close on the W side, and a short dirt road runs NE from Korifoudi to this spot.

1 min, 41.1878, 23.1100 🏕️👣

14 EDESSA RIVER SPRINGS

The bucolic start of the Edessa River, which grows to plunge over nearby Edessa Waterfall (see entry). A rickety wooden footbridge crosses the spring-fed lily pond, surrounded by cows munching in meadows dotted with tall deciduous trees. A delightful spot for a lazy picnic.

➜ Head NW from Vrita and turn R onto a track after around 1.4km, just as you see the pond on your R. Park when the bridge comes into view. There's just enough turning space.

1 min, 40.8103, 21.9057 🏊🏞️♨️

MOUNTAINS

15 MOUNT PAIKO

An easily accessible peak with a luscious forest ascent and superb panoramic views, which you share with a blue metal hiker statue. Particularly special in autumn.

➜ Drive W from Kastaneri about 3.5km and turn L onto a track on a R bend (40.9836, 22.3568). Fork R and continue 4.7km to park by a thinner track on a R hairpin (40.9636, 22.3337). Walk the thinner track 1.5km curving L then R up to the peak.

30 mins, 40.9557, 22.3343 🏕️👣

12

17

16 MUSES PLATEAU

Mount Olympus, also known as the Throne of Zeus, is Greece's highest mountain. This green plateau is an awesome base for exploring it and the other rugged peaks nearby, one of which is adorned with a tiny stone church. There are multiple amazing, and very long hiking routes in; given the distance and the spectacular scenery, stay for a night or two in Giosos Apostolidis Refuge (see entry).

→ One great option starts from parking at Gortsia, where you can rent a mule (40.1034, 22.4417). A busier but shorter option starts at Enipeas Waterfall parking (see entry).
5–7 hours, 40.0976, 22.3692 ▲🚶🝣

SACRED PLACES & RUINS

17 CHORIGI CASTLE

Not a true castle, but a squat plateau above a rock outcrop rising from the fields that's naturally nearly as effective. Remains of an ancient settlement and burial have been found on the summit. A lovely vantage spot for sunset, and popular with climbers. Watch out for snakes.

→ Heading W from Chorigi on the main road, exit with the first R (doubles back R) and then turn R again at 750m to park SE of the hill. A path skirts clockwise up.
5 mins, 41.0145, 22.7084 🝣▲▲

18 OLD VRONTOU

The scattered remnants of this village, destroyed in the Second World War, lie on a plateau in the shadow of Mount Olympus and are now populated by roaming cows.

→ Drive 3.6km SW from the edge of Vrontou, as if for Agia Kori Waterfalls (see entry), but take a signed fork R (40.1676, 22.3977). Curve R, then fork R again to drive through the ruins.
2 mins, 40.1740, 22.3921 🝣

19 ST DIONYSIOS CAVE

A tiny church hidden in the corner of a dramatically overhanging cave deep in the forest. The walk is divine, crossing a pristine river en route.

→ Follow the road from NW Litochoro for about 15km, twisting through the mountains, and take a switchback L for the Old Holy Monastery of St Dionysios of Olympus. Zigzag down 1.4km to the car park. Take the stairs down from here, turn L and follow the trail E for 1km. You can also walk NE from Enipeas Waterfall (see entry).
20 mins, 40.0941, 22.4379 ✝🚶

20 EVORA

Pontic cuisine, of the Greeks who lived in Pontus (now in Turkey) since antiquity, is common in northern Greece. This relaxed, traditional taverna is a fine place to sample it. Order a selection, including something with buffalo meat.

→ Kato Poria 620 55, +30 2327 023395
41.2960, 22.9750

21 ASYLO

A quick jaunt from Lake Kerkini (see entry) is this unassuming taverna serving fabulously tasty and affordable dishes. Their speciality is chicken fillet and cabbage salad.

→ Sterodromi 620 55, +30 69 4152 4871
41.2115, 23.0461

22 CHATZIVARITI WINERY

A 200-acre family estate specialising in Greek grape varieties and natural and organic wines. The wines and hospitality are superb. Call ahead and arrange a tour.

→ Filiria 613 00, +30 2310 215259
40.8893, 22.4774

23 AGIOS GEORGIOS PERISTEREOTAS TAVERNA

Set amidst lush greenery and overlooked by a striking church, this uniquely located establishment offers heavenly food with perfect Greek hospitality.

→ Rodochori 592 00, +30 69 8787 4986
40.6994, 22.0231

24 BERGIOTIKO

Succulent meats reared on local farms and wines to match is the name of the game here. Owner and grill master Nikos can talk you through the mouth-watering options.

→ Veria 591 32, +30 2331 074133
40.5198, 22.2041

25 AILIAS TAVERNA

Simple and delicious food served with a smile at this scenic crossroads in the forest. The meatballs are lauded, as are the prices.

→ Rizomata 591 00, +30 69 4799 1257
40.3612, 22.2526

26 VIGLATORAS TRADITIONAL INN

A friendly, family-run mountain inn next to Lake Kerkini (see entry), with a wood-burning stove, traditional wooden rooms and shaded courtyard aplenty.

→ Ano Poria 620 55, +30 2327 051231
41.2859, 23.0347

27 CAMPING STOLOS

Pleasant tree-shaded camping on a large sandy beach. A great location for exploring Mount Olympus.

→ Katerini 602 00, +30 2352 061266
40.1852, 22.5617

28 KTIMA BELLOU

A small farm hotel offering a host of agricultural activities, including beekeeping, herbal tea tasting and oil distillation, plus a swimming pool overlooking the forested mountains beyond.

→ Agios Dimitrios 601 00, +30 2351 770021
40.1304, 22.2158

29 GIOSOS APOSTOLIDIS REFUGE

One of three spectacular mountain refuges on or near the plateau. It has 66 beds across five dorms, a restaurant and a lounge with a fireplace. Open June through October, and outside of this range with prior agreement. Follow hiking directions for Muses Plateau (see entry) and plan to spend a day walking in.

→ Litochoro 402 00, +30 2351 082840
40.0949, 22.3614

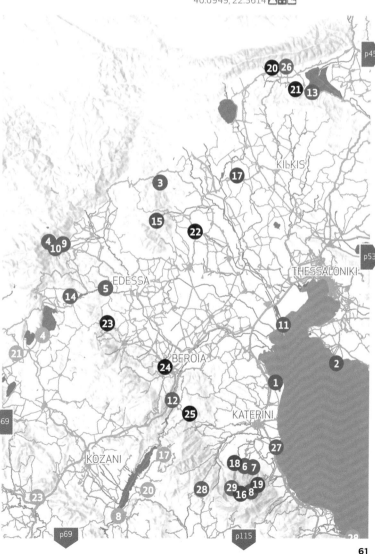

WESTERN MACEDONIA

Our perfect weekend

→ **Behold** the frescoed Hermitage of the Transfiguration of the Saviour, concealed in a shoreline cave.

→ **Tour** the region's finest wines from local vines at Magoutes Vineyard.

→ **Settle** in a waterside glade in Polyfytos Lake Plane Forest, scanning for rare birds and wild horses.

→ **Pitch** a hammock, blanket or tent at Moutsalia Lake, its surface a scene of reeds and reflected mountainscape.

→ **Huddle** in the lamplight with fellow mountain folk at Smolika Refuge, ready for an alpine push to sublime Smolika Dragon Lake.

→ **Forge** up the refreshing Venetikos River, from Portitsa Bridge into the imperiously tall, narrow jaws of Portisa Gorge.

→ **Dive** into the turquoise plunge pool at Balta di Striga Waterfalls, above a tumble of further cascades and rivulets.

→ **Forget** your plans by the Aoos River Weir, invigorated by mountain water and ensconced in a forested gorge.

An arc of natural splendour traces the international borders of Western Macedonia. Lakes, peaks, perches and hermitages abound from the Pindus National Park to the half-Albanian Gramos range and the pioneering Prespa National Park at Greece's nexus with Albania and North Macedonia, complemented by a smattering of lovely spots in the eastern lowlands.

Established jointly by Albania, North Macedonia and Greece in 2000, Prespa National Park is the Balkans' first cross-border protected area – a natural and geopolitical landmark in a politically charged region. It centres around two lakes separated by an isthmus: Great Prespa or Lake Prespa, spanning the three countries, and Little Prespa, mostly in Greece. Its wetlands support egrets, pygmy cormorants and Dalmatian pelicans (the world's largest freshwater bird), and the European brown bear inhabits its mountainous reaches (as well as the region's Arktouros Bear Sanctuary). Bring your binoculars to Agios Achillios Islet in Little Prespa Lake, or to Cape Roti Viewpoint, gazing over to Albania before visiting the hidden Hermitage of the Transfiguration of the Saviour. And stop for Macedonian cuisine at Kontosoros on your way out, if you can.

The Gramos range also crosses into Albania, further south. Lake Gistova, nestled just below its northern ridgeline, is actually bisected by the border. This area was also a communist stronghold during the Greek Civil War; its fall in 1949 hastened defeat. Hike into these wild, storied mountains for a night or two and descend to the warm embrace of Grammos Lodge. Or, if you prefer, ascend to Lake Skirtsi and enjoy similar alpine splendour for less effort, or drive to Lake Moutsalia to bask in a wonderfully pretty enclave amidst the forested eastern foothills.

Even bigger mountains await further south in splendid Pindus National Park, its vertiginous crags extending to Zagori and Eastern Epirus. Lamp-lit Smolika Refuge gives fabulous access to heart-shaped Smolika Dragon Lake, sitting spectacularly on Greece's second-highest mountain, Smolikas. Myth holds that the lake was created by a rock fight between two dragons, one on Smolikas and the other on Tymfi. Versions vary, but locals here will tell you that the Smolikas dragon prevailed by tricking its opponent by throwing salt balls instead of rocks. Either way, this place is the jewel of a spectacular crown making up this part of the region. From the atmospheric gorge swims beneath Portitsa and Kagelia bridges to the deep-blue depths of Balta di Striga Waterfalls, you won't need to travel far to find more gems.

4

LAKES

1 CAPE ROTI VIEWPOINT

A lonesome wooden bench at the end of a forested trail to the tip of Cape Roti looks out across Lake Prespa to both Albania and North Macedonia.

→ Head W from Lemos between the two lakes for about 7km, turn N and continue 6km to park in Psarades. Walk around the inlet and about 800m N on the track; the easy cape trail starts where the track bends L (40.8311, 21.0224).
30 mins, 40.8377, 21.0162 🏔

2 HERMITAGE OF THE TRANSFIGURATION OF THE SAVIOUR

Hidden in a cave at the base of Cape Roti, this frescoed 13th-century hermitage gazes across Lake Prespa to Albania.

→ Following the path to Cape Roti Viewpoint (see entry), turn L, signed Hermitage of Metamorphosis. You can also rent a boat for a quick trip from Psarades; just head to the jetty and ask for Panagiotis.
30 mins, 40.8336, 21.0174 🏔✝

3 SMALL PRESPA LAKE

In the middle of Prespa National Park, this lake enjoys a magnificent mountain-range backdrop. It's best experienced by crossing the footbridge to the central islet, which holds an ancient basilica ruin, a monastery and a strikingly large white cross.

→ Parking at the N end of St Achillios Bridge (40.7943, 21.0735), 9km SW from Lemos.
20 mins, 40.7796, 21.0887 🏔✝🚴🚶

4 LAKE VEGORITIDA

An expansive lake framed by snow-capped mountains, even in summer. A wooden jetty extends far into the water – great for drying off after a swim.

→ On the SE edge of Agios Panteleimonas, just SE of the sports field. There is a shaded place to park, popular with campervans, just above the jetty.
5 mins, 40.7211, 21.7515 🏊🏔

5 LAKE GISTOVA

Half in Greece, half in Albania, this breathtaking alpine lake is the highest in the Balkans.

→ Follow the track SW from Gramos village for 4.7km to 40.372, 20.816. It's a steep, stunning 3km hike from here W to the ridge then S to the lake. The path is tricky to find at points, so a map is highly recommended.
3 hours, 40.3646, 20.7905 🏔⛰🥾⁉🎒🌺

6 LAKE SKIRTSI

A tiny, little-known mountain lake at an altitude of 1800m, surrounded by scrubby alpine meadows and undulating peaks.

→ There is a marked 2.5km trail NW from Aetomilitsa village.
60 mins, 40.3263, 20.8337 🏔⛰🏊🎒🌺

7 MOUTSALIA LAKE

An alluring emerald lake lined with reeds and dotted with boulders, reflecting the enveloping trees and Gramos mountains. There are a couple of picnic tables.

→ Fork L as you head NW out of Chrysi (40.2763, 20.9739) and follow the main track 15km to parking by the lake, turning R at the one obvious fork around 13.5km.
2 mins, 40.3090, 20.9163 🏔⛰🎒🌺

8 LAKE POLYFYTOS PLANE FOREST

Pause for a picnic at this wondrous forest of plane trees extending into the shallows of Lake Polyfytos, supporting rare bird species. Enjoy an amble in the dappled woodland, pausing to watch the wild horses.

→ Drive 5.5km SE from Aiani to cross the Rymnio bridge, take the first paved R and

then the first R after 750m into the forest (40.1254, 21.8626). Park in the trees.
1 min, 40.1246, 21.8565 🏕🏔🚶

9 SMOLIKA DRAGON LAKE
A jaw-dropping alpine lake situated on the second-highest mountain in Greece, surrounded by lush grassland, wild flowers and roaming horses.

→ There is a well-marked path from Smolika Refuge (see entry), taking you through spectacular scenery.
90 mins, 40.0903, 20.9094 🏕🏔🚶🛖🌿🐾

10 FLEGGA DRAGON LAKES
Two small mountain lakes full of frogs and alpine newts, cradled near the top of Mount Mavrovouni. Lying at an altitude of 1950m, the lakes have water all year round, flowing underground from the higher lake to the lower lake. The hike up is stupendous.

→ A well-marked 10.5km trail starts from the Mount Mavrovouni Refuge (39.8461, 21.1484), N of Aoos Springs Lake, reachable in a normal car.
2 hours, 39.8765, 21.1219 🏕🏔🚶🛖🐾🌿

11 AOOS SPRINGS LAKE
A sprawling artificial lake cradled by alpine forest. It's well worth taking time to explore, whether on foot or by car, to find your own secret spot on one of the many jutting peninsulas.

→ An easy road encircles the lake and makes for a great dive.
2 mins, 39.8428, 21.1031 🏊🏕🏔

12 LAKE ZORIKA
A small, waterlily-covered lake by a remote stretch of forested mountain road. Stop by with a hammock and a picnic to soak up the peace and scenery.

→ From the W end of Aoos Springs Lake (see entry) follow the fork W (39.8282, 21.0581) for 7km and park right by the lake.
1 min, 39.8291, 21.0120 🏊🌿

RIVERS

13 PORTITSA BRIDGE
This 18th-century cobblestone footbridge spans the entrance to a sheer, wafer-thin gorge. Wading the waters below the arch and between the gargantuan walls is a real thrill.

14

→ A steep trail descends 1.4km from the S end of Spilaio (40.0025, 21.2826). You can also drive in a 6km anti-clockwise loop along a track starting from NW Spilaio, keeping L at 1.4km and 2.8km, to park just before the bridge.
3 mins, 39.9961, 21.2854 🚴🛶🌊🚶

14 KAGELIA BRIDGE
A remote stone bridge at the base of a wooded valley, spanning beautiful fast-flowing waters. It would be rude not to have at least a quick dip from one of the sandy micro beaches.

→ Drive 800m SW from Trikomo and turn L onto the signed dirt road (39.9774, 21.3130). Park shortly after and walk the clear path 1.5km downhill to the bridge.
30 mins, 39.9706, 21.3123 🌊🚴

15 VOVOUSA BRIDGE
The Aoos River meanders through picturesque Vovousa village beneath this beautiful old stone bridge. It was once so travelled that there were four inns at its ends; today it makes a lovely spot for a dip and a coffee.

→ There are steps down to the water to the E of the bridge, by the cafe in the village square.
3 mins, 39.9366, 21.0492 🌊

16 AOOS RIVER WEIR
A delightfully hidden river pool, created by a small weir, in a sumptuous stretch of forested mountain river, just a quick jaunt across the meadow from Valia Cada Refuge (see entry). Bring your swimmers and a book and let the hours drift by.

→ Head 2.7km S from Vovousas and park on the L by the refuge. A handful of breaks in the trees will lead you to the river.
5 mins, 39.9173, 21.054 🍴🛶🌊🚴🏕️

15

WATERFALLS

17 SKEPASMENO WATERFALL
Pretty cascades and a 20m cataract, with pools for swimming, hidden in the forested mouth of a lush, looming gorge.

→ Drive 1.3km NE from the bridge at the NW edge of Velventos and turn R. Continue 1.5km and take the track L through the gap in the wall L (40.2671, 22.0915). Follow this straight for 1km and park by the hut at the end. A footpath leads 100m to the falls.
5 mins, 40.2643, 22.1037 🌊🌊

18 BALTA DI STRIGA WATERFALLS
A dreamy water world. A 25m waterfall fills a large, cold plunge pool that spills into

17

further cascades and rivulets, with rustic decking to relax and steps to explore.

➜ Park in the centre of the village of Ilicochori (39.9801, 20.9104) and follow the signs 2.5km down to the waterfall. Returning takes about twice the time.

30 mins, 39.9750, 20.9172 🏕️🚶‍♂️🏊‍♂️🅱️

VIEWPOINTS

19 GRAMOS PEAK

This 2520m peak sits right at the border with Albania, affording incredible alpine panoramas in all directions. Wilderness and serenity abound – keep an eye out for brown bears.

➜ Continue 3km S along the ridgeline (and the national border) from Lake Gistova (see entry).

4 hours, 40.3483, 20.7795 📷🏔️🚶‍♂️🅿️🚗

20 SERVIA CASTLE

Still-substantial Byzantine castle ruins atop a hill fortified since antiquity, with never-ending views over local villages, forested lakes and mountains in the distance. A calming place with easy access.

➜ You can drive winding lanes roughly 1km S from the SW edge of Servia and almost to the castle, approaching on its W flank, but take care as you approach as the road gets rough.

3 mins, 40.1758, 22.0010 🏔️🚶‍♂️

LOCAL FOOD & DRINK

21 KONTOSOROS

Head here for excellent Macedonian winter cuisine, Greek classics with fusion twists and a superb wine cellar. There is also a guesthouse attached.

➜ Xino Nero 530 72, +30 2386 081256 40.6918, 21.6263 🐚

22 TAVERNA THOMAS

A stylish stalwart of northern Greek cuisine, and a crucial stop for any foodies in the region. Best known for delicious meat dishes, *trahanoto* (gourmet pasta made with Greek yoghurt) and a thorough, beautifully displayed selection of local wine.

➜ Sklithro 530 75, +30 2386 031206 40.6247, 21.5016 🅱️

23 MAGOUTES VINEYARD

Enjoy a wine tasting in the atmospheric cellars of this well-regarded winery, which grows local historical grape varieties in an impressive, stony landscape.

➜ Siatista 503 00, +30 2465 023236 40.2503, 21.5555 🍴🏊

24 PEKLARITIKO STEKI

Here in the heart of the mountains you will find an old school renovated into a guesthouse and traditional taverna, serving impeccable local and seasonal dishes. Wash down the meat-focused menu with the owner's own wine.

➜ Pigi 441 00, +30 69 8228 5455 40.0689, 20.7843 🏊

25 THEOCHARIS TAVERNA

Excellent home cooking served in Smixi's beautiful square under the generous shade of the plane trees. The baked mushroom and mushroom soup are particular highlights.

➜ Smixi 510 32, +30 2462 085230 40.0575, 21.1255 🍴🏊

26 SERENE STONE HOUSE

Peace and quiet abound from this beautiful stone house in the countryside, on the edge of a forest a short stroll from Prespa Lake. The owner and friends have thoughtfully renovated and custom-built furniture. Sleeps four.

→ Oxia 530 77, +30 69 4662 6243
40.7393, 21.1306 🏔️🔲

27 GRAMMOS LODGE

This wood-and-stone mountain lodge is a superb basecamp for exploring the surrounding mountains – particularly Gramos Peak (see entry) and Gistova Lake. Simple rooms of four bunks with a shared living area.

→ Gramos 520 51, +30 2467 890111
40.3933, 20.8359 🏕️🏔️🔲

28 AETOMILITSA HOSTEL

A rustic hostel in a tiny village providing an excellent basecamp for exploration of the surrounding mountains. Good food, friendly owners and affordable private rooms and dorm beds.

→ Aetomilitsa 440 15, +30 2655 031345
40.3093, 20.8536 🏔️🛏️🔲

29 SMOLIKA REFUGE

Secluded in a towering forest at the foot of Mount Smolikas, the highest peak in the Pindus Mountains, this simple mountain refuge is perfect for exploring the range. After sunset, the interior is illuminated solely by oil lamps. Generous hosts, a great pizza night and room for 24 people in four bunkrooms.

→ Paleoselli 440 19, +30 69 8176 6031
40.0697, 20.8898 🛏️🔲

30 VALIA CALDA REFUGE

Built in 2001 as a gathering place for adventurous folk wishing to explore Pindus National Park, this hostel sleeps 50 people across five bunk dorms, and has a restaurant. It's surrounded with sublime natural beauty, including the Aoos River Weir (see entry), basically in the back garden.

→ Vovousa 440 14, +30 2656 022200
39.9148, 21.0553 🔲

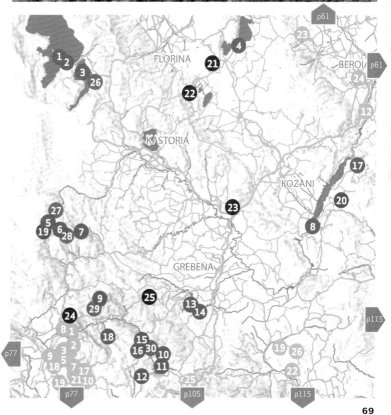

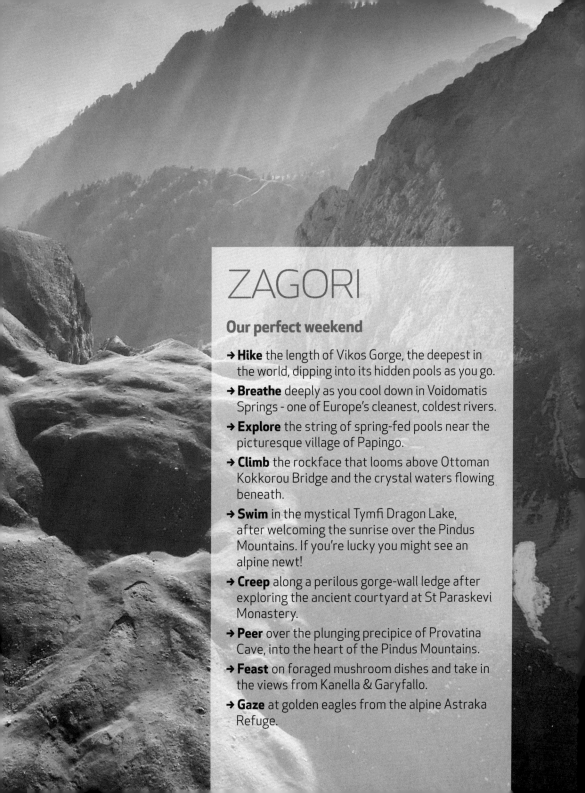

ZAGORI

Our perfect weekend

→ **Hike** the length of Vikos Gorge, the deepest in the world, dipping into its hidden pools as you go.

→ **Breathe** deeply as you cool down in Voidomatis Springs - one of Europe's cleanest, coldest rivers.

→ **Explore** the string of spring-fed pools near the picturesque village of Papingo.

→ **Climb** the rockface that looms above Ottoman Kokkorou Bridge and the crystal waters flowing beneath.

→ **Swim** in the mystical Tymfi Dragon Lake, after welcoming the sunrise over the Pindus Mountains. If you're lucky you might see an alpine newt!

→ **Creep** along a perilous gorge-wall ledge after exploring the ancient courtyard at St Paraskevi Monastery.

→ **Peer** over the plunging precipice of Provatina Cave, into the heart of the Pindus Mountains.

→ **Feast** on foraged mushroom dishes and take in the views from Kanella & Garyfallo.

→ **Gaze** at golden eagles from the alpine Astraka Refuge.

Little known to the throngs flocking to Athens and the islands, lush Zagori is home to some of Europe's most remarkable mountain landscapes. Three hours from Thessaloniki, you can descend into the world's deepest gorge, swim in pristine river pools beneath ancient stone bridges and climb to mythical alpine 'dragon lakes', named after duelling dragons that supposedly once perched on neighbouring Tymfi and Smolikas peaks.

Zagori is famed for its network of 18th-century villages, hidden away against lush mountain backdrops. Friendly tavernas like Mesochori and Thoukididis, proudly serving wild mushrooms and other foraged foothill delicacies, await at every turn. The villages are centred around splendid plane trees, and connected by a labyrinth of cobbled tracks and signature arched Ottoman bridges that once enabled trading routes. Kokkorou, Konitsa and Klidonia are arguably the finest, especially if you're after a swim.

Zagori's dizzying alpine landscape of forested ravines and snow-capped crags is criss-crossed by old mule tracks – a hiker's dream. With Saxonis Houses in pretty Papingo as a jumping-off point, venture into the mountains for a few days. Astraka Refuge is a splendid hiking base, close to the wondrous Tymfi Dragon Lake and Provatina Cave. Keep an eye out for golden eagles and brown bears!

The revitalising Papingo Rock Pools await upon your return, one of this region's many enchanting wild swims. You can find more by exploring Zagori's spectacular central artery, Vikos Gorge – at 1km the world's deepest. Following the river below the sheer limestone walls by foot brings you to Voidomatis Springs and Vikos Gorge Pools, where the spring air whirs with butterflies. For a more hair-raising perspective, opt for Agia Paraskevi Monastery's precipitous ledge or a striking ascent of Vradeto Steps.

RIVERS, SPRINGS & LAKES

1 AOOS RIVER

An abundance of refreshing dipping spots lie along this secluded stretch of river. In autumn, the surrounding forest theatrically frames the river with gorgeous yellows, oranges and reds. There is a via ferrata trail, too; Active Nature (+30 69 3766 7799) offers trips if you don't have the kit.

→ Park at either end of Konitsa Bridge (see entry) and follow the path that hugs the river upstream on the far side of the village.
45 mins, 40.0232, 20.7761

2 TYMFI DRAGON LAKE

This perfect bowl of a mountaintop lake, sitting among dramatic summits at 2050m, should be the crux of any trip to this area. At sunrise, climb the neighbouring peak to watch the range awaken before descending for a dip alongside alpine newts.

→ From Astraka Refuge (see entry) you can follow the clear path winding its way up the opposing valley wall to the lake.
4 hrs, 39.994, 20.7867

3 PAPINGO ROCK POOLS

A string of exhilaratingly cold natural limestone pools between extraordinary cliffs. Local daredevils jump into the first, or continue upstream for further delights. A fabulous family day out.

→ On the road to Mikro Papingo, about 1.2km beyond Papingo, you will meet the Rogovo River at a sharp turn just above the pools. Park in the layby before the bridge, cross and look for the wooden sign to the L. You will need canyoning equipment to travel more than 100m beyond the first pool.
5 mins, 39.9737, 20.7257

4 ANGASTROMENI SPRINGS

A picturesque, gorge-bottom chapel sitting beside a meandering spring. Enjoy the rich interior and bask in the turquoise waters before climbing back up.

→ Follow the path for Voidomatis Springs (see entry) from Vikos. Towards the end of the descent, at 39.9457, 20.7127, take the turn that doubles back L.
90 mins, 39.9486, 20.713

5 VOIDOMATIS SPRINGS

The river here is one of Europe's cleanest and coldest, at a gasping 5°C, making it an ideal spot to either cool off after a long hike or invigorate yourself to get started.

→ The path, signed for the Church of Theotokos Koimesis, starts from just S of Vikos village at a stone shrine and winds down to the springs. Alternatively, a steeper and more dramatic descent from Mikro Papigo (39.9677, 20.7292) takes an hour.
45 mins, 39.9458, 20.7149

6 VOIDOMATIS RIVER

Perhaps the most visited point of this wonderful river threading through Zagori, the Aristi Bridge is a launch point for rafting, canyoning, canoeing and river-trekking trips. Explore in either direction on foot for a secluded nook. For a perfect picnic, head downstream about 1km to 39.9530, 20.6880.

→ Parking is in a clearing by the N end of the bridge.
2 mins, 39.9444, 20.6874

7 VIKOS GORGE POOLS

Even in summer there are a number of pools just off the main path here in the heart of the gorge, behind a thin veil of trees. Float on your back and feel small as you let the world's deepest gorge engulf you.

→ From Vikos take the trail to Voidomatis Springs (see entry) then follow the path along the base of the gorge for a further 2km.
90 mins, 39.9165, 20.7492 ⬛⛰🧗🏕

BRIDGES

8 KONITSA BRIDGE

This majestic arched bridge, built in 1870, spans the aquamarine Aoos River, above frolicking locals and dogs. The hanging bell once warned of winds that made it too dangerous to cross with valuable freight.
→ The bridge is at the S end of Konitsa village, with places to park on both sides. For the S bank, follow the L sign for the bridge 1km S of Konitsa on the EO20 and continue 900m to end.
5 mins, 40.0364, 20.7451 ⬛🐾🏊

9 KLIDONIA BRIDGE

There has been a stone bridge crossing the turquoise Voidomatis River between sheer cliffs here for centuries; this one has stood since 1853. Below there is a delightful, shade-dappled pebble beach.

→ The bridge is signed to the L on a bend on the EO20 1km S of Klidonia. Turn L after 250m and continue to parking just before the bridge.
2 mins, 39.9678, 20.6634 ⬛🐾

10 KOKKOROU BRIDGE

First built in 1759, this is arguably Greece's finest Ottoman stone-arched bridge. It crosses cool, crystal swimming waters beneath towering rockfaces with bolted climbing routes. An idyllic scene for photographers, musers and adventurers alike.
→ Take the only road between Dilofo and Koukouli and you can't miss it as you head across the Voidomatis River on the road bridge.
1 min, 39.8622, 20.7753 ⬛🐾📷

11 PLAKIDA BRIDGE

The striking triple arches of this bridge create a picturesque river crossing. Be sure to include it in any tour of Zagori's signature bridges.
→ Park in the signed layby about 500m W of Kipi village and take the short winding path down to the bridge.
2 mins, 39.8617, 20.7864 🐾📷

13

12 LAZARIDIS BRIDGE

A classic, grass-covered Zagori gorge bridge with an overhanging rockface above, popular with rock climbers.

→ Park in the layby at the sharp bend by the road bridge just W of Kipi and walk the signed path into the gorge for 50m to the bridge.

2 mins, 39.8654, 20.7894 🚵🏊

WILD WONDERS

13 PROVATINA CAVE

First discovered in 1965 by British speleologists of the Cambridge University Caving Club, this vertical cave is one of the world's deepest, at 400m – a precipice opening dramatically into the mountain face. Try throwing a rock down!

→ Follow the path from Mikro Papingo towards Astraka Refuge (see entry). After about 4.5km, 1km before the refuge, there is a marked path with a sign to the cave. After another 1km the (hard to follow) faded path doubles back on itself and brings you to the entrance.

90 mins, 39.9639, 20.748 🥾🧗🏕️📷🔭🧗

14 VIKOS GORGE VIEW POINT

One of a number of superb viewpoints in the area for beholding the mighty Vikos Gorge. Beloi and Oxya viewpoints at the other end are just as spectacular.

→ Park in the shaded square of Vikos village, at the end of the road. Walk back 150m to the edge of the village and take the cobbled path L uphill to viewpoint.

5 mins, 39.9513, 20.7083 🏔️

15 STONE FOREST

Follow the maze of paths between these otherworldly layered rock formations, standing tall like trees. Kids will love to clamber around.

→ Park in the layby at the bend in the road 5km N from Monodendri.

1 min, 39.8934, 20.7434 🚵

16 ST PARASKEVI MONASTERY

This tiny, frescoed chapel is squeezed into a courtyard clinging to the lip of Vikos Gorge. The daring can explore beyond the monastery and tiptoe carefully along a narrow footpath notched into the sheer cliff face.

11

15

→ The winding, paved path to the monastery heads NE from Monodendri, signed from the main square at 39.8821, 20.7489.
15 mins, 39.8866, 20.7543 🏔️✝️🔻

17 VRADETO STEPS

An arresting ancient stone staircase hewn into the gorge, with commanding views. Until the road opened in the 1970s it was the only way into or out of Vradeto.

→ From Vradeto, head 250m E from the village to a trailhead at 39.8971, 20.7808, and continue 400m to the top of the steps. Allow 90 mins to climb back up from the bottom. To view the steps from across the gorge, park E of Kapesovo at 39.8895, 20.7865, just after a L fork signed Vikos Gorge. Walk 100m down the track into the gorge.
60 mins, 39.8952, 20.7861 🏔️🚶🔳

LOCAL FOOD & DRINK

18 SALVIA

Fine dining with a fine view, in a resort where tradition meets experimentation. Be sure to finish with the baklava. Or experience the full magic with a cooking class, where you will pick your ingredients from their garden.

→ Aristi 440 16, +30 2653 041330
39.9338, 20.6701 🍴🔳

19 MESOCHORI

Vaggelio and Panos will welcome you with open arms to this traditional Zagori taverna, sitting on a cute square. Get ready to savour seasonal dishes prepared with fresh ingredients foraged from the surrounding land.

→ Kato Pedina 440 07, +30 2653 071238
39.8794, 20.6753 🦌

20 ANEMI

A warm bar-restaurant-guesthouse-hostel fusion. Get cosy by the fire, use the loom, catch some music or meet fellow diners. A lovely mountain base either way.

→ Kato Pedina 440 07, +30 2653 072003
39.8789, 20.6747 🏇

21 KANELLA & GARYFALLO

Mushrooms are the star of the show here, with every dish built around the local delicacy (at slightly premium prices). A cosy interior opens onto another stunning view.

→ Vitsa 440 07, +30 2653 071671
39.8737, 20.7504 🔳

22 THOUKIDIDIS

A short menu using only the best local, seasonal and homegrown ingredients, including mushrooms picked from the overlooking mountains. Situated in a quaint village, with rooms available too.

➜ Kapesovo 440 10, +30 69 7998 3798
39.8884, 20.7804 ▨▨

STAY

23 ASTRAKA REFUGE

Perched at 1950m between Astraka and Tymfi peaks, this refuge (sometimes called Tymfi Refuge) is open from May to October. It's the perfect base for exploring Zagori's Pindus Mountains. Leave your bags and feast at the restaurant before going in search of golden eagles. Bunkroom accommodation for 50.

➜ Climb out of Mikro Papingo along the well-marked 03 route for 6km. After an hour you will emerge from shady woodland onto exposed hillside. There are water taps en route, but bring enough at the start. Call ahead on +30 69 7322 3100.
39.9789, 20.7686 ▨▨

24 SAXONIS HOUSES

Snuggled in the quintessential Zagori village of Papingo, this ivy-clad guesthouse oozes rural mountain charm. Join mountain activities organised by owner Vasilis in the day and recline by the living-room fire in the evening. Rooms sleep two to four.

➜ Papingo 440 04, +30 69 3715 1624
39.9691, 20.7174 ▨▨

25 ROKKA GUESTHOUSE

This charming guesthouse was the region's first to embrace agritourism, off the back of its sheep farm. Take the loom workshop, tour the farm and enjoy fabulous homemade food with fruit, vegetables, nuts and seeds from the surrounding land.

➜ Elafotopos 440 07, +30 69 4248 5213
39.9015, 20.6906 ▨

26 KIPI SUITES

Unpretentious mountain luxury in a stylish boutique hotel with staggering, signature Pindus Mountain views.

➜ Kipi 440 10, +30 2653 071995
39.8647, 20.7942 ▨

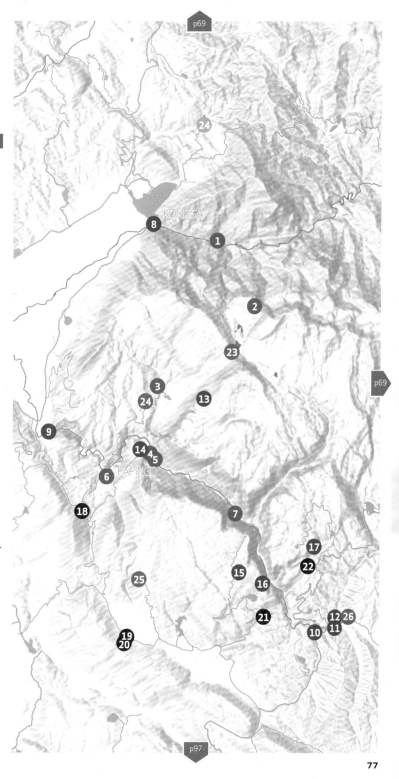

CORFU

Our perfect weekend

→ **Sample** Corfiot agrotourism with a farm-to-table feast and cottage stay at Bioporos Organic Farm, on the shoreline of protected Korission Lagoon.

→ **Marvel** an afternoon away at Corfu's coastal jewel in the crown, gorgeous Giali Beach.

→ **Captain** a boat for the day to explore the hidden beaches, emerald waters and secret sea caves around Palaiokristitsa.

→ **Stroll** the hillside donkey path of Makrades as the sun sinks, finishing with a cooling skinny dip.

→ **Savour** both sunrise and sunset from Porto Timoni's spectacular twin beaches.

→ **Dream** among the trees in one of Vradi Estate's enchanting woodland cottages or cabins.

→ **Plunge** through dense forest to hidden Vrachli Beach, on Corfu's northeastern tip.

→ **Journey** to Othonio's paradisal Aspri Ammos Beach, and explore around the corner to the remarkable Calypso Sea Cave.

From the low-lying south to the crescendo of its northwestern peaks, luscious Corfu promises a wonderful array of secret adventures. Dotted with hidden caves and secluded bays, and with no shortage of homegrown cuisine and cultural artefacts scattered across the hills, this is a place where you could happily linger for some time.

The twisting cobbles of Corfu city's Venetian Old Town, a designated UNESCO World Heritage Site, make a fine starting point. The Corfu Food Tour – a walking sampling of spinach pies, caramelised almonds, figs, noumboulo, olive oil, honey and more – is a delicious way to explore and get acquainted. On the edge of town, Mon Repos pier offers a refreshing swim on the fringes of a verdant estate.

Corfu's western coastline is a string of wonders, many hidden down sleepy, sandy tracks. Although Porto Timoni Beach might protest, the jewel in the crown is comparatively unknown Giali Beach – a boulder-pocked crystal bay snuggled between steep cliffs. Further north, the abundant hidden beaches and sea caves around Palaiokastritsa promise a fantastic boating day, perhaps followed by a moonlit drink and dip in La Grotta Bar, on terraces above tempting sea pools. And in the middle of it all, Bioporos Organic Farm's pioneering agrotourism, alive with animals on the shore of Korission Lagoon, makes a splendid basecamp.

To the north-east Corfu grows higher and wilder, the adventuring a little more intrepid. Nissaki Cave and nearby Grava Tou Damou Cave both require some questing, the first on land and the second across water. Loutses Hollow, above the Ionian, conceals an impressive cave in its sunken depths. And the thickly forested cape east of Kogevinas harbours hidden gems, Vrachli Beach chief among them.

Corfiot adventure extends beyond the island itself, to the magical outpost of Othonoi, the largest of the Diapontian Islands to the north-west. Aspri Ammos Beach, and Calypso Sea Cave burrowing into the sheer rock formations protecting it, make a memorable excursion, seemingly a million miles from anywhere.

8

SEA CAVES

1 CALYPSO SEA CAVE

An imposing, swimmable sea cave on remote Othonoi, with two entrances and a beach inside. It is by the spectacular Aspri Ammos beach (see entry), but hidden behind a sheer outcrop.

→ Accessible only by boat, which you can arrange at Avlakia marina in Othonoi port. You'll need to swim from the boat, not the beach.
5 mins, 39.8418, 19.3791

2 CANAL D'AMOUR

A series of carved limestone inlets with protected water, beaches, jumping ledges and swimming caves. Though busy and loudly marketed, tucked as they are behind Sidari's bustling hotels, they remain a beautiful coastal feature and a pleasant respite from the town.

→ There are multiple signed paths from Sidari high street to the wider beach (walk L from there to the inlets) and the inlets themselves, which are behind Zafiris Hotel Spa Resort. There is also a quieter inlet to the E (39.7960, 19.7023) when walking R from the main beach).
5 mins, 39.7973, 19.698

3 GRAVA TOU DAMOU CAVE

This secret sea cave, with three mouths leading to a little beach, lies on a tree-lined stretch of coast riddled with karst formations to explore.

→ 400m from the N end of Ipsos beach, only accessible by water. You can adventure swim (hugging the coast), hire a boat from Ipsos or rent a kayak or paddleboard from Dassia Ski Club further S on Dassia beach (+30 69 8978 3729).
30 mins, 39.7076, 19.8501

4 BLUE EYE CAVE

An underwater archway you can swim through, framing fish silhouetted against a magical blue light when viewed from the shore side. Remember your goggles!

→ Accessible only by boat. Hire at Alipa port in Palaiokastritsa: Dinos (+30 69 7375 4561) and Mariolis Boat Rental (+30 69 8774 1960) are both good. Boat tours also often stop here.
2 mins, 39.6714, 19.7141

BEACHES

5 ASPRI AMMOS BEACH

This sumptuous white-sand beach, lapped by bright turquoise water and backed by towering cliffs, is the jewel in the crown of Othonoi island. The Calypso sea cave (see entry) is nearby.

→ Accessible only by boat, which you can arrange at Avlakia marina in Othonoi; the same boat may take you to the sea cave.
1 min, 39.8423, 19.3832

6 VRACHLI BEACH

A secret shingle beach deep in a forested peninsula, shaded by an overhanging canopy. Beyond the odd boat pulling in quietly to moor, nothing will interrupt your views across the Ionian Sea to Albania.

→ Park at Avlaki Beach and take the path at its NE end to Avlaki East Beach. Turn R and walk 200m inland, then turn L on a bend (39.7815, 19.9456). Walk 500m through thick forest to Vrachli Beach.
10 mins, 39.7853, 19.9448

7 ARIAS BEACH

Thick trees along an overgrown path protect this sleepy pebble beach. Driftwood dots the shoreline and Albania's Butrint National Park lies over the shallow, clear water.

→ Follow directions for Vrachli Beach (see entry) but ignore the final L turn. Instead, continue 400m and turn L into the forest

(39.7787, 19.9480). From here it's 100m to the beach.

10 mins, 39.7795, 19.9484 🏊🚶🏃

8 PORTO TIMONI BEACH

A stunning peninsula that narrows between two back-to-back protected beaches, rewarding wild campers with sunset and sunrise. The approach path has breathtaking views and continues to the tiny cave chapel of St Stylianos.

→ There is parking in Afionas village, including on scrubby land at the S end where the path begins (39.7208, 19.6589). Follow it 850m S to the beach.

10 mins, 39.7152, 19.6578 🏊🚣🏖✝🏕🅰🅱

9 LIMNI BEACH

This double-sided white-pebble beach connects the land to an outcrop with a small cave and snorkellable rock pools. Overlooking Palaiokastritsa to the N, it is relatively quiet thanks to the somewhat tricky access.

→ On the road from Liapades down to Liapades Beach, fork L uphill opposite the supermarket (39.6710, 19.7368). Turn R at the T junction after 200m, then fork L and follow the road just over 1km up and over the ridge, to where a path signed 'Limni' starts (39.6640, 19.7281).

5 mins, 39.6655, 19.7239 🏊🚣🏃❓

10 LLIODOROS BEACH

Tranquility awaits on a magical beach in a deep, protected bay hiding beyond a series of dense olive groves.

→ From Liapades start following directions for Limni beach (see entry), but turn L at 39.6665, 19.7290, just after a sharp R. Park here to walk 3km, or further along the progressively narrowing track. Turn R 350m from the start (39.6647, 19.7318), and follow the main track just over 2km to the beach, keeping L at 1km (39.6559, 19.7308).

40 mins, 39.6561, 19.7241 🏊🚣❓🏃

11 STELARI BEACH

This long sandy beach with aquamarine waters is accessible only by boat. Artful rock formations extend around the north-western end, pocked with small caves and jumping ledges.

→ Rent a boat from Alipa port in Palaiokastritsa: Dinos (+30 69 7375 4561) and Mariolis Boat Rental (+30 69 8774 1960) are both good for a wonderful day along this coastline.

2 mins, 39.6466, 19.7343 🍴🏊🚣🏊🏃

12

12 GIALI BEACH

The jewel in the crown of Corfu's coastline. A paradisal cove of turquoise water cocooned by sheer cliffs. Large boulders offer climbing and jumping opportunities. Bring your snorkel, book and lunch and bliss the day away.

→ From Giannades village follow country lanes SW to park by the Chapel of the Prophet Elias at 39.6248, 19.7544. Follow the track heading SW towards the sea for 700m to a dramatically steep, rope-and-ladder final descent.

15 mins, 39.6212, 19.7559 🍴🏊🏼‍♂️🥾♿🛶🏊

13 MIRTIOTISSA BEACH

A micro beach tucked at the bottom of a steep lane, busy but beautiful. Swimmers, many naked, glide between large rocks rising from the crystal water. Fantastic swimming and secluded shallows on either side make it worthwhile (as does the taverna above).

→ Heading SE out of Vatos village, turn uphill, signed Church of St Nikolaos. After about 1km, the beach turning is signed R. Parking after 1km opposite Elia Taverna makes the most sense, given the steep, narrow descent to the beach.

3 mins, 39.5957, 19.7995 🍴🏊🏼‍♂️🥾♿🛶B

14 SKALA HARBOUR

Small breakwaters protect this picturesque double bay guarding local fishing boats and swimmers alike in the clear, calm shallows.

→ From the coast road to Skala, about 2.8km S of Pentati, a steep, paved road turns R and descends to the beach. Park a little above the final section (39.5081, 19.8511), if you're worried about re-ascending.

1 min, 39.5106, 19.8499 🛶🏊

15 ST NIKOLAOS BEACH

A picturesque church sits on this small sunset-facing beach. A rock-carved channel welcomes the sea at high tide and black seaweed lines the water's edge.

→ On the coast road about 650m S of Skala, park on the road amidst the olive groves (39.4954, 19.8538). A track opposite leads to a short, rough path on the R by the only building.

3 mins, 39.4959, 19.8513 🏊✝️

16 PSARAS BEACH

An unassuming shingle beach with calm water, tree shade and a view of the mainland. Tucked just off the coastal lane, it's ideal for a break as you travel along the island.

16

18

→ Park in a small layby by the shore just over 1km SE from Psarat (39.4674, 19.9557). Walk back W about 30m to a short path R to the beach.

2 mins, 39.4678, 19.9544 🏊🚶

17 GREAT DANCE BEACH

There is local fishing activity at the N end of this quiet, expansive beach. Clearer waters and cleaner sand than the neighbouring beach beneath Kritika Terrace (see entry).

→ In Vitalades turn S off the main street opposite Pizza Agrotica and follow it 2km to a sandy car park at the top of a track (39.4019, 20.0055). Unless you have a 4x4, park here and walk just over 1km down to the beach.

15 mins, 39.3973, 20.0048 🚶🏊🚶

18 KRITIKA BEACH TERRACE

Stop at the hillside picnic area, gazing over a sweeping beach dotted with fishing paraphernalia and across the twinkling sea to Paxos, or stroll down to the beach. A fine spot to watch the sun disappear with a hamper and a bottle of red.

→ From the convenience store in Kritika, head W for 150m and turn L. Follow the road 900m and park in a layby on the L (39.3868,

20.0474). Walk 150m to the table or a further 500m down to the beach.

2 mins, 39.3854, 20.0464 🏊🚶🏞🏕🏊

CAPES, LAGOONS & PIERS

19 DRASTIS CAPE

Though foot access to this wind-sculpted cape is prohibited, the evening light on its limestone arcs is magnificent. Walk one switchback down for peace if the viewpoint is crowded, and continue to a small natural harbour for swimming rocks and cape boat tours.

→ Follow signs N from the Church of St Nikolaos in Peroulades, and park after 600m (39.7936, 19.6726). Continue on foot 190m to the viewpoints.

5 mins, 39.7984, 19.6741 🍴🚶🏞🏕Ⓑ

20 KASSIOPI CAPE

A pretty cape beyond busy Bataria Beach. Plenty of nooks to enjoy, with patches of long, yellow grass and smoothed rock slabs leading to sea pools.

→ A small coastal road runs 1.5km around the larger headland from Kassiopi village. Park in the village for a longer walk, or in a small parking area at the neck of the cape.

1 min, 39.7943, 19.9196 🚶🏊Ⓑ

21 MON REPOS PIER

The grounds of 18th-century Mon Repos Estate are themselves worthy of a stroll, but even better is this stone pier protruding into a shallow, wooded bay. Locals and tourists gather between dips, and pine-shaded benches sit on the outcrop above.

→ The estate entrance (€4; open 8.30am – 3.30pm) is on Feakon (39.6077, 19.9229). Follow a wooded path via the museum to the pier. Alternatively, a scruffy alley leads from opposite the back of a cemetery on Analipsi (39.6007, 19.9248) down steps to a rocky beach; head L to the pier. Free road parking either way.

10 mins, 39.6031, 19.9267 🏊🚶🚴🚶🌲

22 KORISSION LAGOON

This protected wetland is abundant with flamingos, turtles, orchids and other flora and wildlife. A short canal through the enclosing sandbar joins it to the sea, flanked by a cedar forest and dune-backed beaches sprinkled with windsurfers and campervans.

→ A sandy track with ample parking runs from Chalikounas between the beach and lagoon, ending at the canal and cedar forest.

1 min, 39.4404, 19.9013 🏕🚶

CAVES

23 LOUTSES HOLLOW

An atmospheric chasm with vertical walls, carved into the arid foothills overlooking north-east Corfu. Birdsong floats above the vegetation, and a considerable cave burrows into the N wall. The jagged lip presents sumptuous sea views.

→ Take a paved mountain road S from Loutses village, signed Anapaftiria. Turn R after 450m, hairpin L in another 750m and continue to a short trail just above the hollow, with parking beside the road.

1 min, 39.7772, 19.8906

24 NISSAKI CAVE

Thick olive groves hide the secret entrance to this little-known cave. It descends a gentle but slick 75m into blackness, its floor and roof adorned with stalagmites and stalactites. Proceed with appropriate equipment, a good light and caution.

→ In the coastal village of Katavolos, on a bend 20m uphill from the Shell garage, follow a 'House On The Rocks' sign down a driveway. Take the narrow path along the R side of the house. The cave is 20m beyond, downhill on the R.

5 mins, 39.728, 19.9121

25 ROVINIA CAVE AND THE HOLE OF HA

At the southern end of this pleasant beach is an imposing arched cave. A ledge runs from the cave's back corner up a makeshift ladder to a forested perch overlooking the beach. A trail continues to the Hole of Ha, a roofless sea cave popular with scuba divers. A fun escapade.

→ On the road from Liapades down to Liapades Beach, take a L fork uphill opposite the supermarket (39.6710, 19.7368). Turn R at the T junction after 200m, then fork R and continue to the beach. The road steepens near the end. Parking at the beach is €3 per day, or find a roadside spot. Walk time varies depending on where you park.

5 mins, 39.6703, 19.727

26 GRAVA GARDIKI CAVE

This small cave, nestled in a fantastically pock-marked cliff in an olive grove, was occupied by humans as much as 20,000 years ago. It overlooks the silver-green blanket of southern Corfu – including a Byzantine fort about 350m away.

→ The cave and fortress are signed 1.5km SE of Agios Matheos, near the Revoil garage. Proceed 1.2km (turn L for the fort at 800m) and park at the start of a small footpath

(39.4781, 19.8812). Follow it 100m uphill into the olive grove, trending slightly R.
2 mins, 39.4792, 19.8816 ⬛️🔺️🏊️

RUINS & WALKS

27 OLD SINIES

Abandoned in the 1960s, this remote, crumbling village lies in the shadow of Pantokrator, Corfu's highest peak. Wandering through its church and homestead carcasses is an evocative experience.

→ Follow the road N from Corfu Aquamarine Hotel in Nissaki, zigzag up for 1.7km to a L (39.7316, 19.8900), continue 700m up to a L on a switchback corner (39.7350, 19.8883) and then 4.3km to a final R into the village. Without a 4x4 or quad you may want to walk the final 2km. Alternatively drive up to the telecoms station and monastery atop Mount Pantokrator, and hike 45 mins down its E face (75 mins back up).
30 mins, 39.7444, 19.8819 ♿️👤️❓️🏊️

28 MAKRADES DONKEY PATH

One of Corfu's old donkey paths, or kalderimis, skirting steep hillsides with spectacular views due west. A wonderful stroll, ideally as the sun sets, with the option to descend for a cooling sea dip at secluded rock pools.

→ Follow the road W (bearing N) out of Makrades village for about 1km to a trailhead (39.6912, 19.6813) with some parking. Follow the path N around a hillside, turn L at a bigger track and L again after 600m (39.6943, 19.6792) to rock pools (1.5km in all).
20 mins, 39.6916, 19.6807 ⬛️🔺️👤️

29 ANGELOKASTRO

A Byzantine acropolis spectacularly sited on a precipitous outcrop, giving a magnificent panorama of Corfu's north-western coast. Probably built in the 13th century, it was never conquered, even during multiple Ottoman sieges.

→ Signed from the road just S of Makrades. Follow it 1.3km to a small parking area. Entrance is €3, free for children.
2 mins, 39.6782, 19.6868 ⬛️🔺️♿️🅱️👤️

30 VIRGIN MARY MONASTERY

Wild clematis and bryony are reclaiming the ruins of this small 17th-century monastery, which are perched on the southern tip of the island between thick forest and cliffs tumbling into the ocean below.

→ The monastery is signed S of Kavos (39.3775, 20.1137). Continue 1.7km, keeping L at fork after 1km, to parking (39.3668, 20.1124). Walk on 800m along the forested, cliffside track to the monastery, bending R after 500m.

10 mins, 39.3641, 20.1074 🖼️🏔️🚶🏃

LOCAL FOOD & DRINK

31 ST ANDREAS TAVERNA

A much-loved taverna hiding down a winding lane on Corfu's northern shore. Fantastically fresh seafood and sea views across to Albania.
→ Karousades 490 81, +30 2663 031488
39.7978, 19.7516 🏖️⚓

32 O FOROS

Enjoy delicious traditional recipes at excellent prices in this charming taverna. It's tucked away in Old Perithia, Corfu's oldest village, abandoned in the 1960s but undergoing a sleepy, picturesque resurgence.
→ Perithia 491 00, +30 69 5595 0459
39.7647, 19.8749 🌀

33 CORFU BEER

A family-run microbrewery producing ales, lagers and IPAs with natural ingredients. There is a free tour on Saturdays, and a beer festival featuring local and international musicians every September.
→ Arillas Magouladon 490 81, +30 2663 052072
39.7494, 19.6568 🍴

34 TOULA'S SEASIDE

Right on the shore at Agni beach, this is a world-class dining experience fusing Mediterranean and Corfiot cuisine, specialising in fish dishes. Justly expensive.
→ Kerkira 490 83, +30 2663 091350
39.7362, 19.9293 🏖️⚓💶

35 LA GROTTA BAR

This popular but mellow bar is perched in an inlet above a natural swimming pool with a diving board. Visit at night, when it's quieter and the water is illuminated.
→ Palaiokastritsa 409 83, +30 2663 041006
39.6738, 19.7188 🍽️🏖️⚓🅱️

36 THEOTOKY ESTATE

A lush vineyard cradled in rolling hills, owned by the politically renowned Theotoky family. Enjoy estate wine tasting, guesthouse accommodation and estate-pressed olive oil.
→ Ropa Valley 491 00, +30 69 4559 3016
39.6279, 19.7864 🍴

37 CORFU FOOD TOUR

Take a delightful three-hour ramble through historic Corfu's food markets, traders and artisans. Savour Corfiot pies, oils, butters, meze, yoghurts and more. Skip breakfast!
→ Daily tours (Sunday on request) at 10am and 6pm, €70pp. Start at the Statue of Schulenburg in front of the Old Fortress, +30 69 4589 4450.
39.6236, 19.9257 🚶💶

38 AMBELONAS

A vineyard and restaurant nestled in the rolling hills near Corfu. Sit beneath shady vines and savour local dishes accompanied by choice estate wines, or take a Corfiot cooking class culminating in a five-course meal. A cultural programme of talks, workshops, films and exhibitions runs through the year.
→ Agia Triada 491 00, +30 69 3215 8888
39.6063, 19.8512 🍴🐾

39 SAVVAS TAVERNA

This family taverna serves simple, tasty food from a delightful terrace overlooking the Straits of Corfu. Stroll through the gardens or take a dip in the azure waters after eating.
→ Notos 490 80, +30 2662 051742
39.4441, 20.0068 🏖️⚓

STAY

40 VRADI ESTATE TREEHOUSE

A cabin on stilts surrounded by trees, with a beautifully lit open-plan room. A balcony crafted from knobbled branches overlooks a hammock, working stables and a vegetable garden you're free to pick from. The enchanting estate offers other cottages, forest houses and rooms set in pastured woodland.
→ Ano Korakiana 490 83, +30 69 4670 8707
39.6977, 19.8028 🐾☕

41 ONCE UPON A WOODENHOUSE

A cute, minimalist wooden cabin hiding in the leafy Corfu city suburbs. Space for four across a mezzanine and sofa bed.
→ Kanali 491 00
39.6065, 19.8922

42 PELEKAS OLIVE GROVE OASIS

Enjoy fruit from the trees, herbs from the garden and sunrise from the lookout tower at this small glamping oasis. Two tents, a hammock tent and a wooden cabin - all sleeping two - and a simple, shared kitchen and toilet, with everything solar-powered.

→ Pelekas 491 00, airbnb.com/
rooms/50701095
39.5913, 19.816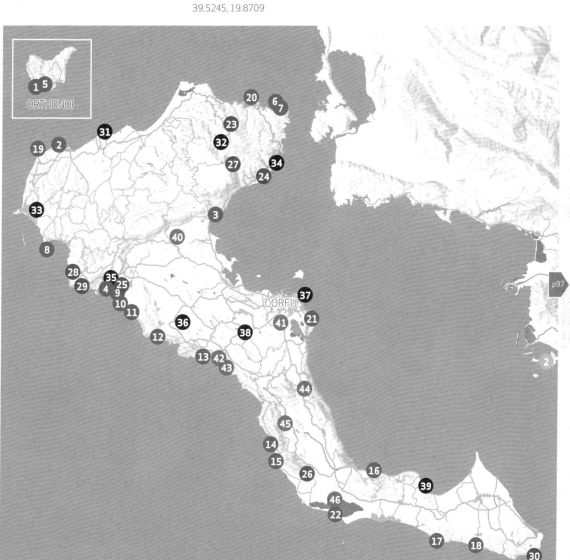

43 SUNROCK BACKPACKERS HOSTEL

The recent arrival of paved roads turned this old hippy stopover into a relaxed hostel enjoying a spectacular panorama from a quiet hillside. The rooms are simple, breakfast and communal dinner are included and the beach is a walk away. Cash only.

→ Kontogialos 490 84, +30 2661 094637
39.582, 19.822

44 ST NICHOLAS RANCH

Two simple mobile homes, each sleeping up to six, set by a horse paddock among rolling hills dotted with poplars. Host Eleftheria will be happy to arrange a guided ride.

→ Benitses 490 84, +30 69 8681 1444
39.5483, 19.9008

45 KATO PAVLIANA CABINS

Two magical double storey wooden cabins, each sleeping two. Large windows, wooden interiors and quirky features. Shared pool.

→ Kato Pavliana 490 84, +30 69 3732 7076
39.5245, 19.8709

46 BIOPOROS ORGANIC FARM

Bees and free-roaming donkeys, sheep and chickens populate this idyllic family farm pioneering Corfiot agrotourism. The organic restaurant uses farm produce, and you can take traditional workshops and cooking classes. Two houses sleeping five are reasonably priced, with free camping for farm volunteers.

→ Vrakaniotika 490 80, +30 2661 076224
39.4526, 19.9045

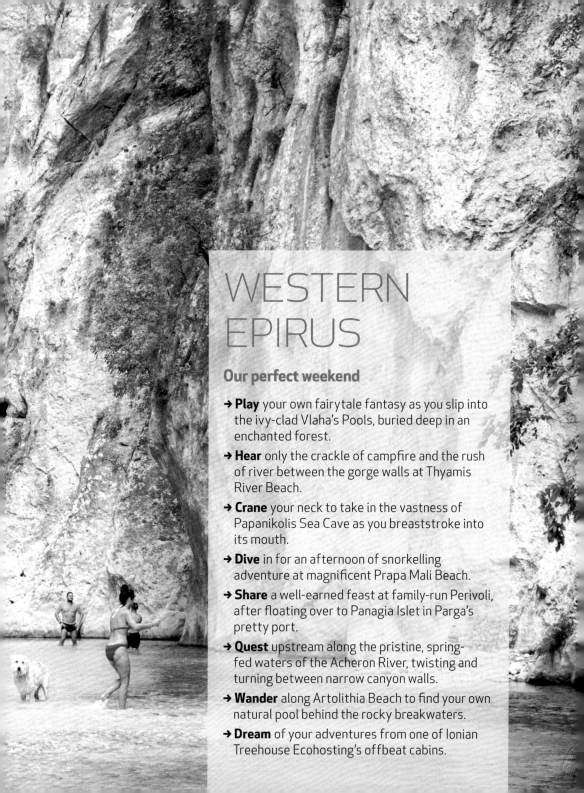

WESTERN EPIRUS

Our perfect weekend

→ **Play** your own fairytale fantasy as you slip into the ivy-clad Vlaha's Pools, buried deep in an enchanted forest.

→ **Hear** only the crackle of campfire and the rush of river between the gorge walls at Thyamis River Beach.

→ **Crane** your neck to take in the vastness of Papanikolis Sea Cave as you breaststroke into its mouth.

→ **Dive** in for an afternoon of snorkelling adventure at magnificent Prapa Mali Beach.

→ **Share** a well-earned feast at family-run Perivoli, after floating over to Panagia Islet in Parga's pretty port.

→ **Quest** upstream along the pristine, spring-fed waters of the Acheron River, twisting and turning between narrow canyon walls.

→ **Wander** along Artolithia Beach to find your own natural pool behind the rocky breakwaters.

→ **Dream** of your adventures from one of Ionian Treehouse Ecohosting's offbeat cabins.

Western Epirus includes the region's long western coastline and the first rumbles of mountain terrain that explodes inland in Eastern Epirus and Zagori. It may lack the majesty of its neighbours, but its shoreline is a string of charming ports, delightful beaches and atmospheric sea caves, and the river adventures and sacred sanctuaries of its inner undulations hint at the wild wonders nearby.

The village of Syvota may be the jewel in the coastal crown, nudging out into an archipelago of deep-green islets. Hire a boat and putter about for a splendid day. Blue Lagoon Beach grabs the headlines, but its beauty is often buried beneath a carnival of jostling boats; the golden curl of Diapori Beach, sheltered in a channel between Mourtos and Agios Nikolaos islets, is far more calming. For something spicier, navigate to Mourtos' seaward side for a stirring swim into the jaws of Papanikolis Sea Cave. Back on dry land, you may have time for sunset at Dei Plus Beach, guarded by forested headlands and jumping rocks. Retiring to Sivota's Secret Villa will complete the romance.

Further south, the tiny town of Parga is another lovely jumping-off point. Panagia Islet makes a fine micro-expedition in the heart of the handsome harbour; you can swim or float across to its church and bathing nooks from St Giannakis Beach. Follow it with hearty local dishes from Perivoli's pretty garden or Sakis' sunset-facing street tables. Next morning, head south and paddle or pedal out to Aphrodite's Cave, where the ancient god of love and beauty is reputed to have bathed in the shimmering sea caverns. And perhaps continue to Alonaki Fanariou Beach, in a magnificent bay encircled by aromatic pine headlands.

Delving inland, Western Epirus whispers of the alpine splendour west and north, and nowhere more so than where the Souli mountains rise from the plains into a great horseshoe valley. Contemplate the vistas from Kougi Monastery and Kiafa Castle – the first a site of legendary resistance against Albanian potentate Ali Pasha, the second a relic of his rule. But the essential stop here is Acheron Springs, where the heavenly spring-fed waters of the Acheron River wind through a delectable canyon. Greek mythology holds this to be one of the five rivers of the underworld, transporting newly dead souls to Hades. But don't fear; life reigns here.

BEACHES

1 THYAMIS RIVER BEACH

A large river beach of big smooth pebbles in the heart of the grand valley of the Thyamis River – believed by some to have passed its name to the Thames in England with ancient Celtic migrants. Beware the fast current if swimming.

→ Follow the main road S then W 2.5km from Pente Ekklisies and park just before the bridge in the layby on the R, before the gate (39.5898, 20.4586). The beach is 50m beyond the gate.

5 mins, 39.5908, 20.4576 🅿🏕️🚶🅅

2 KORFU BEACH

You're unlikely to be disturbed at this lovely pebbled bay, secluded from the busier beaches to the east by a quiet headland.

→ Follow the coast road W from Nea Selfkia to the W end of Makrigiali Beach. Fork L and drive 2.9km along the track, ignoring a L on a R hairpin. Park on the side of the dirt road behind the beach.

2 mins, 39.5179, 20.1706 🚗🏊🅿🏕️🚶

3 DEI PLUS BEACH

This small, rounded cove is a low-key gem, protected by rocky, tree-lined headlands on either side that double up as great jumping spots. Hidden around the corner from better known Dei Beach, it is often called Dei Plus.

→ Follow the coast road NW from Syvota marina about 1.5km. There is space for a couple of cars at the sharp R bend (39.4178, 20.2302). Walk 150m downhill through the scattered trees.

5 mins, 39.4171, 20.2295 🍴🚗🏊🅿🏕️

4 DIAPORI BEACH

This tiny wave-shaped beach, curled in a channel between the islets of Mourtos and Agios Nikolaos, makes a great pit stop on a boat trip around Syvota's lush archipelago.

→ Boat access only, with good options in Syvota; try Sivota Boat (+30 69 4565 9465).

1 min, 39.4024, 20.2246 🚗🏊🅿🅱

5 STAVROLIMENA BEACH

A deep, picture-postcard cove with shallow, pristine waters, backed by trees for shade. A fine alternative to the more developed Arillas Beach nearby.

→ Follow the coastal road 1km or so S from the parking area behind Arillas Beach, bearing

R on a big L bend after 500m and continuing 550m to pull off carefully near the track (39.3489, 20.2872). Walk the short trail down.

3 mins, 39.3493, 20.2864 🚗🏊

6 PRAPA MALI BEACH

A remarkably secluded sandy beach with rock pools for snorkelling, surrounded by lush, steep hills. Popular with campers.

→ Head SE from Karavostasi and turn R after around 1.2km (39.3314, 20.3026). Unless you have a 4x4, park at the junction in 1.7km (39.3276, 20.2979). Walk 1.3km down the R fork to either end of the beach. The path is well-marked.

20 mins, 39.3251, 20.2925 🚗🏊🚫🏕️🚶

7 AGIOS SOSTIS BEACH

Remote, calm waters harbouring a large jumping rock (with a rope to climb up). Combine with a trip to nearby St Sostis Church (see entry).

→ By car, follow the tracks from Chrisogiali in the E for 4km and park on the hairpin by the church. It's also a 2.5km walk from Sarakiniko Beach to the W; you can drive this route with a 4x4, but will need to park at the R turn after 1.4km with a normal car.

5 mins, 39.2852, 20.3544 🍴🚗🏊🅿🏕️🚶⛵

8 PANAGIA ISLET

A picturesque pine-clad islet and popular wedding spot in the waters of Parga port. Take flip-flops or shoes in a dry bag to explore the church and various bathing spots.

→ Quickest, and most fun, access is by wading, swimming or floating 100m from the W end of St Giannakis beach.

10 mins, 39.2816, 20.4019 🏊🚶

9 ST GIANNAKIS BEACH

An idyllic cove with a small beach, calm snorkelling waters and a shaded cantina for refreshments.

→ Head E from Agia Kiriaki, fork R after around 1.7km (39.2823, 20.4617) and follow the main track to parking set back from the beach, behind the cafe.

2 mins, 39.2797, 20.4663 🏊🚶🐾

10 AMONI BEACH

This rocky cove shelters a true micro beach, with pockets of sand enough for only a few. A cute alternative to the more popular Skala Beach nearby. If you're up for a 150m swim there's a delightful sea cave.

→ Around 2.8km SW of Valanidorrachi on the road S of the river, with space for a few cars

in a sandy area behind the beach. Sea cave at 39.2120, 20.4924.

1 min, 39.2116, 20.4949 🏊🚶

11 ALONAKI FANARIOU BEACH

A sumptuous semi-circular cove guarded by steep, tree-lined cliffs, with a huge rock in the centre for adventurous swimmers and jumpers and a chilled cafe. The beach gets busy, so arrive early or come for a sunset dip.

→ Drive as for Amoni Beach (see entry) but turn L around 1.8km from central Valanidorrachi (39.2109, 20.5061). Continue 500m to parking amid trees on the cliff behind the beach.

5 mins, 39.2060, 20.5052 🍴🏊🚶🅱

12 ARTOLITHIA BEACH

A chain of protective rocky breakwaters creates a calm swimming area here. Head south along the beach for further seclusion.

→ On the coastal road about 4.3km NW from Pidima Kiras turn L and park in the clearing as you arrive at the N end of the beach.

3 mins, 39.1145, 20.6074 🏊🚶🅱

14

13 KASTROSIKIA BEACH

Uninterrupted sandy beach stretching for 2km. Just to the south of Pidima Kiras village is the seemingly endless 10km Monolithi Beach, also well worth a stop.

→ Park anywhere along the coastal road that runs along the length of the beach NW out of Pidima Kiras, and walk down through the shrubs.

2 mins, 39.1014, 20.6301 🏊🚣▲🚶

SPRINGS & WATERFALLS

14 VLAHA'S POOLS

This enchanted waterfall and pool on a Kalamas River tributary is draped in moss and ivy, and hidden deep in thick forest beneath higgledy-piggledy boughs.

→ Take a narrow lane NW from W Voutsaras (39.6687, 20.5870). Keep L past the buildings then fork R at 1km. The road is unpaved and rocky, so take care. The footpath starts at a small sign marking a walking route on the L 1.6km after this (39.6834, 20.5757). Follow the path for 15 mins to the pool. There is a rope for easy access and a bench for soaking it all up.

15 mins, 39.6796, 20.5698 🏊🚶🌀

15 SOUILI WATERMILL

A picturesque abandoned watermill with a tumble of rivulets running through it and down the old steps to a small river. Take a stroll downstream beneath shady plane trees to an unfussy, family-run cafe.

→ Drive N then E from Glyki, starting with steep switchbacks, to a sharp R at 9.6km signed for mills. Follow it 1.4km and park by the mill.

2 mins, 39.3581, 20.6305 🚶

16 ACHERON SPRINGS

A renowned spring-fed river running through a delectable narrow canyon. Paddling and wading your way upstream and back, past bubbling springs and small pebble beaches, is a wonderful experience. The water is icy at the start, near the springs, but warms as you quest. Allow two hours for a full exploration.

→ The canyon extends E from Glyki. From the car park just to the E of the village, follow a path along the L bank for 200m to the entry point.

10 mins, 39.3277, 20.6234 🏊🚶 B

SEA CAVES

17 PAPANIKOLIS SEA CAVE

A towering sea cave gazing south from

15

17

Mourtos Islet into the Ionian. It's an exhilarating swim inside, but be careful of boats and choppy water.

→ By boat only, with good options in Syvota. Try Sivota Boat (+30 69 4565 9465).
2 mins, 39.3992, 20.2174 🏖️🛶🏊🔺▽❄️

18 APHRODITE'S CAVE

According to legend, Aphrodite used to bathe in this deep sea cave. Its shimmering waters make for a wonderful mini expedition, but try to pick a calm day.

→ Boat access only, except for extremely strong swimmers. You can rent a pedalo or kayak for roughly €15 per hour from Lichnos Beach, 500m away.
15 mins, 39.2782, 20.4455 🏊🏖️🛶🏖️❄️

SACRED PLACES & RUINS

19 OSDINA CHURCH

A late-Byzantine construction, this church is the region's oldest building, part of the remains of an ancient settlement revived in that era. You can see why it was built here, sprawled along the ridge with huge views over the Thyamis River valley.

→ Head SW from Pente Ekklisies village as if for Thyamis River Beach (see entry), but turn sharp R onto a track signed 'Citadel' after 1.9km (39.5892, 20.4611). After 600m fork L and park at the end. Walk 200m S to the church.
5 mins, 39.5915, 20.4593 🔺✝️🚲

20 KOUGI MONASTERY

This legendary hill ruin, with stunning vistas, was the site of heroic resistance to Ali Pasha by the last of the local Souliot population. Monk Samuel, who built the monastery in 1793, destroyed it in 1803, so it didn't fall into the hands of the Ottoman army.

→ Drive 2.2km N from Samonida, take the L hairpin at the café and park by the church at the end. Continue walking the trail S up to the ruin.
5 mins, 39.3479, 20.6442 🔺✝️

21 KIAFA CASTLE

This hulking ridgeline castle was built by Ali Pasha, the Albanian Ottoman ruler, in the late 18th century. The plateau above the squat fortifications surveys the nearby valleys and the plains beyond.

→ Park 1.5km S of Samonida, just before the tarmac turns to dirt track. Hike the signed path R and upwards. The path grows faint towards the end, but the direction is clear.
15 mins, 39.3365, 20.6516 🔺🚲🔺📷

22 ALI PASHA CASTLE

A hilltop castle enjoying a sensational coastal panorama over the bay of Parga. Allow time to explore the secret nooks, courtyards and windows, some shaded by invading trees.

→ Head NW from Anthousa, take the first L after 1km and then the first L tarmac fork up after 800m. Park at the end by the castle.

3 mins, 39.2985, 20.3679 🏯🏞

23 ST SOSTIS CHURCH

A tiny, icon-filled cave church built into an angular rock cleft, with views out over the sea.

→ Park as for St Sostis Beach (see entry), and walk 100m W into the cleft.

2 mins, 39.2839, 20.3529 ✝

LOCAL FOOD & DRINK

24 TAVERNA O THEIOS

Delicious Greek dishes with fun creative twists and a magnificent hillside view make this a must for foodies in the Parga area.

→ Parga 480 60, +30 69 4058 6147

39.3129, 20.3564 🏞🏔🐚

25 SAKIS

Oft considered Parga's best taverna. The seating spills onto the street and the terrace enjoys a stunning view over the town and bay. Best enjoyed at sunset, with a reservation.

→ Parga 480 60, +30 2684 032262

39.2844, 20.3982 🖥🏞🏕🅱

26 PERIVOLI

A family taverna where hearty local dishes are served with a warm welcome and a big smile. Live music often floats between lemon trees in the charming garden terrace. Book ahead or expect a small wait.

→ Parga 480 60, +30 2684 032082

39.2839, 20.4133 🅱

27 REEF CAFÉ

A simple café set in a delightful garden overlooking the sea, with steps down to the shoreline.

→ Preveza 481 00, +30 2682 056223

39.1303, 20.5885 🏞

STAY

28 SIVOTA'S SECRET VILLA

This plush villa has an infinity pool and hanging chair on a patio overlooking the archipelago. A special place for two.

→ Sivota 461 00, +30 69 8665 3117

39.4004, 20.2436 🏞

29 SOFAS CAMPING

A charming, tranquil campsite with its own beach, a cool beach bar and delicious food served up by the delightful Eleni and Zacharias and family. Open April to October.

→ Perdika 461 00, +30 69 8497 2369

39.3786, 20.2821 🏕

30 MIKRI AKTI

This secluded apartment is simple and airy, with sea-sunset views from the balcony and terrace and a small path down to a pristine, almost-private beach. Sleeps six.

→ Perdika 461 00, airbnb.com/rooms/33521721

39.3676, 20.2778 🏞🏕

31 MERAVIGLIA SLOW LIVING

A sleek, carefully crafted beachside resort designed for slow living. Suites of stone walls and terrazzo floors are set among rosemary and lavender gardens, each with its own sea-view infinity pool and some with jacuzzis.

→ Mytikas 481 00, +30 2682 440120

38.9872, 20.7060 🏖€

32 IONIAN TREEHOUSE ECOHOSTING

A collection of fairytale treehouses and cabins on stilts, built with wonky charm in a grassy garden.

→ Preveza 481 00, +30 69 7480 5145

38.9790, 20.7299 🏕

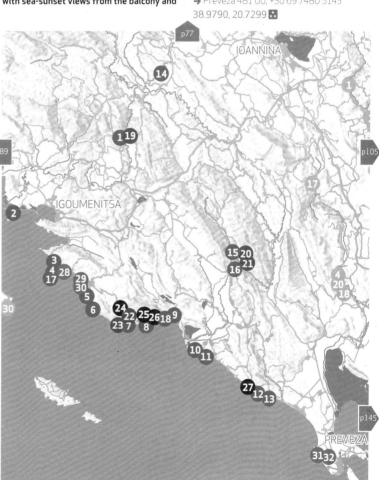

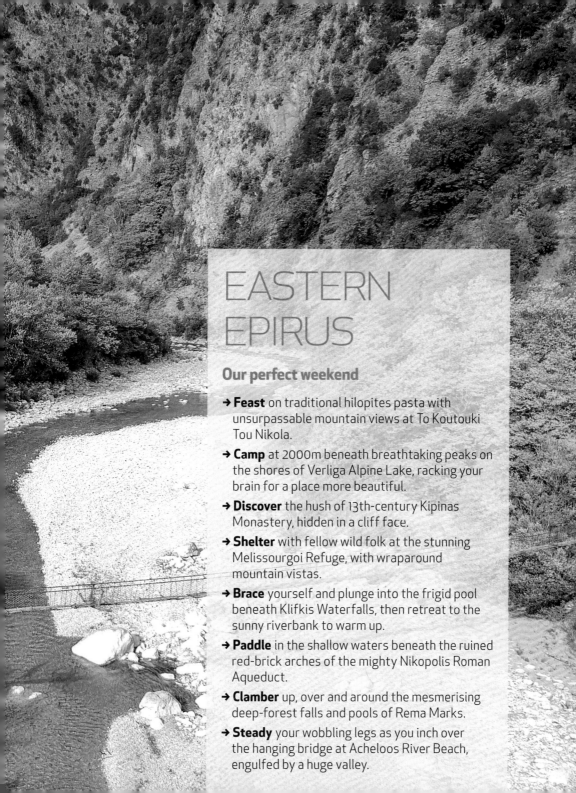

EASTERN EPIRUS

Our perfect weekend

→ **Feast** on traditional hilopites pasta with unsurpassable mountain views at To Koutouki Tou Nikola.

→ **Camp** at 2000m beneath breathtaking peaks on the shores of Verliga Alpine Lake, racking your brain for a place more beautiful.

→ **Discover** the hush of 13th-century Kipinas Monastery, hidden in a cliff face.

→ **Shelter** with fellow wild folk at the stunning Melissourgoi Refuge, with wraparound mountain vistas.

→ **Brace** yourself and plunge into the frigid pool beneath Klifkis Waterfalls, then retreat to the sunny riverbank to warm up.

→ **Paddle** in the shallow waters beneath the ruined red-brick arches of the mighty Nikopolis Roman Aqueduct.

→ **Clamber** up, over and around the mesmerising deep-forest falls and pools of Rema Marks.

→ **Steady** your wobbling legs as you inch over the hanging bridge at Acheloos River Beach, engulfed by a huge valley.

Eastern Epirus is a jagged mountainous scar formed as the mighty Pindus range, the 'spine of Greece', marches south from glorious Zagori (part of Epirus, but meriting its own chapter). The cascading forest and sparse peaks of Tzoumerka National Park – packed with waterfalls, alpine lakes and crystal rivers – dominate a geography so severe that Epirus remains remote and under-developed. Simply existing here feels adventurous.

The northernmost wonder here is Verliga Alpine Lake, dwarfed by looming Mount Lakmos. In spring the snow thaws to reveal the first meanders of Greece's second-longest river, the Achelous, flowing from a pristine lake in a sublime meadow of colourful flowers. Trek to this paradise, camp for a night or two among other mountain pilgrims, then replenish with fresh *hilopites*, traditional Greek pasta, at To Koutouki Tou Nikola in Metsovo.

To the south lies the heart of the National Park, between Kakarditsa and Tzoumerka (or Athamanika) peaks. Pick your basecamp wisely, because you'll have lots of exploring to do. Pramanta and Melissourgoi shelters are both glorious examples of Greek mountain-refuge culture, and full of like-minded folk. Or opt for the cosy timber of Kalivas Chalet and its jacuzzi, swaddled in deep cedar forest. Wherever you stay, plunge into the frigid canyon beneath Klifkis Waterfall, perhaps as part of a rafting trip, and hike the sweeping valley leading to Kefalovrysso Waterfall. And be sure to leave time to marvel at the mountain scenery, stroll the surrounding trails and explore the local villages.

Spectacular alpine adventures continue south-east of the National Park. The twin cascades of Souda Waterfalls roar in a glade surveying more stirring vistas. And the fairytale forested descent to Rema Marks, a delight in itself, ends at a sequence of beguiling falls and pools linkable by scrambling an inspired trail of red dots. Both are on the outskirts of village-at-the-edge-of-the-world Theodoriana, staring cinematically into an enormous dead-end valley flanked by giants. Stop on the way in or out at Achelous River Beach, where a rickety hanging footbridge spans the rushing mountain water, a little too long and wobbly for comfort. Recover on the cobble beach below.

The smaller peak of Xerovouni, to the south-west, guards a string of less vertiginous but fascinating delights. The circular spring-fed waters of Louros Lake are ablaze with vegetation and colourful reflections, especially in the autumn. So too is the water flowing beneath the grand, crumbling arches of the Roman Aqueduct of Nikopolis, remnants of a remarkable construction that once ushered water over 50km south. Most striking of all is neighbouring Kokkinopilos, a mind-bending landscape of red-clay dunes more befitting of a guidebook to Mars.

2

RIVERS & BRIDGES

1 TSIMOVO BRIDGE
A dramatically collapsed bridge above the rushing Arachthos River, engulfed by the sheer mountain valley.

→ About 4km E on the main road from Charnokopi village, winding down into the valley. Park at the W end of the parallel active bridge.

1 min, 39.576, 20.9768 ⛺🚵

2 POLITSA BRIDGE
This arched stone bridge crosses a popular starting point for rafting adventures down the Arachthos River. Lounge on the beaches either side or jump from the rocks just upstream and bob beneath with the current.

→ Just over 8km E from Lazena. Fork L as you leave the village heading E, turn L on a L hairpin after 1.8km and continue to the new bridge running parallel. Park on the E end.

5 mins, 39.5115, 21.0070 🛶⛺🚵

3 ACHELOUS RIVER BEACH
A bright-blue mountain river rushing through a dramatic valley between cliffs and pebble shores, beneath a hanging footbridge with rickety wooden slats. A memorable setting

and a hair-raising crossing; a float followed by a snooze is the relaxing option.

→ Drive 2.5km downhill on a winding road from Panagia village and park on the road just above the bridge. A short path leads down.

5 mins, 39.3879, 21.2743 🏊⛺⛰️🔄⛱️🐚

4 ROMAN AQUEDUCT OF NIKOPOLIS
The grand red-brick ruins of a Roman aqueduct that guided water over 50km south to Nicopolis, once the capital of the Roman province of Epirus Vetus. Paddling in the shallow river beneath the overgrown arches is a delight.

→ Easily accessible. Park by the road either side of the bridge on the road heading NW out of Agios Georgios.

2 mins, 39.2709, 20.8488 🏊🚵🐚

WATERFALLS

5 VATHYPEDO WATERFALLS
A beautiful pair of waterfalls filling a cold pool in a secret valley below Vathypedo village.

→ Park in Vathypedo. The short path down to the waterfalls starts on the SE edge of the village (39.6297, 21.0626).

5 mins, 39.6297, 21.0634 🏊⛱️

6 KOUIASSA WATERFALLS
Walk along a gentle string of small cascades and dipping pools babbling in a lush forest. Along the path you will find an old watermill, now a riverside café.

→ Take the road N towards Kalarites, and park at a R hairpin at the deepest point in the valley about 4km short of the village, 500m due S of it (39.5787, 21.1245). The path starts here up a flight of stone steps.

10 mins, 39.581/, 21.1172 🏃🚶

7 KAMILI WATERFALL
This crushing 50m cataract has a stellar viewpoint, and makes a fine picnic pit stop on the way through the dramatic valley.

→ Just SW of Matsouki. For the best vantage spot, park in a small clearing on the R 200m after crossing the iron bridge heading S (39.5622, 21.1581). Walk 50m along the marked path to the viewpoint.

2 mins, 39.5629, 21.1592 ⛺

8 KLIFKIS WATERFALLS
This lofty waterfall creates a magical plunge pool with a tiny swimmable canyon, just before it meets the Arachthos River. The water is frigid, but you can quickly warm up on the sun-drenched pebble shore.

→ Park 2.5km E of Kalentzi (39.4960, 21.0058) and walk for 1km down the steep, clearly signposted switchbacks to avoid a hair-raising drive.

30 mins, 39.4972, 21.0100 🚶🅱

9 KEFALOVRYSSO WATERFALL

A towering ribbon of water, Greece's highest at 350m, plunges down the cliff face above a sweeping mountain valley at the end of an amazing hike. It can run dry in the summer, so ask at Melissourgoi Refuge (see entry) to avoid disappointment.

→ A tough but well-marked uphill trail starts at Melissourgoi Refuge.

60 mins, 39.4988, 21.1271 🏔🚶🧗

10 TZOUMERKA WATERFALLS

A spectacular pair of easily accessible, 100m waterfalls that run from October to June, raging from between two cliff faces in late spring. The café at the start of the short hike boasts impressive views.

→ Switchback steeply N from Kriopigi, taking the R off the sixth L bend (39.4599, 21.1174). Continue 700m E, bending S to park at the café and follow the path to the base of the falls.

5 mins, 39.4580, 21.1240 📷🏔

11 SOUDA WATERFALLS

After a short forested hike the trees scatter to reveal an enchanting scene, with two cataracts springing free from the cliff into pools with jagged alpine views. Allow time to soak up the beauty here.

→ Head NW from Theodoriana for 1.3km and park by an easy trail heading L (39.4430, 21.1974). Hike W uphill through the forest, following the red arrows.

20 mins, 39.4402, 21.1890 🏔🚶📷

12 REMA MARKS WATERFALLS

An otherworldly string of cascades and pools tumbling through a dark, magical forest. Red dots mark a memorable scramble from the bottom pool upwards. This is a must.

→ Drive around 2.5km S from Theodoriana and park in the layby L (39.4262, 21.2160). Walk the main track E, downhill, ignoring two L turns and bearing R at a scrubby open plateau. A good, marked trail descends into the lush forest.

30 mins, 39.4266, 21.2246 🚶🏔🧗📷

13 CAPTAIN'S BATHS

A magical forested footpath leads you to a pool, great for a dip, fed by a crescent of small falls.

→ Turn S off the main road on a hairpin bend

18

about 1.8km W of Athamania (39.3687, 21.2028). Park at St Marina Church at the end of the short track and follow the signed path.

30 mins, 39.3666, 21.1969 🏕️🏔️🎒🔆

14 MELATES WATERFALL

Flowing reliably in spring only, this unknown fall with an accompanying plunge pool is hidden in a wild forest.

➔ Cross the bridge from the church in Melates to the opposite bank, turn L and park after 600m (39.2474, 21.0982). Follow the path N for about 500m (39.2505, 21.0995) then head up the riverbed for 50m to the falls.

20 mins, 39.2506, 21.1006 🏞️🥾🏊

15 MEGARCHI WATERFALL

A hidden waterfall with horizontal rock layers and hanging greenery. It often runs dry in summer.

➔ A rough track starts in the middle of a fork in the road around 650m E of Megarchi (39.1386, 21.0784), and winds 1km to a L hairpin (39.1420, 21.0870). Walk E from here for 550m along a track turning into an overgrown riverbed.

20 mins, 39.1436, 21.0927 🏞️🥾🏊

LAKES

16 VERLIGA ALPINE LAKE

True mountain paradise. This majestic watercourse, already at 2000m but dwarfed by the fearsome face of Mount Lakmos, flows in swooping meanders through lush alpine meadow to feed the Achelous River. A supreme camp spot, best enjoyed in spring when crocuses bloom amidst the snow patches.

➔ With a 4x4 there is a drivable 12km track system from Chaliki. But by far the best option is to hike from Chaliki along a well-marked trail and camp for a night or two.

4 hours, 39.6730, 21.1282 🏞️⛰️🏕️🥾🎒🔆

17 LOUROS LAKE

Almost perfectly circular and fed by springs, this lake is alive with vegetation. The remarkably clear water is dappled with water lilies and the reflections of surrounding trees. A lovely picnic spot, especially in autumn.

➔ On the NW edge of Vouliasta village, with parking right by the lake under the trees.

1 min, 39.4323, 20.8415 🔆

16

17

18 ZIROU LAKE

A beautiful lake cradled by green hills. Find a scenic taverna on the southern edge and kayak rentals on the eastern shore; the west bank is explorable by foot only.

➜ A track runs SW from Pedopoli Zirou, just off the E951, along the edge of the lake. Park at the restaurant at the end or anywhere on the side of the road.

2 mins, 39.2385, 20.8516 🖼️🐾🛶🚶

MONASTERIES & CLAY DUNES

19 KIPINAS MONASTERY

Hewn deep into the surrounding rock in 1212, with a retractable entrance bridge, this cave monastery served as a secret school during the Turkish occupation and a hidden arsenal throughout the Greek Revolution. Stunning inside and out, but typically closes around 4pm.

➜ There is space for a handful of cars in a layby 2km E of Mistras, on the L just past the monastery. It's a 100m walk up to the monastery.

5 mins, 39.5674, 21.1304 🖼️✝️🛶🚶

20 KOKKINOPILOS

Step onto Mars at this unique, eerie pocket of steep red-clay dunes. Avoid rainy conditions – and white trainers, if you want them to stay that way.

➜ On the E951 2km S from the Agios Georgios turning, park in the layby by the Tunnel of Kokkinopilos (39.2567, 20.8474). Walk 100m S to rough stairs on the R up to the dunes.

1 min, 39.2567, 20.8436 🖼️🐾

LOCAL FOOD & DRINK

21 TO KOUTOUKI TOU NIKOLA

The locals' local. Amazing regional dishes, at good prices and with the best mountain views in town. Try the *hilopites* (a traditional Greek pasta) served in chicken broth.

➜ Metsovo 442 00, +30 2656 041732
39.7716, 21.1827 🖼️

22 DELFA'S TAVERNA

One for the meat eaters. Big, fresh, delicious portions served with a smile. Don't be put off by the simple exterior: the wood-stone interior is delightful, and the food does the talking – loudly. A real gem.

→ Anilio 442 00, +30 2656 041474
39.7595, 21.1875 🌐

23 AKANTHOS

Traditional Greek specialities courtesy of Napoleon and Lambrini, in an authentic taverna, shop and garden brimming with character.
→ Kalarites 440 01, +30 69 7226 5961
39.5839, 21.1226 🏔

24 TO KAFENEION

Hearty, affordable local dishes with a terrace view to die for in a small mountain village. You might be lucky and catch some live music.
→ Kentriko 471 00, +30 69 7679 5846
39.3473, 21.0644 🏔🏔

MOUNTAIN STAYS

25 GRAND FOREST METSOVO

A stylish, modern mountain retreat on the fringe of a black-pine forest, boasting a spa, sauna and infinity pool with panoramic vistas.
→ Metsovo 442 00, +30 2656 029001
39.7748, 21.2047 🏔🏔€

26 PRAMANTA MOUNTAIN REFUGE

Stay in a family-run shelter in the incredible landscape of the Tzoumerka mountains, between cascading firs and jagged peaks. The cabin offers mixed dormitories with shared bathrooms, yummy meals and homemade lemonade.
→ Pramanta 440 01, +30 2659 300645
39.5089, 21.1246 🏔🏔🏔

27 MELISSOURGOI REFUGE

Greece's alpine refuges are not to be missed, and if you only make it to one, this should be it. An epic basecamp for hikers, with simple dorm bunks, foraged food and a staggering Pindus Mountains setting.
→ Melissourgi 440 01, +30 69 7437 4172
39.5050, 21.1415 🏔🏔🏔🏔

FOREST RETREATS

28 THEASIS IGLOO

A collection of unique cabins with conical roofs lost deep in the forested foothills of the Tzoumerka mountains. Delicious food served at the restaurant on site.
→ Ktistades 470 43, +30 69 4868 2910
39.5073, 21.0807 🏔

29 KALIVAS CHALET

This striking timber A-frame chalet has been built beautifully by the owner across three levels, with room for four. Wake up surrounded by cedars, firs and oaks, and finish the day in the jacuzzi or sauna.
→ Ktistades 470 43, +30 69 3079 7829
39.5061, 21.0817 🏔

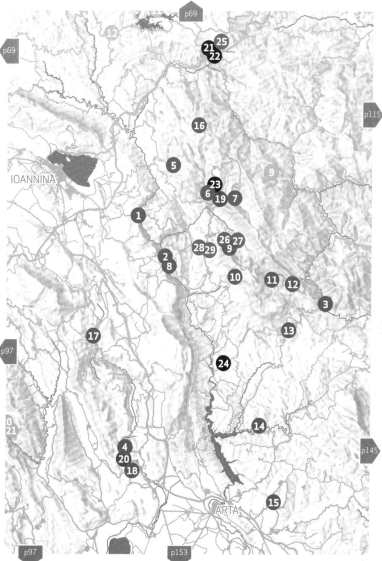

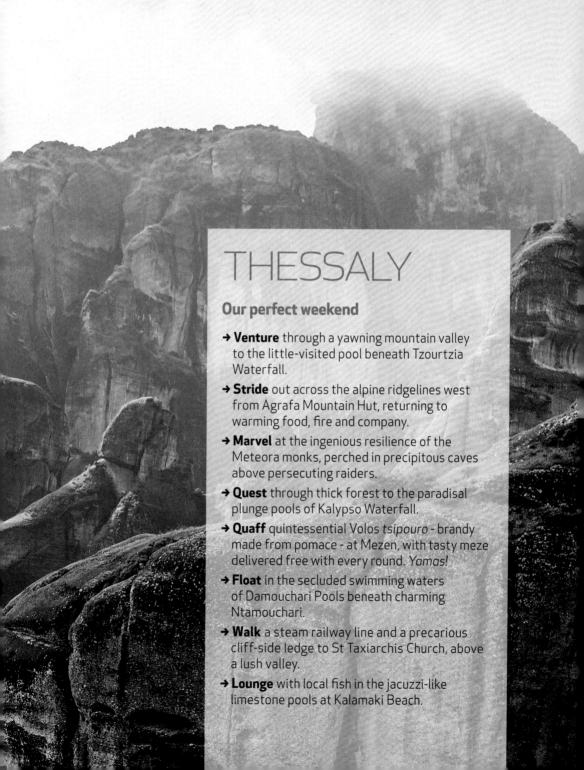

THESSALY

Our perfect weekend

→ **Venture** through a yawning mountain valley to the little-visited pool beneath Tzourtzia Waterfall.

→ **Stride** out across the alpine ridgelines west from Agrafa Mountain Hut, returning to warming food, fire and company.

→ **Marvel** at the ingenious resilience of the Meteora monks, perched in precipitous caves above persecuting raiders.

→ **Quest** through thick forest to the paradisal plunge pools of Kalypso Waterfall.

→ **Quaff** quintessential Volos *tsipouro* - brandy made from pomace - at Mezen, with tasty meze delivered free with every round. *Yamas!*

→ **Float** in the secluded swimming waters of Damouchari Pools beneath charming Ntamouchari.

→ **Walk** a steam railway line and a precarious cliff-side ledge to St Taxiarchis Church, above a lush valley.

→ **Lounge** with local fish in the jacuzzi-like limestone pools at Kalamaki Beach.

Thessaly is a land of two edges, from a wild perspective. Its vast lowlands, the fertile 'breadbasket of Greece', lie between soaring flanks: to the west, the colossal Pindus range; to the east, mounts Olympus, Ossa and Pelion, where the Pelion Peninsula follows the Aegean to the Sporades archipelago before curling around the Pagasetic Gulf. Alpine perches, crashing waterfalls and wild beaches riddle these mountainous wings, and one of Greece's most unmissable wonders awaits just as they relent above Trikala.

The heights of Tzoumerka National Park, part of the wider Pindus range, mark Thessaly's western border with Epirus. Alpine adventure abounds here, ideally from the warm-hearted hearth of either Koziakas Shelter or Agrafa Mountain Hut, both alive with kindred spirits. Every surrounding trail feels guidebook-worthy at times, but quest through the valley to Tzourtzia Waterfall for a special slice of solitude.

Thessaly was the famous arena of the Battle of the Gods, where the Olympians usurped the Titans, but other spiritual struggles mark this land. On the Pindus fringes lies Thessaly's pièce de résistance: jaw-dropping Meteora, where a migration of monasteries cling dizzyingly to an uprising of otherworldly rock formations. Between the 12th and 14th centuries, as Ottoman raiders took control of the Thessaly plains, monks found preposterous refuge amidst precipices and caves reachable only by precarious pulley systems and retractable ladders – some still visible. Only six monasteries survive today, but Meteora's monastic community remains second in importance only to Mount Athos. The Rock of the Holy Spirit is one sublime vantage point here, but explore fully. You can retreat from the crowds with delicious traditional cooking at Monaxia or by venturing north to Gavros, bordering a similar landscape nicknamed 'Unknown Meteora'.

Eastern Thessaly harbours the region's densest concentration of natural delights, mostly in the Ossa and Pelion foothills – the latter home of the mythical centaurs. One could spend weeks following mountain rivers through this tangle of forested villages, visiting secret waterfalls and plunge pools, like neighbouring Plakotoura and Poros. For mission headquarters, consider The Lost Unicorn, a beguiling hotel crammed with quirks and wrapped in greenery. One of Greece's grandest living beings, the gigantic Tsagkarada Plane Tree, stands outside.

Wondrous beaches appear where the Pelion foothills spill into the Aegean. Fakistra Beach cowers beneath cliffs in a small cove, with Panagia Megalomata Church hiding in a coastal cave over the headland. Kommos and Melani beaches await further south, two pristine boulder-strewn expanses of sand, the latter a free-camping mecca in the summer. Or perhaps continue round to Tzasteni Beach, a sleepy place at the point where the peninsula grows more peaceful. Slumber nearby in the dreamy nook that is Koukouleika Treehouse, and walk or sail the next day to a fresh-fish lunch at waterside Taverna Da Angelo.

BEACHES

1 TZASTENI BEACH

A postcard cove where wildness seems to reclaim the Pelion Peninsula. A cluster of white, blue and orange houses on the spit mirrors the colour of the clouds, water and sand. A calming place.

➜ Park on a L hairpin 2.2km W from Marathias on the coastal road. Follow the track, then a footpath branching L down to the beach.

3 mins, 39.1265, 23.1627 🏊‍♂️🛶🦀

2 MELANI BEACH

This long sandy beach connects to the two segments of Potistika Beach to the north, dotted with big jumping boulders all the way. The whole string is popular with wild campers, and the middle section in particular is nudist friendly.

➜ Around 2.5km E of central Argalasti, fork R onto Epar.Od. Argalastis-Ormou Paltsis (39.2315, 23.2451) and follow it 7.2km to a hairpin L. Follow this NW to parking by the beach.

2 mins, 39.2554, 23.3050 🍴🛶🏊‍♂️🚫▲B

3 KOMMOS BEACH

A delectable beach of golden sand and huge boulders for jumping, quieter than neighbouring Melani (see entry) thanks to the trickier access.

➜ Head NW 600m on the coastal road from Potistika to a track on the R (39.2675, 23.2859). Follow it 250m (parking is easiest closer to the road or at Carla's taverna) to a footpath heading R just after a L bend. It descends 100m to the beach.

10 mins, 39.2707, 23.286 🍴🛶🏊‍♂️🛶▲

4 PANTAZI AMMOS BEACH

Tall scrubby hillsides provide evening shade on this long pebble beach with boulders.

➜ Follow the paved road N then E from Syki, ignoring turns for 4.5km to the S end of the beach. Park in the small area before the steep descent to the sand.

2 mins, 39.2948, 23.2766 🍴🛶🦀

5 KALAMAKI BEACH

A distinctive flat-pebble cove with many submerged limestone platforms that fill to form jacuzzi-like pools, often filled with fish. There's also a natural spring and a canyon to the rear that's fun to explore.

➜ Follow the road NE from Kalamaki for around 3km to parking above the S end of the beach, and walk about 100 steps down.

5 mins, 39.3485, 23.2264 🛶🏊‍♂️🦀

6 LIMNIONAS BEACH

An end-of-the-line beach populated with fishing bric-a-brac and a few campers in summer, guarded by a large wooded headland. Swim round to the right for a secret cave beach.

➜ Head NE from Xorychti and hairpin L at 2km. Continue 2.7km to a R hairpin. If you're nervous on rough tracks, park here and walk the final 1km S, passing a church.

20 mins, 39.3640, 23.2074 🛶🏊‍♂️▲▲🚗🦀

7 FAKISTRA BEACH

The little sandy beach of this enticing bay is dwarfed by towering cliffs. There is a seasonal waterfall to the rear, jumping rocks to the side and Panagia Megalomata Church (see entry) over the headland.

➜ Zigzag downhill from the big collection of signs between two supermarkets in Tsagkarada (39.3880, 23.1725). Turn R after 2.4km, then ignore turns until parking by a gazebo above the beach. The trail R of the gazebo is short but steep; wear good shoes.

10 mins, 39.3897, 23.1934 🛶🏊‍♂️†B🦀

8 DAMOUCHARI POOLS

Secret, tree-lined sea pools created by jutting rock formations, with plenty of spots for jumping and stairs to climb back out again.

→ Park in the open area with the olive tree in Ntamouchari and follow the track N into the trees, L of the church. Bend R then immediately L, where a track descends L. Follow it to the pools.

5 mins, 39.4063, 23.1780 🍴🛶🏖🐚

WATERFALLS

9 TZOURTZIA WATERFALL

A thundering cascade and plunge pool in a remote mountain valley at the end of a splendid alpine journey. Revel in the green solitude.

→ 4x4 advisable. On the SE edge of Agia Paraskevi turn uphill from road to track (39.5657, 21.2617). Hairpin L then zigzag up, bending R at 6km behind a church after a second riverbed crossing. Fork R 1.8km after the church and continue 1km (39.5842, 21.2329). Here a steep, technical 1km trail descends R to the falls, marked by red dots.

30 mins, 39.5840, 21.2372 🛶⛺🏔🚶🔥🌲🐚

10 PALAIOKARYA STONE BRIDGE

This handsome arched stone bridge, built in the 16th century to connect Thessaly with Epirus, crosses the river of the same name between two mesmerising artificial waterfalls – a tall one upstream, and a smaller cascade below. There is a paved picnic area and even some climbing routes for good measure.

→ Heading SW from Loggies Kotroniou, bear L off the EO30 after 3km then take a short dirt track L after 850m to parking near the bridge.

2 mins, 39.4312, 21.5276 🛶🧗🐕🌲🅱

11 KALYPSO WATERFALL

A spellbinding forest pool filled by two falls dancing down a series of lush forested ledges rising far above. Leap in from the sidelines to celebrate a successful quest.

→ Leaving Karitsa SE, fork R twice in close succession, the second onto a dirt track. Follow 1.7km, turn L on a R hairpin and continue 1.6km. Park and follow a trail R into an open section (39.8204, 22.7802), bending 1km L then R to the falls, marked but at times faint.

20 mins, 39.819, 22.7743 🛶🐕🏃

12 PLAKOTOURA STREAM

Water thrown from a cliff charges on through a series of river rapids in a narrow cleft hidden in a wild section of forest. You can explore the river carefully upstream by heading right when you meet the waterfall.

→ Drive SW from Karavoma hamlet (SW of Makrirrachi) for 4km via tight switchbacks, and park where a track heads L on a R hairpin. Walk 500m through orchards and turn R (39.4075, 23.0888) onto a forested trail, which narrows for 200m before opening onto slippery rocks with waterfall views.

20 mins, 39.4057, 23.0885 🚶🏃🅥

13 POROS WATERFALLS

A string of forested pools and cascades darting between rocky channels along a 200m stretch river. Start at either end and explore between to find a pool of your liking and linger a while.

→ From Makrirrachi head N, bending W, for 5km on the main road and turn L signed Volos. Immediately bear L onto a narrow downhill track. Park in a layby after 800m and walk on 300m to a L bend. For the upstream end bear R 150m downhill into the trees (39.4113, 23.0966). For the downstream end turn R 250m after the L bend.

10 mins, 39.4121, 23.0982 🛶🐕🚶

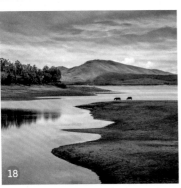

14 MEGA REMA LAGOON

A shallow pool receding into a waterfall nook at the end of a pleasant woodland track.

→ Follow a dirt track SW from Kissos from 39.4025, 23.1296, forking L after 750m. You can drive most of the way or park in the village and make it a pleasant 4.5km round walk.

10 mins, 39.3917, 23.1208 ⬛🏊🚶🏃

15 KISSOU WATERFALL

Perfect for a spontaneous dip, this plunge pool surrounded by massive mossy boulders lies just off a bend in the road.

→ On a sharp R bend and bridge on the 34 heading W from Mouresi, just before you enter Kissos. Park in a big layby on the Kissos side of the bend.

1 min, 39.3979, 23.1292 ⬛

16 KATAFIDI WATERFALL

Varying greatly with the season, this tall waterfall curves over layered rock into a canyon-bottom pool, a short walk from the pretty village of Vizitsa.

→ Park by the main road in the centre of Vizitsa (39.3332, 23.1321) and follow an alley R of the Life-Giving Spring Church opposite. It descends just under 1km, through the buildings before trending R to the falls, marked with occasional red dots and signs.

20 mins, 39.3312, 23.1274 ⬛🏊🚶

WATERSIDE STROLLS

17 KEFALO RIVER WALK

This paved path follows a dashing forest river via rocks, waterfalls and small pools for 1.25km. A pleasant four-season stroll for all.

→ The trail starts on the R as you exit Gorgogiri SW, just before a L bend (39.5482, 21.5800). Allow 90 mins for a full, leisurely return journey. You can also reach the upper section by parking 1.9km beyond the L bend, on the first L hairpin.

10 mins, 39.5507, 21.5705 ⬛🔭🚶

18 LAKE PLASTIRAS

An enormous artificial lake with a tendrilled, grassy shore, here dotted with copses. Stroll the banks, swim, rent a kayak or grab a coffee at Plaz Pezoulas just south.

→ Drive E from Kalyvia for 1.7km to the café. Park there or just before it on the L, near the kayaks.

2 mins, 39.3108, 21.7311 ⬛🚲🐕🛶

(25)

NATURAL MONUMENTS

19 GAVROS

Fantastical rock formations nicknamed 'Unknown Meteora', just a short drive north of the famous UNESCO site (see entry). Take a few hours to explore the trails weaving between the wondrous formations, and seek out the cave church on the northern side.

→ Park in the main village square and take the lane heading E, just R of a church. Turn R, L, R to join a lane that bends R into the rock formations.

5 mins, 39.7971, 21.5981 🗺️🔲🔲⛪

20 MOUNT OSSA PEAK

An accessible 1978m peak with a cave church marking the summit. The panoramic vista takes in Mount Olympus to the north, the Aegean in the east, the Pelion range in the south and interior Thessaly to the west.

→ Drive 12.5km on the main road N then NE from Spilia to Kissavos Shelter, keeping R after about 4km. A marked trail ascends SE before bending R to the summit.

90 mins, 39.7957, 22.6851 🗺️🔲⛪🔲🔲🔲🔲

21 TSAGKARADA PLANE TREE

A gargantuan plane tree single-handedly shading a pretty village square. At over 1000 years old, it's reckoned to be the oldest of its kind in Europe. Its trunk measures 17.5m around and one of its colossal branches requires its own stone support. Have a coffee and bow to this beast of nature.

→ In Tsagkarada village square outside The Lost Unicorn Hotel (see entry).

2 mins, 39.3868, 23.1745 🔲🔲

WATCHTOWERS & WORSHIP

22 ROCK OF THE HOLY SPIRIT, METEORA

This UNESCO World Heritage Site is a cultural and geological wonderland of Eastern Orthodox monasteries cloistered precipitously in a landscape of titanic and otherworldly rock towers. Explore it fully, including this secret enclave, where a cave chapel opens onto a hideaway garden with a ladder leading to a glorious perch overlooking Kastraki, all accessed by an improbably spectacular trail through a giant cleft.

→ Walk to the E edge of Kastraki (39.7165, 21.6238), where cobbled steps ascend L of Pyrgos Adrachti hotel past a red cross. Follow

the trail 500m, through a meadow beneath a hulking cliff on the L, into a boulder field, where a path branches L and ascends 250m via a handrail to the chapel. Climb the shorter, less dodgy ladder to the viewpoint.

30 mins, 39.7182, 21.6239 🔲🔲⛪🔲🔲🔲🔲

23 PHARSALUS ACROPOLIS

The impressive wall and watchtowers of an ancient city acropolis, with Byzantine remodelling, arrayed along a forested bluff, with sweeping views all the way to Mount Olympus on clear days. The woodland walk up is a delight.

→ A dirt track signed 'Acropolis' starts on a hairpin at the SW edge of Farsalus, just SE of the sports field (39.2915, 22.3780) and winds 2km through the forest. Alternatively, drive 2.6km SE from Farsala, bear R onto a paved track and immediately R again onto a dirt track. Follow it 2.4km NW through fields, bend R, fork L just after a building and park after 400m by another fork at the SE end of the bluff.

40 mins, 39.2880, 22.3873 🔲🔲🔲🔲

24 ST TAXIARCHIS CHURCH

A quintessentially wild Greek Orthodox chapel surveying a luscious valley from a

narrow path hewn into a cliff, itself requiring a blocky scramble and a splendid walk along the Pelion railway line. A little steam train runs the line between Ano Lechonia (10am departure) and Milies (3pm departure); it's well worth buying a ticket.

→ Park at the cute train station on the W edge of Milies. Walk the pretty railway line for roughly 1km to cross an iron bridge, then take a trail R into the forest. After 200m turn L up to the base of a blocky scramble to the ledge path. If you reach the corral you've gone too far.
30 mins, 39.3262, 23.1366 ⛰️✝️🏃🥾🐚

25 PANAGIA MEGALOMATA CHURCH

A teeny church and a hidden school in which a hermit monk used to teach children to read, built side by side into an overhanging coastal cave with meditative sea views. Preposterous neighbours in the best sense.

→ Park as if for Fakistra Beach (see entry). Walk the track L of the gazebo and turn immediately R onto a footpath to the church.
10 mins, 39.3911, 23.1927 ⛰️✝️🐾🏊🐚

LOCAL FOOD & DRINK

26 MONAXIA

Quintessential Greek grandmother cooking – delicious, hearty, unassuming – served by her granddaughter in a shady patio cradled in rolling pastoral foothills. A fabulously relaxed jaunt from famous Meteora (see entry) in the distance below.

→ Vlachava 422 00, +30 2432 076820
39.7711, 21.6619 🍴

27 STATIRIS

A superb but unassuming *tsipouro* joint in Tirnavos, its fresh fish popular with locals. Be sure to swing by if passing through town.

→ Tirnavos 401 00, +30 2492 022445
39.7382, 22.2873 🐚

28 PSAROLAKOS BEACH BAR

Seasonal beach bar that attracts a boho crowd to its cosy corner. Bean bags, quirky wooden shades, chill music and cocktails.

→ Psarolakas 400 07, +30 69 8821 0000
39.8524, 22.7709 🏊🏖️💲

29 MEZEN

The place, or *tsipouradika*, to sample Volos' signature *tsipouro*: brandy made from pomace, the grape remnants leftover from the winemaking process. Order a *tsipouro* and get a free meze dish – probably delicious morning-fresh seafood.

→ Volos 382 21, +30 2421 020844
39.3599, 22.9484 🅱️

30 KRITSA

Exceptional food, all local recipes with local ingredients, served in a classic village square beneath a plane-tree canopy. Particularly satisfying after walking the scenic Centaur's Path nearby, named after the mythical beasts thought to live on Mount Pelion.

→ Portaria 370 11, +30 2428 099121
39.3906, 22.9990 🅱️

31 TAVERNA DA ANGELO

An idyllic seafront seafood taverna in a deep inlet, only accessible by foot or boat. The octopus and crayfish pasta are excellent, especially followed by a turquoise plunge.

→ Trikeri 370 09, +30 69 7975 0866
39.1160, 23.1014 🏊🏖️

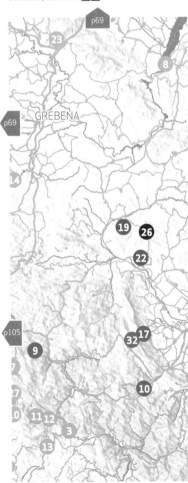

32 KOZIAKAS SHELTER

In a storybook alpine meadow just below the peak of Mount Koziakas, this family-run shelter offers warming food, friendly hosts and mountain activities galore on the doorstep. Open year round, with dorm beds for around 30 and plenty of tent space outside.

→ Ethikes 420 32, +30 69 7766 2569
39.5451, 21.5312

33 AGRAFA MOUNTAIN HUT

Explore the Agrafa range from this cosy stone refuge, with a fireplace, delicious food, cooking facilities and dorm beds for 24. Fabulous alpine views and trails head west towards Voutsikaki peak (secret Kaimakia Cave, with a river flowing from it, lies at 39.2772, 21.6527, for experienced hikers with a good digital map).

→ Limni Plastira 431 50, +30 69 8858 6292
39.2789, 21.6833

34 SELINA

A collection of 19th-century mansions converted into a hostel and hotel in the Mount Pelion foothills above Volos. Private suites and dorm rooms are complemented by a delightful terrace, a cinema room and wellness activities. Popular with solo travellers and remote workers.

→ Makrinitsa 370 11, +30 69 4426 2594
39.4011, 22.9877

35 THE LOST UNICORN

A charming 19th-century mansion hotel smothered lovingly by an extravaganza of vines, flowers and trees, including the mammoth Tsagkarada Plane Tree (see entry) in the square outside. A fine restaurant, a library, a rich cultural programme and quirks galore, from antique curios indoors to a treehouse in the sprawling garden.

→ Tsagkarada 370 12, +30 2426 049930
39.3865, 23.1747

36 KOUKOULEIKA TREEHOUSE

Look down on a sleepy bay from your balcony at this dreamy cabin on stilts for two, ensconced in thick olive trees. An outdoor shower and a private swimming platform complete the retreat.

→ Koukouleika 370 06, airbnb.com/
rooms/586064686216624430
39.1448, 23.1999

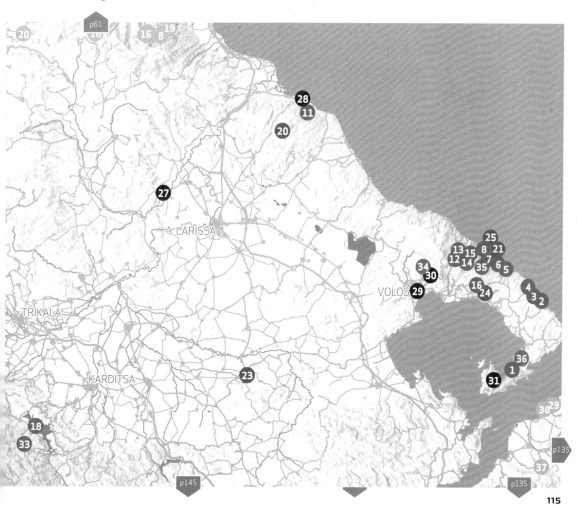

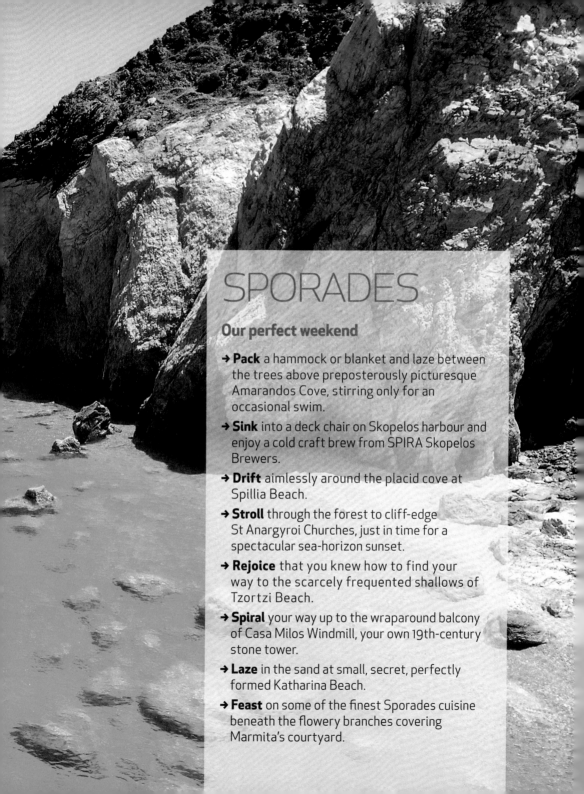

SPORADES

Our perfect weekend

→ **Pack** a hammock or blanket and laze between the trees above preposterously picturesque Amarandos Cove, stirring only for an occasional swim.

→ **Sink** into a deck chair on Skopelos harbour and enjoy a cold craft brew from SPIRA Skopelos Brewers.

→ **Drift** aimlessly around the placid cove at Spillia Beach.

→ **Stroll** through the forest to cliff-edge St Anargyroi Churches, just in time for a spectacular sea-horizon sunset.

→ **Rejoice** that you knew how to find your way to the scarcely frequented shallows of Tzortzi Beach.

→ **Spiral** your way up to the wraparound balcony of Casa Milos Windmill, your own 19th-century stone tower.

→ **Laze** in the sand at small, secret, perfectly formed Katharina Beach.

→ **Feast** on some of the finest Sporades cuisine beneath the flowery branches covering Marmita's courtyard.

Legend holds that the gods created the Sporades – 'the scattered ones' – by tossing pebbles into the Aegean. Skiathos, Skopelos and Alonnisos are three of the archipelago's four permanently settled islands, all spreading from charming port towns into undulating canopies of deep green, dotted with ruins and religious retreats and spilling onto divine beaches and bays of deep blue.

Skiathos is the most bustling Sporades island, its eponymous port popular with young partygoers. But don't be deterred: blissful pockets survive where the alleyways meet the water, like the swimming waters at Plakes Rocks and the charming waterside terrace at Bourtzi cafe. And beyond the outskirts wildness rules, criss-crossed by a network of well-marked Skiathos Routes for keen walkers. Sandy tracks snake through forests to a string of wonderfully secluded beaches along the northwestern shore. Agistros Beach is the pick, or Mandraki Perches for a secret sunset. Further east, near Skiathos Castle, lies the island's most famed beach, Lalaria, its pristine pebbles and magnificent sea arch the crowning moment of a boat ride along a wild coastline of treats.

Skopelos is supposedly Greece's greenest island, blanketed in virgin pine forest. Walking to Sedoukia Tombs to enjoy panoramic vistas over the island's heart is a fine way to orient yourself – as is reclining with a craft beer at harbourside SPIRA Skopelos Brewers. Forests and bays interact to delightful effect on Skopelos. Pines ring resplendent Amarandos Cove in the south, as if appreciating its glassy waters. The protected inlet at Spillia Beach lies beyond deciduous woodland and olive groves near St Ioannis Church, the most famous of Skopelos' 360 churches, monasteries and convents thanks to *Mamma Mia!*. And Hovolo Beach, with Ftelia Beach beyond for intrepid scramblers, awaits along a narrow sandy beach walk, legs lapped by waves, beneath cascading hillside pines.

Alonnisos is the quietest of these islands, its olive groves and apricot orchards threaded with gentle trails. Even the primary port town of Patitiri, from which you can stroll to the rock plateaus of Gremisa Beach, rarely rises above a gentle clamour. The valley walk from pretty Alonnisos Old Town to secluded Mikros Mourtias Beach is even better – especially if returning, via a sunset drink at Hayiati, to Casa Milos Windmill, built in 1850 and recently converted to sleep six. From Patitiri, Alonnisos extends gently north-east, following the National Marine Park of Alonissos and Northern Sporades. Europe's biggest protected marine area, this is home to the Mediterranean monk seal and rare dolphins and seabirds, and is partly explorable by boat. Finish any outing in this direction with sunset at the St Anargyroi Churches, roosting in the clifftop pines gazing back towards Skopelos.

8

BEACHES

1 AGISTROS BEACH, SKIATHOS

One of three long, sandy beaches with calm crystal waters at this end of the island, with pine forests spilling down the hills behind. Partially organised with shaggy umbrellas, but still well worth a stop.

→ For the most scenic route, follow the good, sandy coastal track clockwise from the NW of Koukounaries around the headland, although you can cut straight across and turn R. Either way, fork L 700m after the second of two close crossroads leading to the other bays, before a hairpin R (39.1647, 23.4078). Park in a clearing above the beach.

3 mins, 39.1679, 23.4097 🏖🏊🅱

2 KATHARINA BEACH, SKIATHOS

A small, pristine beach of soft yellow sand tucked away from the world beneath the coastal road and a buffer of lush greenery, and reached with the help of a rope. Nudist friendly.

→ Drive SE from Koukounaries and park by the road 400m after passing Maratha Beach. Take a short, steep, rope-assisted path R.

3 mins, 39.1430, 23.4114 🏖🏊🌊🚫

3 LALARIA BEACH, SKIATHOS

Sheer white cliffs giving way to white pebbles and turquoise water, with a swimmable sea arch at one end. Dreamy, though it does get busy in peak season.

→ Boat access only. Rent from Skiathos Boat Hire (+30 69 4419 4251) at Vassilias Beach, or take a tour with Privé (+30 69 7769 9849).

2 mins, 39.2067, 23.4783 🏖🏊🚣🅱

4 MEGAS GIALOS BEACH, SKIATHOS

Two shingle arcs curving the length of a wide, wild bay beneath steep green hills.

→ Park at the brief widening in the road 800m N from Kalivia (39.1903, 23.5031). Continue on foot for 300m to a sharp L turn and very steep descent.

15 mins, 39.1931, 23.4959 🏖🏊🌊🏊

5 PSAROCHOMA BEACH, SKIATHOS

A pair of gorgeous black-sand beaches separated by a tumble of rocks.

→ Park 400m N of Xanemos, in the clearing behind the N beach. Walk S between the buildings and beach to the stone steps.

5 mins, 39.1801, 23.5117 🏖🏊⛺

6 SPILIA BEACH, SKOPELOS

A serene cove with sand and shingle sheltered by a deep inlet and a dramatic wedge-shaped rock. A couple of caves provide shade.

→ From Glossa head E across the island, then zigzag SE, for around 4.5km in total. Park on the L by the church on the bend (39.1735, 23.6478) and follow the track heading W, parallel to the road. Fork L, pass through some buildings and criss-cross N steeply down through olive groves to the beach.

15 mins, 39.1760, 23.6452 🏖🏊🌊🏊☀

7 ST IOANNIS BEACH, SKOPELOS

After a sweaty climb up to St Ioannis Church (see entry), you may need a cool dip. Don't worry, this convenient little beach will provide it, in some style.

→ Continue 700m from Spilia Beach parking (see entry) and park at the end. Follow a short, steep path down from the L of the taverna.

2 mins, 39.1728, 23.6498 🏖🏊🅱

8 HOVOLO BEACH, SKOPELOS

A delightful stretch of pebbles beneath steep white cliffs and tumbling forest, with small pockets of morning shade. Swim, or climb very carefully, beyond the

jumping rocks at the southern end for more paradisal beaches.

→ Park at the S end of Elios Beach, where the buildings give way to trees, just S of Neo Klima. Skirt between the water's edge and the cliff S and be prepared to get your feet wet.

5 mins, 39.1329, 23.6451 ▼ ⭐ 🏖 🖼 🚶 ▼

9 FTELIA BEACH, SKOPELOS

This heavenly micro-beach lies beneath a lime-green canopy, bordered by twisted boughs and tiny sea caves.

→ Foot access is difficult but possible by climbing over the steep rocks at the S end of Hovolo Beach (see entry), walking along divine Ekatopenindari Beach and rounding another rock outcrop. Alternatively, rent a boat from Neo Klima; Wind Boat (+30 69 7729 6448) is a good option.

15 mins, 39.1285, 23.6485 ⭐ 🏖 🏄 🖼 ▼ 🐚

10 MILIA BEACH, SKOPELOS

A splendidly long pebble beach with classic Sporades views along the tree-lined coast. Organised in sections, including a kayaking agency at the northern end; head south to escape the crowds.

→ Head NW along the coast from Panormos for 1.5km, with a sharp bend R, then take a hairpin turn off L and park in the clearing behind the beach.

3 mins, 39.1152, 23.6528 ⭐ 🏖 🖼 🅱

11 VIRGIN MARY BEACH, SKOPELOS

Tucked around an unassuming corner at the far end of Skopelos marina, in the shadow of beautiful Virgin Mary Church, is this quiet and easily accessible pebble beach.

→ Park near the marina and at the very N end head round to the R of the church rock, where there are steps over to the beach.

2 mins, 39.1248, 23.7295 ⭐ 🏖

12 MIKROS MOURTIAS BEACH, ALONNISOS

A nudist-friendly pebble beach in a deep and pretty green bay at the end of a valley descending from Alonnisos Old Town.

→ Walk or drive from the Old Town: follow a 1.5km footpath from the S end of town, at the Knowledge Awareness Center, or drive a 2km dirt track heading SW from the big car park NW of town (keeping L at the first two junctions).

20 mins, 39.1435, 23.8382 ⭐ 🏖 ⊘ 🚶

15

13 GREMISA BEACH, ALONNISOS

A truly tiny cove hidden in the forest along a stretch of coastline replete with waterside rock plateaus.

→ There is a small signpost and path from a bend in the road around 1.3km SW of Patitiri, 100m NE of a parking layby at 39.1352, 23.8558. The final few steps of the 50m path are steep, with a rope to assist.

5 mins, 39.1356, 23.8572 🏊🚣👤🐚

14 SPARTINES BEACH, ALONNISOS

A secluded little bay in a gap between crumbling cliffs on the edge of a pine forest. The wind can make the water choppy.

→ Park in Votsi and follow the trail starting from a corner at the NE edge (39.1528, 23.8748). Wind for 200m through the forest down to the beach.

5 mins, 39.1543, 23.8779 🏊🚣⛺

15 TZORTZI BEACH, ALONNISOS

Perhaps the definition of a hidden gem: a short stretch of white pebbles sloping into shallow crystal waters, all backed by olive trees providing shade.

→ Turn E off the main road about 2.8km N from Votsi. Follow 1.6km, keeping L at a fork at 750m, and park in a large clearing at the end with trees in the middle (39.1652, 23.9021). Walk the dirt track on the L as you enter the parking area for 100m, then turn R onto the trail and weave down to the beach through the trees.

10 mins, 39.1668, 23.8999 🏊🚣👤🐚

16 KOKKINOKASTRO BEACH, ALONNISOS

A semi-organised beach with a charming beach bar and striking red headland. Keep walking to the southwestern end for some solitude.

→ Park as for Tzorti Beach (see entry). Take the second track on the R as you enter the parking area, which leads to stairs down to the beach.

5 mins, 39.1641, 23.9033 🏊🚣🅱

12

ROCKY PENINSULAS

17 PLAKES ROCKS, SKIATHOS

The alleyways of Skiathos lead to a pine-lined peninsula with winding stairs down to rock ledges for lounging and jumping.

→ Park in town and walk as far S as you can, W of the harbour. There is also a large triangular car park along the town's SW coast, from which you follow the coast SE.

10 mins, 39.1588, 23.488 🍴🏊🐚

13

18

18 AMARANDOS COVE, SKOPELOS

A rocky cove hugging a crystal sea pool on a peninsula gradually re-greening from a wildfire. Come for a late-afternoon swim and stay for sunset beneath the iconic pine trees, ideally with a hammock. A tiny sea cave also hides on the southern side of the peninsula.

→ Driving SE from Agnontas, almost immediately take a hairpin R onto a track and drive 1.3km to a L hairpin. Park here and follow a short path R to the cove. Cave at 39.0739, 23.7080.
3 mins, 39.0747, 23.7067 ▣⏇🏖

CHURCHES, CASTLES & TOMBS

19 SKIATHOS CASTLE

Built in 1360 as shelter from pirate raids, this was the main settlement on Skiathos through various occupations until 1829, when the island became part of independent Greece and it was abandoned. Its ruins are dotted with cacti gardens extending along a promontory with fantastic coastal views over Kastro Beach below.

→ Follow tracks NW from NE Skiathos for around 6km to a junction at 39.1978, 23.4605. Drive the fork N 1.2km to a parking area at the end. Walk the L fork 200m further.
5 mins, 39.2095, 23.4605 ▲⛰

20 ST IOANNIS CHURCH, SKOPELOS

200 carved stone steps lead up to this small church sitting atop a squat sea stack. Visit early in the morning; *Mamma Mia!* has made this a film-pilgrimage destination.

→ Best road access is from Glossa; park as for St Ioannis Beach or, if crowded, as for Spilia Beach (see entries).
15 mins, 39.1748, 23.6514 ▲✝B▣

21 SEDOUKIA TOMBS, SKOPELOS

A handful of impressive ancient rock-cut tombs, possibly Roman, lying at the stony summit of a forested hiking trail, with panoramic views over neighbouring Alonnisos.

→ Approach by car from the S, turning N off the road from Skopelos to Neo Klima at about 7km, at 39.1284, 23.6806. Fork L, then the trailhead is on the R after 950m, immediately following an industrial clearing. Red-paint dots mark the easy path.
20 mins, 39.1364, 23.6909 ▲⛰🚶

22 ST ANARGYROI CHURCHES, ALONNISOS

There are riches to be found at this rarely visited pair of churches, dedicated to the 'penniless saints'. They roost high on a tree-covered hillside with fabulous sea panorama, especially at sunset, and the approach is a delightful woodland jaunt.

→ Follow roads N from Votsi for about 3km to park in the small clearing on the side of the dirt road at 39.1715, 23.8779. There is a wooden sign to the church on a tree.
10 mins, 39.1737, 23.8769 ▣▲✝🚶

VIEWPOINTS

23 MANDRAKI PERCHES, SKIATHOS

A secretive sandy path leads through dense trees to a number of hidden openings onto cliff perches above Mandraki Beach. A great spot for sunset, best experienced from the swing of a hammock.

→ Drive as if to Agistros Beach (see entry) but turn N to the shore at the second crossroads. Park behind Elia Beach and follow the path heading W over a headland, via a clearing, into the trees. You can also head to Mandraki Beach from the first crossroads and delve N into the trees from the taverna at the S end.
5 mins, 39.1681, 23.3996 ▣▲🚶

24 KALOVOULOS VIEWPOINT, ALONNISOS

At the end of a steep ascent, a small shelter waits on this remote wooded peak, looking out over the western edge of the island with

huge sea-and-sky views to Skopelos.

→ Park in the large car park by the cemetery at the NW edge of the Old Town and head NW. Turn W opposite the church, take the first L and the trailhead is on the R after 100m (39.1514, 23.8393). The 1km track heads directly up the hill until a sharp R for the final 100m climb.

20 mins, 39.1487, 23.8323 ⬛🏔🚶

LOCAL FOOD & DRINK

25 LIGARIES TAVERNA, SKIATHOS

This remote beachside taverna offers fresh grilled seafood beneath a flowery trellis, complete with a sunset vista and friendly service.

→ Skiathos 370 02, +30 6981 536030
39.1803, 23.4448 🏖

26 MARMITA, SKIATHOS

A narrow street opens up into an enchanting plant-filled courtyard offering the best Greek food, and possibly the biggest smiles, on the island.

→ Skiathos 370 02, +30 2427 021701
39.1645, 23.4883 🏖

27 BOURTZI, SKIATHOS

An iconic café at the tip of an islet by Skiathos port, serving delicious cocktails and refreshments on a garden terrace with steps down to a private swimming platform.

→ Skiathos 370 02, +30 2427 023900
39.1608, 23.4911 🏖

28 KORALI, SKOPELOS

Dinner at Korali in the sleepy, picturesque bay at Agnontas is a sublime experience, with outrageously fresh seafood served to your table on the beach.

→ Agnontas 370 03, +30 2424 022407
39.083, 23.7115 🏖🏊🏕

29 ANATOLI, SKOPELOS

A gem at the very top of the town, up a series of steep steps. Sea views from the terrace and live music led by owner Giorgio and his trusty bouzouki. Reserve in the summer.

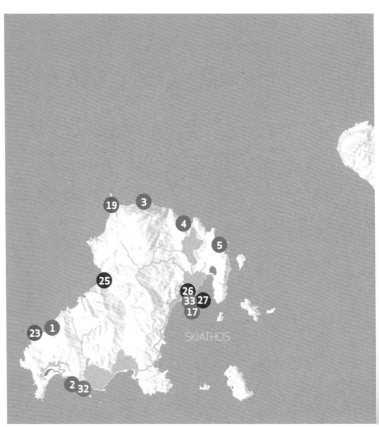

→ Skopelos 370 03, +30 2424 022851
39.1246, 23.7277 ▲B

30 SPIRA SKOPELOS BREWERS

A visit to this microbrewery in Skopelos port, established in 2018, is a delight. Recline in one of the deck chairs set up on the harbour and people-watch with a crisp ale. There is also a great cocktail bar (Vrachos) overlooking the harbour, should you fancy a change.

→ Skopelos 370 03, +30 6978 252848
39.1231, 23.7284 ⑪B

31 HAYIATI, ALONNISOS

Café by day, piano bar by night. The common factor is the sensational vista from the veranda over the coast towards Skopelos.

→ Alonnisos, 370 05, +30 2424 066244
39.1487, 23.8436 ▲

32 FOLIA VILLA, SKIATHOS

Shrouded in hillside pine trees, this airy house boasts a short staircase down to two small private beaches and a large wraparound terrace with sea views, including a dedicated sunset deck. It sleeps five between one bedroom and the sitting room.

→ Troulos 370 02, +30 69 4425 1795
39.14, 23.4161 ▨▨▨

33 KOULA'S HOUSE, SKIATHOS

A low-key hideaway in Skiathos town with easy access to the bustling alleys and even easier to the Aegean, via stone steps descending to a small swimming platform with a ladder into the water. Rooms and apartments sleeping two to four.

→ Skiathos 370 02, i-escape.com/koulas-house
39.1604, 23.4887 ▨▨

34 CASA MILOS WINDMILL, ALONNISOS

A wonderful stone windmill, built in 1850 at the base of the picturesque Old Town, with four floors linked by a spiral staircase and a panoramic terrace up top. Sleeps six.

→ Alonnisos 370 05, airbnb.com/rooms/6343068
39.1505, 23.8437 ▲

35 ALTHEA TRADITIONAL HOTEL, ALONNISOS

Simple, elegant rooms offering an incredible perspective over the island from your private pool.

→ Alonnisos 370 05, +30 2424 066255
39.1501, 23.8452 ▲

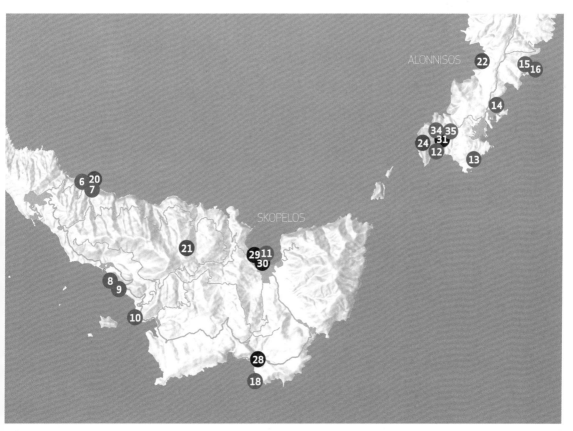

EVIA

Our perfect weekend

→ **Soak** in the plunge pool of spectacular Drymonas Waterfall, surrounded by lush forest.

→ **Salivate** over Marditsa's sumptuous mutton burger and homegrown delights.

→ **Trek** your way to the magnificent Purple Cave, its shimmering water framed beneath a huge collapsed mouth.

→ **Clamber** along the hulking ruins of Armena Castle, arrayed across an imposing ridgeline.

→ **Stock** up on beach beers at the fantastic Septem Microbrewery.

→ **Stargaze** by the fire on remote Archampoli Beach, reached by a wild headland walk.

→ **Leap** into calm, crystal waters from the unique, little-known Zarakon Rock Spit.

→ **Enter** Evia's finest *drakóspita* on the peak of Mount Ochi, emerging to sensational panoramic views.

Greece's second-largest island, after Crete, is just an hour or so from Athens and connected to the mainland by two suspension bridges. Yet its alpine heights, rugged coastline, gushing spring waterfalls and mysterious drakóspita, or dragon houses, are overlooked by most international tourists in favour of more 'islandy' islands. It's a trend worth bucking.

Hulking ranges trace Evia's long spine like a dragon's back, riven by gorges such as Nileas beneath Mount Dirfi to the north and Dimosari by Mount Ochi to the south – both offering fantastic seasonal swims and year-round walks. Beyond the barren south, the mountains also cradle sumptuous waterfalls like Manikiatis and Drymonas, with inviting pools beneath. And with dreamlike basecamps like Lavender Farm Cottage or The River House on the Red Rock hiding in the foothills nearby, there's no need to rush.

Evia's mountains are also scattered with peculiar historical relics. On Mount Ochi's southeastern foothills, above Mili, lie the fallen Roman Columns of Karystos, giant relics of ancient marble mining. And Ochi peak holds arguably the finest of Evia's mysterious drakóspita: ancient hilltop buildings with uniquely corbelled roofs, their purpose and origin unknown. Their unmortared limestone slabs are so impressive that it is said dragons must have built them, hence the name. Another group, Styra Dragon Houses, sits in the woodland beneath domineering Armena Castle, its mighty stone blocks arrayed along a grand ridgeline dominating central Evia.

Hiding beyond these peaks and ridgelines, Evia's eastern and southern beaches rival those anywhere in Greece. Remote, gorge-mouth Archampoli Beach awaits at the end of a wild coastal walk, while secluded Damianos Beach is a wild camper's dream, along a trail crossing dense headlands and secret beaches. And the enveloping bay of Thapsa Beach feels like Evia's Shangri-La. All warrant full days and full nights spent in sun-drenched, fire-warmed reverence.

If Evia takes more travelling than most Greek islands, one reward is gastronomic variety. Family-run Vriniotis, perched above the North Euboean Gulf, is the pick of Evia's wineries. In the south, Septem Microbrewery produces a range of craft beers to stock up on for beach trips. And fittingly for an island derived from the words for 'good' and 'ox', Evia's tavernas specialise in sensational meats. Mardista's mutton burger is to die for, as are the dishes at O Platanos Karystinakis and Taverna O Tseligas, all paired with an abundance of homemade vegetables, cheeses and garden delights.

BEACHES

1 DAFNI BEACH

Cascading pine hills provide morning shade on this thin, arcing beach. The water is clear and cold, fed by Mount Kantili's streams. Stroll away from the tavernas for solitude, and be sure to stay for sunset.

→ There is a car park on the L just before the end of the road from Dafni. Follow the path down to the beach.

2 mins, 38.6336, 23.4922 🏊🏖🛶

2 VITHOURI BEACH

Pebble beach, deep inlet and towering rockfaces at the end of a winding valley track. There's a small cave to the rear offering shelter for a night around the campfire.

→ From a hairpin bend and bridge just SE of Glifada village, turn N on the road down into the valley. Turn sharp L after 1.5km, then fork R after another 900m. Continue 2.5km to park at the beach.

1 min, 38.6876, 23.8202 🏊🏖🏕🛶

3 LIVADAKIA BEACH

A sweeping beach, wild and peaceful, backed by luscious mountains. The tranquillity attracts the odd hardy camper.

→ Head SW from Lamari village, and after 600m turn R steeply uphill. After 2km take a hairpin R, and in another 2km fork R to descend switchbacks 1.5km to beach. It's driveable to the beach, but rough; proceed with caution.

1 min, 38.6753, 23.8976 🏊🏖🏕❓🛶

4 KOKKINIA BEACH

This smaller, pebblier, similarly beautiful neighbour of Trianisia Beach (see entry) is nestled beneath towering green hillsides.

→ As for Trianisia Beach, but head L at the final fork. Rough but passable with caution in a normal car.

1 min, 38.6783, 23.8925 🏊🏖❓🛶

5 DAMIANOS BEACH

The last of a string of magical pebble beaches tucked between green headlands, popular with naturists and long-term campers. A sea cave through the headland connects the beach dramatically with the open sea beyond.

→ Park at popular Chiliadou Beach (signed from Stropones village). From the W end follow a rough path for 500m across a middle beach and a headland. Serious scrambling required. Otherwise it's boat access only.

20 mins, 38.6724, 23.9118 🏊🚫🏖🏕⛺❓🛶

6 THAPSA BEACH

A splendid sunset-facing bay with placid water, pocked with rocky nooks for campers and served by a relaxed beach bar. High summer can be busy, but the tricky access limits crowdedness.

→ 6.4km W of Kymi on the Artakis to Kimis road (38.6476, 24.0454), take a signed track N. Follow it 5.2km, ignoring a couple of R forks and smaller tracks, to Tsilaros Beach (see entry). Continue on a steep red track another 1.5km W to Thapsa Beach. It's passable in a normal car with confident driving.

1 min, 38.6754, 24.0133 🏊🏖🏕❓

7 TSILAROS BEACH

The quieter and only slightly less majestic neighbour of Thapsa Beach (see entry) is easier to reach, with serene turquoise waters below red rocks and wooded slopes.

→ Follow the route for Thapsa Beach, but stop and park at the first beach.

1 min, 38.6769, 24.0283 🏊🏖🛶

8 KOSKINA BEACH

A small, lazy cove with a shady glade of pine and bamboo creating a calming space for tents and hammocks. There is another beach

with the same name a few kilometres north.

→ Good tracks lead either S from Koskina or E from the main coastal road to a crossroads at 38.3413, 24.1933. Follow the E track 1.75km from here to parking by the beach.
1 min, 38.341, 24.2043 🏊⛴🏕⚓🌊🏖

9 ST DIMITRIOS BEACH

A large sandy beach and estuary, with a pleasant cafe and small sea cave, carved into the rugged north-facing coastline of this southern region. Upstream, the river is a string of cooling pools at the right time of year.

→ Heading N from Agios Dimitrios, bend sharply R above the beach then hairpin L 300m later down to an expansive beachside parking area.
1 min, 38.1416, 24.4477 🏊⛴🍴🌊

10 AMIGDALIA BEACH

Fishing boats and rock pools add character to this boulder-strewn beach below the clifftop village of Amigdalia.

→ A winding coastal lane descends NE from Amigdalia to the beach.
1 min, 38.126, 24.5822 🏊⛴

11 ARCHAMPOLI BEACH

You'll likely be alone at this spectacular pebble beach, which lies at the mouth of wild Archampoli Gorge, protected by a sheer rockface to the south. The foundations of an ancient town are still visible.

→ Park in Thimio hamlet at the end of the track past the church (38.0963, 24.5683). Skirt the fence heading SW into the olive groves, where a path descends L to the gorge floor, taking you back on yourself and joining a sumptuous 1.5km coastal trail to the beach.
35 mins, 38.0923, 24.5777 🏊⛴🚴🚶🌊🏖

12 CAPE KAFIREAS BEACH

A remote cove with a sandy beach and a river running in from a gorge, via explorable pools and falls.

→ Heading E out of Komito village, fork R then bear R onto a rougher track after 2km. After another 1.8km park by a junction (38.0712, 24.5761) and walk down the track R to the beach, unless you have a 4x4.
10 mins, 38.0696, 24.5797 🏊⛴🌊

WATERFALLS

13 KREMASI WATERFALL

Snaking along a rugged riverbed, sometimes cascading, the water eventually falls to fill a cold, wide paddling pool.

→ Follow the road SE from Agdines about 300m to two tracks, L and R. Follow the R track 3km. Walk (50 mins) or drive as far as you're comfortable, via many zigzags (a phone with GPS or a saved map will be helpful), to where the track joins the riverbed (38.9476, 23.2969). The falls are 300m upriver from here.
50 mins, 38.9447, 23.2974 🏊⛴🐚❓

14 DRYMONAS WATERFALL

A dramatic free-falling cataract, cascading from a curved overhang into an enticing forest pool. The water level dwindles by early summer, but the surrounding woodland remains a shaded sanctuary.

→ Take the EO77 SW from Kerasia for nearly 3km. Fork L at 38.8877, 23.3133 and continue for 2.5km, keeping L at a fork just before the parking area. Follow the clear, signed trail with ropes and railings to the falls.
5 mins, 38.8723, 23.2933 🏊⛴🌊🅱

15 MANIKIATIS WATERFALL

The river, sculpted limestone gorge and this stunning waterfall share the same name. The gorge-bottom rocks and pools lead to a deep, dramatically enclosed swimming hole, which stays after the waterfall dries in late summer.

14

→ Follow a lane out of Manikia village past St Marina church 1km to a T junction. Turn L, keep L at the fork after 500m and bend sharp L after another 1.2km. Continue 750m and park by the church (38.5410, 24.0061). Walk N for around 1km along the riverbed.
15 mins, 38.5464, 24.0049 🏊🏃

16 BRIDGE OF LOVERS

A pretty waterfall cascading 10m into a small river by a shaded bend in the road. Perfect for a cheeky river dip on the fly.

→ Right next to the road, just under 1km NW from Platanistos. There is parking and seating.
1 min, 38.0248, 24.5096 🏊🏞

HOT SPRINGS & SEA CAVES

17 EDIPSOS THERMAL SPRINGS

Thermal springs providing warm (sometimes hot!) beach bathing for all seasons, both in the sea and in specially created pools, all for free. Rich in magnesium, calcium and iron, these springs have been cherished since antiquity for their healing properties.

→ Street parking in Edipsos. Pools are below the plaza opposite the S end of Filellinon.
1 min, 38.8526, 23.047 🏊B

18 ZARAKON ROCK SPIT

These layered rock formations provide excellent jumping points into the wondrous waters of a seemingly inaccessible bay hidden over the headland east of Zarakon Beach.

→ Park at Zarakon Beach and follow a track, turning into a path, from the R end of the beach (38.3149, 24.2265) 500m to a high saddle between two coves. It continues, now fainter, skirting the R-hand bay through the undergrowth to the spit.
10 mins, 38.3168, 24.2352 🍴🥾🏊⛅

19 PURPLE CAVE

Breathtaking open-roof sea cave with under-water entrances, popular with divers. Also accessible by bushwhacking and climbing.

→ Tricky foot access; digital map highly advisable. From Mesochoria, follow the road from behind the church and cemetery 5km E and N around hills below a power station to 38.2739, 24.2495, where three dirt tracks leave the road R. Follow the L-most track N about 400m to the end, then continue in the same direction for 150m to meet another track (38.2790, 24.25156). Follow this line N for 800m and turn R (38.2865, 24.2516), picking your way to the sea and cave. Only climb down with extreme caution.
30 mins, 38.286, 24.2555 🏊🐟❓🏞⛅V🥾

8

16

PEAKS & GORGES

20 NILEAS GORGE

Depending on the season, this narrow, rugged gorge can be an adventure swim or a shaded riverbed hike. Wonderful either way, with early summer particularly dreamlike.

→ For easiest access, drive around 1km NW from Agia Anna and take a hairpin L. Descend 3km through switchbacks to a bridge (38.8672, 23.3787), park and scramble down. Head S 1km for the most dramatic section. You can also enter or exit from the S (38.8548, 23.3782), by cutting down from the paths above to the E.
20 mins, 38.8568, 23.3809

21 AGALI GORGE

A verdant gorge with small bridges criss-crossing the river between towering rock slopes. You can hike for hours or enjoy a short stroll.

→ Head E from Agios Athanasios to the football pitch, crossing a road. Keep L after the pitch and park at the end of the track, where the gorge starts.
5 mins, 38.614, 23.8017

22 DIMOSARI GORGE

A gorge abundant with wildlife, fauna and even fossils. The sometimes rugged trail winds through countless cooling pools and waterfalls, right to the sea, but the most beautiful section is further inland.

→ Follow the moderate dirt road along the side of the gorge and park near the end in Lenosei village. Follow a stone path S, uphill, into the gorge. A 3km round trip is rewarding.
10 mins, 38.1099, 24.4836

23 MOUNT OCHI DRAGON HOUSE

One of Evia's highest peaks, Ochi offers panoramic views after just one hour of walking. It is also home to arguably Evia's finest drakóspita, with an intact roof, as well as a chapel and other archeological remains.

→ The hike to the peak starts at Ochi Refuge (38.0529, 24.4645), following red dots and cairns. To reach the refuge, turn N off Epar.Od. Karystou-Amigdalios where it bends around a communication antenna (37.9844, 24.4975). Continue N for 10km, taking the middle route at 1.4km and L route at 7.8km, to park at the bend below the refuge.
90 mins, 38.0597, 24.4667

RUINS & CULTURAL RELICS

24 ST GEORGIOS CASTLE

The ruinous remains of a 13th-century Byzantine castle and the more intact chapel to its saint are both perched on a steep, untracked hill. On a clear day the magnificent panoramic vista includes the Sporades archipelago to the north.

→ Driving E from Kimi, fork L 250m past the hospital and climb for 3km, ignoring R forks and turns until the end. Approaching the monastery, fork R onto a dirt track and curve behind the monastery. Drive or walk past the outbuildings to start scrambling up to the R (38.6603, 24.1047).
10 mins, 38.6618, 24.1029

25 STYRA DRAGON HOUSES

Also called the Palli Lakka dragon houses, this is a group of three of Evia's legendary drakóspita, built with huge unmortared limestone blocks and slabs. Archeology conducted here has confirmed that they were built in antiquity, but yielded no clue as to their purpose.

➜ Follow the main track E from Styra. Turn R at a T junction after about 1.5km and continue another 1.5km, ignoring one L then two R forks, to a parking area at the end. Walk a sharp 100m trail to dragon house.

3 mins, 38.1529, 24.2636

26 ARMENA CASTLE

A spectacular fortress sprawling across a striking ridgeline surveying central Evia and Attica beyond. This powerful position was fortified from the Bronze Age to the 17th century. The huge stone gate is just one highlight.

➜ Easiest access is via a wind-farm track leaving Epar.Od.Lepouron Karistou about 4.5km S from Kapsala (38.1169, 24.2399). Follow it 5.5km, keeping L at the major fork, to park in a layby on the R (38.1501, 24.2679). Take the trail opposite. For a longer but more impressive hike through the hills, follow the route to Styra Dragon Houses (see entry) but follow the first of the two R forks to a trailhead at the end.

10 mins, 38.1457, 24.2621

27 ANTIAS

This picturesque village is the last bastion of a rare and vanishing whistling language, Sfyria. Shepherds developed it to communicate across the mountainous landscape. Chatting with locals might lead you to one of the few remaining language keepers.

➜ The cafe, Kapheneio, is a good place to refresh and enquire.

1 min, 38.0546, 24.5352

28 ROMAN COLUMNS OF KARYSTOS

The Romans quarried the finely patterned marble here 2,000 years ago for prestige structures. Some of the giant pillars, 12m long, remain fallen on the mountainside, atmospheric relics with magnificent views.

➜ Follow road winding NE out of Mili to a reasonable but steep 1.5km path shortly after passing behind the last house (38.0356, 24.4400), marked by red dots.

45 mins, 38.0378, 24.447

LOCAL FOOD & DRINK

29 AKROGIALI TAVERNA

A quiet seaside taverna with a garden, a kids' play area and its own beach – all operated by a friendly family. The seafood is morning fresh.

➜ Vouliki 342 00, +30 2226 040382 39.0234, 23.2558

30 VRINIOTIS WINERY

This delectable family winery is nestled on a hillside overlooking the North Euboean Gulf. The fabulous wines are produced with traditional techniques and new technologies.

➜ Gialtra 343 00, +30 2226 032429 38.8669, 22.9736

31 KANDILI NATURAL FARM SHOP

A tiny farm shop selling organic produce and offering working farm stays. Stop for some fresh vegetables or eggs if you're driving past.

➜ Prokopi 340 04, +30 69 8669 3527 38.7168, 23.5168

32 MARDITSA

Village taverna dining in a courtyard that feels like a family garden of local friends. Home-grown ingredients, hearty cooking and warm-hearted service make this an excellent choice. The mutton burger is the recommendation.

➜ Mili 344 00, +30 2228 022110 38.7225, 23.7388

33 TAVERNA O TSELIGAS

A super rural taverna buried in the verdant Dirfi foothills. The meat is particularly sumptuous. Ideal for a post-beach feast.

➜ Dirfis 340 14, +30 69 8501 9744 38.6747, 23.788

34 SEPTEM MICROBREWERY

An internationally renowned but locally rooted microbrewery producing a broad range of craft beers to suit any palette.

➜ Orologio 340 09, +30 2222 770000 38.5201, 24.1076

35 O PLATANOS KARYSTINAKIS

A wonderful family taverna with a meat-centred menu, beneath a huge plane tree. The homemade cheeses and fire-cooked meats are superb.

➔ Karystos 340 01, +30 2224 024300
38.0324, 24.4348

STAY

36 CAMPING PEFKI

One of Evia's best campsites. Quiet, clean, shaded pitches by the beach, as well as simple, pet-friendly bungalows.

➔ Artemisio 342 00, +30 2226 040469
39.0196, 23.2256

37 LAVENDER FARM COTTAGE

A charming pastel-pink house tangled in the ivy of a lavender farm. The attractive interior opens to a bountiful garden with a rolling pool-to-ocean vista. Fresh hen eggs every morning. Sleeps six.

➔ Galatsades 342 00, airbnb.com/
rooms/25718247
38.8965, 23.1709

38 ELEONAS

This peaceful boutique hotel on an organic olive farm by the coast offers a farm-made breakfast every morning and walking trails, yoga, sports equipment and outdoor adventures.

➔ Rovies 340 05, +30 2227 071619
38.8191, 23.2253

39 KIRINTHOU ECOLOGICAL FARM

A rustic one-bedroom house built with traditional and sustainable materials on an organic pomegranate farm, with daily home-grown produce and opportunities to learn about the estate. Simple decor, no TV or wifi and space for two.

➔ Kirithnos 340 04, airbnb.com/
rooms/30358925
38.8116, 23.46063

40 MAKRIGIALOS BEACH CAMPING

Free beach camping among a community of wild tent dwellers, with access to a small shop, a taverna and smaller bays nearby.

➔ No booking, simply parking available at the beach.
38.7523, 23.682

41 THE RIVER HOUSE ON THE RED ROCK

A fairytale abode snuggled deep in a forest of fir and cherry trees, with room for sixteen. Host Giánnis is happy to facilitate adventurous activities, from mushroom walks to music evenings and open-air film nights.

➔ Seta 340 06, airbnb.com/
rooms/50005920
38.5646, 23.9354

CENTRAL GREECE

Our perfect weekend

→ **Plunge** into the vibrant blue Achleous River from the white ledges by Templas Bridge.

→ **Ogle** at the enormous mountain panorama from St Andreas the Hermit Church, burrowed into a wild bluff.

→ **Quest** up a gorge, via an eerie cave and a thrilling via ferrata traverse, to the Black Cave Waterfalls.

→ **Marvel** at the ethereal spectacle of glimmering waterfalls raining down in the heart of Panta Vrechei Gorge.

→ **Escape** the Delphi extravaganza in the pastoral simplicity of Stone House, up in the Parnassos foothills.

→ **Steel** yourself for the vertiginous and exposed Karagianni's Path, on the spectacular hike up to the peak of Mount Giona.

→ **Ponder** from a private perch in secret Harvali Cave, rising above the canopy with views to Evia.

→ **Dine** on hearty mountain fare in a distant alpine glade at Arvanitsa Restaurant, adorned with historical curios.

Lacking the name recognition of more illustrious neighbours and islands, Central Greece is easy to overlook. But avoid the temptation. The region may lack coastal splendour, but where the eastern plains soar into massive Mount Parnassos north of legendary Delphi, a northwesterly procession of giant peaks begins, hiding dramatic gorges, tendrilled lakes, storied ruins and astonishing caverns. In antiquity this region was the home of the Muses, sacred to Dionysus and Apollo, and in modern times it became host to one of the first National Parks in Greece.

Despite a lack of beaches, there are wild swims aplenty here. Paddle at the grand gorge junction where Dipotama Bridge crosses the rushing Krikeliotis River by its confluence with the Karpenisiotis, and float lazily under arched Kefalogefyro Bridge, which spans the Mornos River in a pretty canyon. Lake Trichonida - Greece's largest natural lake, and a core nesting site for rare and threatened bird species - does harbour quiet beaches. Then there are Central Greece's mind-bendingly big dammed reservoirs. Kastraki Lake Pier pokes tentatively into one, and ruined Velouchovo Castle juts into Mornos Lake on a striking promontory; both make fine dips.

Waterfalls are the high watermarks here, though – especially the sublime trio ensconced by Panetoliko, Kaliakouda and Chelidona peaks. Ordinarily, the shimmering river-canyon walk, or wade, beneath Mikro Panta Vrechei Gorge's string of mossy waterfalls would be unique. But *mikro* means 'micro', for the gorge is named after its more spectacular cousin, Panta Vrechei Gorge (the rest means 'always raining'). It's possibly Greece's most wondrous gorge walk, though neighbouring Black Cave gorge might stake a claim. It boasts a lower cascade pool, a delightful river, the mysterious Black Cave and a secret second fall beyond a thrilling via ferrata traverse and short canyon wade. Visit them all and retire to Katafygio Chalet, a romantic log cabin in the forested Mount Kaliakouda foothills, to consider which is finest.

Drier gorge adventure awaits in Asopos, where you can hike either the gorge itself – steadily narrowing, often with a running river to navigate – or the hair-raising trail following the tracks and tunnels of a 100-year-old railway line forging along the gorge edge. Or do both, staying for a night of local specialities at Litsa Taverna and funky accommodation at Vasilikia Mountain Farm & Retreat, by Oitis National Park.

Central Greece's parade of peaks also harbours remarkable caves, two with somehow little-known churches. The vista over Kremasta Lake from St Andreas the Hermit Church, following a fabulous bluff walk, is mind-boggling; and Arsalis Church's cave belfry, reached incredibly by via ferrata, surveys Ypati with similar splendour. Corycian Cave bears a more mysterious human imprint. Its secret chambers were once a place of worship to Pan, god of the wild, and supposedly home to the Corycian nymphs and a one-time prison of Zeus himself. It sits in the Mount Parnassos foothills above mythic mecca Delphi, centre of the world to the ancient Greeks. Savour this area with a night or two at plush Kanella Ski Lodge (Parnassos has Greece's best skiing) and the infectious culinary passion of chef Yannis at To Tsoukali.

LAKE DIPS

1 KASTRAKI LAKE PIER

Among the reeds on a meandering peninsula extending into the bright-blue water of Kastraki Lake is this cute covered pier. Stop for a dip and a picnic if passing by.

→ Leave the lakeside road 11km N from Kastraki on the S-most lane heading into Mpampalio hamlet (38.8228, 21.3244). Keep R and park in the open space on the first, narrow section of the peninsula. Walk onwards and L.

2 mins, 38.8238, 21.3302 🏖🌀

2 LAKE TRICHONIDA BEACH

A small, lonesome beach tucked below the road on this varied lake shore. A nice spot for a more private swim than the pier down the road.

→ Park in the layby above the beach around 2.4km NW of Kapsorrachi and walk the 200m trail down. The pier is at 38.5089, 21.6096.

5 mins, 38.5208, 21.5986 🏖⛺🚶

3 PETROCHORI BEACH

A quiet pebble beach at the end of Lake Trichonida, backed by a row of gnarled olive trees.

→ On the road skirting NW of Petrochori, turn W onto a track just E of the lakeside viewing point (38.5498, 21.6463). Follow the switchbacks down to the beach, keeping R (though L at the church). Alternatively, take the coastal lane S from Loutra past inviting waterside laybys (38.5713, 21.6163).

1 min, 38.5449, 21.6398 🏖🚶

RIVER BRIDGES

4 TEMPLAS BRIDGE

The bright Achelous River runs under this arched stone bridge, with fun rock formations for jumping. Though built in 1909, the bridge echoes the older style of the region.

→ Descend from Vrouviana to the E for 3km, until the road meets the river. Park at either end of the old bridge.

1 min, 39.1007, 21.4342 🍴🚶

5 DIPOTAMA BRIDGE

An old stone bridge crossing the rushing Krikeliotis River at a meeting of mighty gorges. The broad pebbly riverbanks are great for a paddle, a picnic or some kayak spotting.

→ You drive right past it on the new bridge 9km S of Gavros, on the road to Prousos. Pull off at either end.

2 mins, 38.7793, 21.6811 🏖⛺🚴

6 BANIA BAILEY BRIDGE

Because the original stone bridge here was destroyed in the Second World War, this scenic iron Bailey bridge with wooden slats was laid to reconnect the remaining ends across the rushing Evinos River in 1954. Rattle your way over and head down to the waters below, popular with rafters.

→ Cross the bridge heading N, out of Gefira Mpania village, fork R then take the first R and park in the open area on the R to access the river beach below the bridge. Rafting can be booked with Outdoor LAB (+30 69 3674 6764).

2 mins, 38.4521, 21.7012 ⛺🚴🚶🏖🌀

7 KEFALOGEFYRO BRIDGE

An arched stone river bridge in a secluded gorge. A lovely walk and an even better picnic and dip, when the water level is right.

→ Heading N from Kato Dafni, after 6km take the first R after St Paraskevi Church (38.4646, 21.8765). From here a 3km track turns E and skirts the riverbank, fading to a

rough trail. Drive what you can and enjoy the rest as a walk.

60 mins, 38.4737, 21.9035

WATERFALLS

8 KLEISOURA WATERFALL

A tall, thin waterfall carved into a cornered cliff. You'll almost certainly be alone.

➔ Turn L off the highway heading S just past Fragkouleika. Park between the buildings and river around the L bend. Follow the riverbed S for around 200m. You can also pick your way through the scrub on the E side of the river, but it's a pathless maze.

10 mins, 38.5131, 21.3827

9 BLACK CAVE WATERFALLS

A secret waterfall and plunge pool reached via a lower, more accessible waterfall pool (also fantastic), an exciting *via ferrata* traverse and a short upstream paddle, just below Black Cave (see entry). The jewel in the crown of this fabulous gorge adventure.

➔ Drive S 1.7km from Prousos and park at the trailhead in a layby just before a L bend with signs and benches (38.7340, 21.6513). The trail leads around 700m into the gorge, steep in places. The lower waterfall is at 38.7325,

21.6471 and the via ferrata traverses L upstream just below the cave.

20 mins, 38.7323, 21.6449

10 MIKRO PANTA VRECHEI GORGE

The smaller, similarly beautiful cousin to Panta Vrechei Gorge (see entry). Walk, paddle or wade along the slender canyon, its ivy-draped walls glimmering in the spray, to a series of magical pools and falls.

➔ Park at the Holy Trinity Church at the N end of Tornos, behind which a marked path starts. Follow it 1.6km NW down into the gorge.

30 mins, 38.7516, 21.669

11 PANTA VRECHEI GORGE

Possibly Greece's most magical gorge walk. Paddle, wade and even swim along the pristine Krikeliotis River, beneath a rickety footbridge and into a narrow, twisting canyon that ushers you towards a kaleidoscopic hideaway of shimmering mossy falls. Panta Vrechei means 'always raining', named for the springs in the cliffs above, though optimal water flow is from early summer to September. Bring sensible shoes and prepare to get wet.

➔ Easiest access is from Prousos to the S, via Tornos, Kastania, Prodromos and Roska,

though don't risk it in a normal car after bad weather. The gorge walk starts at Krikeliotis bridge, 4km N from Roska, with parking on the N side (38.7589, 21.7594). The main falls are a roughly 35-min walk W.

40 mins, 38.7579, 21.7467

12 KAPNOCHORI WATERFALLS

Two tall, little-known waterfalls. The upper fall feeds the lower one, which in turn fills a shallow pool flowing into a series of cascading chutes, all accessible by a funky via ferrata hike.

➔ Park on the E side of the river bridge between Kapnochori and Ypati, by a map board. Follow the trail S along the L side of the river, curving R before turning L (38.8617, 22.2325). Turn 90 degrees uphill for the lower fall, or more gently L, to walk almost parallel to the river, for the upper fall (at 38.8594, 22.2332). Both trails are similar distances, and have slippery via ferrata sections.

20 mins, 38.8596, 22.2335

CAVES

13 BLACK CAVE

This large cave, half-enclosed by a crumbling wall, awaits at the end of a wondrous

river-gorge trail that takes in the Black Cave Waterfalls (see entry). Its history and purpose are obscure, but it's all the more dramatic for that.

→ Park and walk as for Black Cave Waterfalls, passing the lower one; the cave is just above the via ferrata.

20 mins, 38.7324, 21.6456 🚗🏃🚴🏊📷

14 CORYCIAN CAVE

A domed cave overlooking the arable plains north of Delphi. It is named after the Corycian nymphs said to have once inhabited its depths, and was certainly a sacred place back as far as the Neolithic. Each of its three chambers is more difficult to access than the last. Bring a strong torch, good shoes, sensible clothes and explore, being careful of the slippy ground and loose rocks.

→ On the main road around 3.5km N from Kalyvia Livadiou Arachovas hairpin L onto a track (38.5404, 22.5301). Fork R after 800m and continue 2.5km to parking by the cave. Some people hike N from Delphi.

2 mins, 38.5157, 22.5215 🏔🕇🚴🔽📷

15 HARVALI CAVE

A gaping cave, with inner perches you can scramble to, rising above the canopy on a steep forested hillside, giving terrific views over Kamena Vourla to the Malian Gulf.

→ Easiest with a vehicle. Leave Karia village at the E edge, on the more northerly of the two tracks (38.7494, 22.7870). Fork L and L again, and park 2.5km after the second fork, on the second R hairpin (38.7630, 22.7908). The road gets boggy in the wet, so drive with caution without a 4x4. Hunt out the sign in the trees for a trail leading N to the cave. It descends to join the highway outside Kamena Vourla (38.7738, 22.7931); this would be a stiff hike up, climbing over 500m.

15 mins, 38.7658, 22.7900 🏔🚴🌲🔽📷

FORTIFIED RUINS

16 THESTIA ACROPOLIS

On a narrow plateau with dramatic panoramic views surveying the surrounding valleys and Lake Trichonida, this ancient acropolis was in use from the Mycenaean to the Greek War of Independence in the 1820s. Today it is surprisingly overlooked.

→ Drive uphill 2km from Ano Vlochos and park at the final switchback before the monastery (38.6543, 21.4855). Iron stairs, starting on the L just before the monastery, lead to the summit.

5 mins, 38.6539, 21.4867 🏔🕇🛹

17 VELOUCHOVO CASTLE

The ruins of a Frankish castle are laid over an earlier village and the acropolis of ancient Kallion, on a promontory jutting into Mornos Lake. The panorama of lakes and receding mountains makes this an awesome perch. Take a dip afterwards at the beach.

→ Drive 2km anti-clockwise round the lake from Callium hamlet and take the second of two neighbouring tracks L (the first L leads to a walkable beach at 38.5500, 22.1644). The L fork (not the fainter track to its L) leads 600m to below the ruins. It's drivable, but some rocky patches might make walking preferable. A short trail starts on the R edge of the rocky promontory.

5 mins, 38.5481, 22.1604 🏔✝♿🔺❄

18 AMFISSA CASTLE

A mostly 13th-century Frankish castle built on the remains of an ancient acropolis in a park overlooking Amfissa. It makes a lovely morning stroll as the town awakens below.

→ Lanes along the W edge of Amfissa lead to a parking area right by the castle. If already in town it's simpler and more pleasant to walk up.

2 mins, 38.5315, 22.3738 🏔♿

19 ANCIENT DELPHI

Considered the centre of the world by ancient Greeks, Delphi is perhaps Greece's most important archeological site. Originally the seat of the Oracle Gaea, and later of Apollo, the complex contains sacred sanctuaries, a theatre, a stadium and an archeological museum, all arrayed above a sweeping valley. Allow a few hours.

→ The archeological complex is just E of modern Delphi on the 48. Park at the Delphi Archeological Museum just after the first sweeping L heading out of town. Adult tickets for the entire site cost €12, or €6 in winter.

1 min, 38.4803, 22.4999 🏔✝♿B

20 VOURLIA CASTLE

Small castle ruins on a promontory with serene views over Agios Isidoros below and the Gulf of Corinth beyond.

→ Turn S off the main road 500m SW of Antikiras, on a hairpin, and continue into Agios Isidoros, turning L along the bay's E shore. The main gate is closed due to a dangerous path. Instead, fork R and park at the end of the track (38.3580, 22.6215). Pick your way on foot through fields and gates to the ruins.

10 mins, 38.3563, 22.6220 🏔♿

26

21 PROPHET ELIAS MONASTERY

A squat, fortified monastery of stone and uncertain age, abandoned but conserved, hiding deep in the rolling hills of Phthiotis. You can explore its courtyards, wooden walkways and 18th-century *katholikon* in splendid isolation.

→ Follow a reasonable dirt track a little over 7km NW from Zeli.

1 min, 38.6781, 22.8249 ✝🏛️⊙

22 LIVADIA CASTLE

A pine-covered hill topped by the ruins of one of four castles in Greece attributed to mercenaries of the 14th-century Catalan Company – although it was fortified since antiquity. There is also a chapel, a summertime amphitheatre and an Ottoman stone aqueduct. A lovely stroll.

→ Park in the car park under the trees at the S edge of Livadia (38.4326, 22.8749). Walk S and W to ruins. The aqueduct is at 38.4263, 22.8703.

5 mins, 38.4311, 22.8729 🏛️✝⛲🚶

GORGE & MOUNTAIN WALKS

23 MOUNT GIONA

Greece's fifth-highest peak is one for experienced hikers, who will love the notoriously steep and exposed Karagianni's Path on the ascent from Sikia. It requires via ferrata, scrambling and a cool head.

→ The dot-marked trail heads E from the basketball court at the N edge of Sikia, bears R up the valleyside and turns R at a grassy saddle at 38.6468, 22.2334 to join Karagianni's Path. At the peak it loops L, down into the valley and back to Sikia, for an approximately 15km loop. Not to be attempted without the right experience, gear and paper or digital map.

8 hrs, 38.6474, 22.2545 ⛰️🚶🏔️🎒📷▽

24 ASOPOS RAILWAY WALK

This breathtaking and at times hair-raising trail encounters tracks, narrow ledges, bridges and tunnels as it traces the 100-year-old railway line that teeters and burrows its way along the edge of Asopos Gorge.

→ Head S from Irakleia for 1km and turn R onto a track opposite a church amid trees (38.7908, 22.4432). Park here or drive up the track a little,

23

25

143

but don't leave any valuables in your car as thieves operate here. Walk the switchbacks up to the coordinates below, 1.6km from the road, where a trail heads L by a board with a QR code route map. From here it's a spectacular 3.5km to Asopos train station. Allow four hours for a full hike from the map board to the station and back.

2–4 hours, 38.7892, 22.4389 ⛰🚶

25 ASOPOS GORGE

This 2.5km river gorge steadily narrows into a thrilling, engulfing canyon. Depending on the water level, pools and flowing falls can add to the excitement.

→ Park by the bridge at the NE end of the gorge, around 1.7km S of Irakleia. Don't leave valuables in your car, as there have been reports of thieves. Allow three hours for a relaxed, full-gorge walk.

5 mins, 38.7894, 22.4433 🏊🚶📹

CAVE CHURCHES

26 ST ANDREAS THE HERMIT CHURCH

A dark, evocative cave church clinging to a hulking ridgeline, with staggering views north over Kremasta Lake and beyond. A powerful outing.

→ Entering Agios Vlasios village from the

S, hairpin R onto a good track (38.9749, 21.3909). Follow it around 5km and park at the abandoned building at the end. A wonderful trail continues for roughly 1km to the church.

20 mins, 38.9922, 21.3829 ⛰✝🚶🌲☀📷

27 ARSALIS CHURCH

A difficult hike is rewarded with a truly special church, built into a gaping cave mouth with a via ferrata belfry and a magnificent perspective over the plains beyond Ypati. A giant cross awaits slightly further up the trail.

→ Heading E out of Ypati, hairpin R onto a paved track (38.8719, 22.2451). Take the first L fork at about 1.8km and park by the church. Continue S uphill on foot and turn L after 400m, just after a solitary outbuilding, onto a smaller downhill path. Head R momentarily along the dry riverbed, then spot the steep, marked trail on your L. Climb it to the church, with a R fork right at the end (L to the cross).

2 hrs, 38.8622, 22.2585 ⛰✝🏠🚶🌲☀📷

28 TZIMIS TAVERNA

A real locals' joint, serving souvlaki, succulent meats and some tasty vegetarian dishes from the edge of town.

→ Nafpaktos 303 00, +30 2634 027466
38.3926, 21.8187 🍴

29 LITSA TAVERNA

Traditional dishes, including many regional specialities, prepared with local ingredients and served on a balcony with green valley views. Fabulous mountain-village dining.

→ Pavliani 351 00, +30 2231 083039
38.7407, 22.3368 🏔

30 FAROPOULOS TAVERNA

A traditional eatery crammed with historical paraphernalia, owned by two friendly brothers dishing up simple, fresh dishes from a small menu. Try the family meatballs.

→ Amfissa 331 00, +30 2265 028823
38.5272, 22.3769 🍴

31 TO TSOUKALI

Invariably creative, tasty dishes made with local, seasonal ingredients by chef Yannis, who exudes such warmth and passion that eating here can feel like enjoying a personal chef.

→ Arachova 320 04, +30 2267 029248
38.4817, 22.5877 🅱

32 ARVANITSA RESTAURANT

An enchanting taverna in a secluded alpine pine glade, with space for kids to play free and historical relics aplenty. The meats, house red and specials are excellent.

→ Kiriaki 320 06, +30 69 7283 1279
38.3215, 22.8549 🥾

33 KATAFYGIO CHALET

A cosy log cabin in the fir-lined foothills of Mount Kaliakouda, with room for seven. Fabulous in summer or winter, and your host can organise all sorts of outdoor activities.

→ Krikello 360 76, +30 69 3249 1199
38.8146, 21.8332 🏔🐾🏠

34 VASILIKIA MOUNTAIN FARM & RETREAT

Situated at 1010m, at the entrance to Oitis National Park, this farm offers characterful and colourful cottages, shacks, barn lofts and even an Airstream caravan, sleeping up to six. The estate has an organic garden, a herb garden, a kids' play area, a taverna and a wooden watchtower.

→ Pavliani 351 00, +30 2231 082992
38.7335, 22.3466 🍴🐾🏠

35 STONE HOUSE, LILIEA

A rustic 19th-century abode of exposed stone, dark wood and traditional decor, with splendid views to distant Mount Parnassos. Room for five.

→ Lilea 350 57, +30 69 4510 7926, airbnb.com/rooms/34953877
38.6322, 22.4961 🏠

36 KANELLA SKI LODGE

A sumptuous lodge with panoramic mountain views, traditional touches and a fireplace, close to famous Delphi. Sleeps four.

→ Arachova 320 04, airbnb.com/rooms/21528158
38.4796, 22.5814 🏠

37 NISI GLAMPING

Eco-friendly glamping domes, caravans, cabins and tents in a waterside glade, with a restaurant and regular events programme.

→ Paralia Rachon 353 00, +30 2238 031809
38.8776, 22.7695 🐾🛶

38 HELICON MUSES

A simple, edge-of-village guesthouse that does everything well. Friendly owners, pleasant rooms, delicious food and views across a shallow valley building to distant peaks.

→ Aliartos 320 01, +30 2268 022100
38.3406, 23.0169 🏠

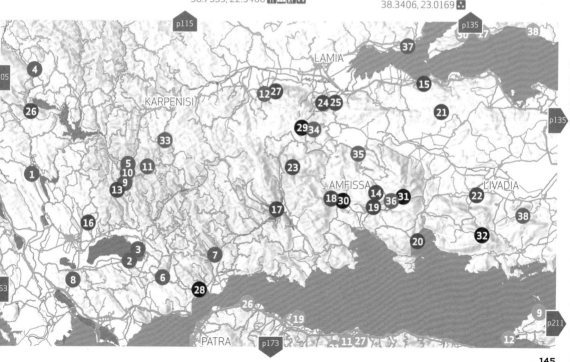

LEFKADA

Our perfect weekend

→ **Escape** to hidden Krioneri Beach for a quiet morning dip to start the day.

→ **Reserve** a table at the impossibly cosy Maria's Taverna and savour her off-menu, home-grown delights.

→ **Voyage** down to Papanikolis Sea Cave and swim through its yawning mouth to the tiny beach within.

→ **Venture** around the headland from famous Milos Beach to its secret neighbour, Hidden Milos Beach.

→ **Feast** on Ta Lytrata's renowned lentil dishes before taking a splendid walk to panoramic Prophet Elias Church.

→ **Bid** farewell to the setting sun from Doukato Cape, with a blanket and a bottle of local wine.

→ **Revitalise** the next day with a shaded gorge stroll and a plunge into the pool below Dimosari Waterfall.

→ **Descend** the hundreds of steps to the wild sands of Egremni Beach, perhaps with a picnic and a sleeping bag.

Sometimes identified as Ithaca, the home that mythical hero Odysseus spent a decade trying to return to, Lefkada lies at the end of a narrow causeway and the floating bridge crossing the Lefkas Canal below the once watchful Castle of Santa Maura. This is an island of village tavernas and mountain vistas that gaze down onto pretty eastern fishing settlements and sweeping western beaches beneath dramatic cliffs.

Your first stop is small Lefkada city, half surrounded by placid wildlife-friendly lagoons. A loop around neighbouring Gyra Lagoon – be sure to stop and spy flamingos, pelicans and other migratory birds – takes in tiny, tucked away Krioneri Beach and the endless sands of St Ioannis Beach. Grivas Castle, an overgrown Ottoman testament to the volatile geopolitics of this region, overlooks the island and wetlands from the east.

Lefkada's eastern coast is lined with fishing villages looking to the mainland and Meganisi island - both once part of Ottoman Lefkada, some relics of which feature in this chapter A boat from Nydri is the best way to travel this coast, punctuated with thin beaches nuzzled beneath forested bluffs. Pause at Ellomeno and Kamari beaches, glide between the emerald nooks of nearby islands and quest south to the magnificent Papanikolis Sea Cave, named after the Hellenic Navy submarine that hid here during the Second World War.

Lefkada's west coast is comparatively wild, with wide-open views across the Ionian Sea. Egremni is arguably the pick of the grand beaches that rule here, and a wonderful wild camp. Doukato Cape, remote and reflective, is also a fine place to watch the sun sink slowly into the water. Its mighty cliffs are said to be where the poet Sappho met her death in antiquity.

Whatever coastal adventures you choose, climb into the foothills to feast. Maria's Taverna – intimate, menuless home cooking at its finest – is essential, perhaps after a refreshing expedition to Dimosari Waterfall. T'Aloni's succulent slow-cooked lamb, homegrown dishes and homemade wine, served from a sunset perch, make a splendid end to any west-coast beach day. And Ta Lytrata's unique menu, based around Eglouvi's renowned lentils, combines excellently with a visit to the panoramic Prophet Elias Church – Lefkada's sacred crown, gazing back down to the coastal delights below.

BEACHES

1 ST IOANNIS BEACH

The northern end of this vast sandy beach is undeveloped, giving way to rolling dunes with tufts of long grass. It lies between surfable waves and Gyra Lagoon, which is popular with migrating pelicans and flamingos. An easy retreat from the activity of Lefkada.

➔ Pull off the road that runs around the lagoon where it curves away from the W coast (38.8485, 20.6865) and park on the dirt track.
1 min, 38.8515, 20.6869 🏖️🅿️🚻

2 KRIONERI BEACH

A secret micro beach with cold, clear water fed by freshwater springs and a big rock for jumping. A tiny hidden gem on the outskirts of Lefkada.

➔ Follow the seafront road to the far SW end of St Ioannis Beach (see entry) and park at the end. Walk the signed path past the church to steps descending to the beach.
3 mins, 38.8328, 20.666 🏖️🅿️🥾🚻🏊

3 HIDDEN MILOS BEACH

Milos Beach is stunning, but very busy during high season. Escape the crowds by adventuring around the corner to this delightful hidden beach, shaded by cliffs and guarded by large water boulders.

➔ Easiest access is from St Nikitas beach to the E by clambering and swimming (100m) or water taxi (€3 pp). But you can also swim or float from Milos Beach to the W (300m). Park in St Nikitas.
10 mins, 38.7911, 20.6113 🏖️🅿️🚻🏊

4 MEGALI PETRA BEACH

Seemingly endless sands running along the base of steep hills, strewn with bouldery nooks (its name means 'big stone'). You won't struggle for privacy or a wide-open sunset.

➔ 'Beach' is signed from the main road in Kalamitsi, down 4km of switchbacks to a parking area and short trail at the beach's N end.
2 mins, 38.7514, 20.5883 🏖️🅿️🚻⛺🏊

5 EGREMNI BEACH

Kilometres of pristine sand and shingle below towering cliffs. Its size and long approach keep it blissfully quiet, despite its renown.

➔ Head S from Athani village for 1km, fork R at the taverna and continue 1.6km down to parking among trees (38.6418, 20.5613). It's a 1.25km road walk plus 400 steps down to the beach.
30 mins, 38.6357, 20.5584 🏖️🅿️🚻🏊

6 ST NIKOLAOS BEACH

A tiny cove at the end of a winding dirt track far below the monastery of St Nikolaos, with fantastic swimming in a deep, narrow bay.

➔ Follow the road S from Athani for 5km and keep L to continue S onto the peninsula for another 5.7km. Keep R at the fork, then after 1km take a sharp L onto a dirt track. Without a 4x4, park here and walk the last 1.5km to the beach.
30 mins, 38.5838, 20.5606 🏖️🅿️🏊

7 KAMARI BEACH

A quiet, narrow beach overlooking the strait from the foot of Lefkada's verdant eastern foothills, popular with campervans. Some hidden micro beaches await a short walk to the south.

➔ Start as for Ellomono Beach (see entry), but just before Desimi Beach (38.6742, 20.7099) turn R and follow the coastal road S for 2.4km.
1 min, 38.6551, 20.7193 🏖️🅿️

8 ELLOMENO BEACH

This small shingle beach with shallow water is backed by forest for late-afternoon shade, and makes a calm spot to watch the boats to and fro between Lefkada and Meganisi.

➔ Head E from Epar.od Lefkas-Vasilikis

(38.6764, 20.6971), signed Menes Hotel Beach and Villa Agni. Fork R after 1km, then keep L for 1.2km above Desimi beach to a T junction on a bend. Head L then keep R, following 1.3km down to the beach. Without a 4x4, park at the open spot after 800m (38.6821, 20.7199) and walk.

5 mins, 38.6851, 20.7238

9 PLAGIA BEACH

A wild beach of white pebbles in a shallow bay, often visited by yachts.

→ Walking 1km from the coast road (at 38.7646, 20.7750) is the adventure option. Boat access is the norm, and Pipis Boats in Nikiana (+30 69 4560 0695) offers a good service.

10 mins, 38.7573, 20.768

WILD WATERS

10 PLAGIA SHIPWRECK

This rocky tidal inlet is scattered with shipwrecks, giving its tiny beaches a unique appeal. Another wreck lies further out at 38.7989, 20.7297.

→ Walk 500m W downhill from St. Georgios Fortress (see entry), using a trail starting

by the westernmost tower. Some very light bushwacking is needed to access the beach.

5 mins, 38.795, 20.7285

11 DIMOSARI WATERFALL

A shady gorge leading to a 12m waterfall which, outside of the height of summer, fills a swimmable pool overspilling into a rocky creek.

→ Take the signed turning for waterfalls from the road through Rachi village, just NW of Kato Rahoula restaurant. Continue 1.5km past the football pitch to a parking area at the end. The falls are a gentle 700m walk beyond.

10 mins, 38.7264, 20.6847

12 PAPANIKOLIS SEA CAVE

A majestic cavern burrowing into Meganisi's southern tail, accessible only by boat. The small beach at the back is swimmable, and diffused light from the mouth creates a breathtaking underwater scene.

→ Only accessible by boat. Nydri is the best starting point, and Lefkas Boats (+30 69 3744 7659) is a good bet. Note that the cave is technically outside the permitted range of some rental boats.

2 mins, 38.6141, 20.7626

16

RUINS & VIEWPOINTS

13 GRIVAS CASTLE

Ali Pasha, Albanian ruler under the Ottoman Empire, built this hilltop castle in 1806 before it was captured in the Greek Revolution of 1821. Its overgrown ruins gaze west to Lefkada, the evening sun burning in the lagoons below. Just across the causeway is the more maintained and explained Castle of St Maura.

→ Unmissable above the main road onto Lefkada, just E of the causeway. Turn off the main road and park after 220m on a R bend. Follow the short path up to the castle.

2 mins, 38.8476, 20.7397 ⬛🐐🐚

14 ST GEORGIOS FORTRESS

Built at the same time as nearby Grivas Castle (see entry), this crumbling fortress has been conquered by goats. The walkable ramparts overlook the water to Lefkada.

→ Signed R from the road heading out of Plagia on its SW edge. Park along the final approach.

1 min, 38.7956, 20.7356 🐐

15 PROPHET ELIAS CHURCH

Every side of this blue-and-white, mountaintop church presents a panorama spanning Lefkada and beyond. A spectacle well worth the walk or drive up.

→ A twisting route runs N from Karya village, starting by the folk museum, for 8.7km. Keep L at 2.6km and ignore all smaller forks. It is still a reasonable road as it ascends to the chapel, but best parking is just before the final, steep 100m. A steep 2km walking trail also starts from the uppermost hairpin above Egklouvi (38.7327, 20.6446).

2 mins, 38.7382, 20.6472 ⬛⛰✝

13

16 DOUKATO CAPE

A snaking cape with plunging cliffs and a lighthouse stationed at Lefkada's southernmost point. A place of solitude and dramatic light, especially as the sun sinks into the lapping ocean. The best views are from the coordinates.

→ There is one road down the peninsula. Park on the bend and scramble up the small slope. You can also continue 1km to the lighthouse.

1 min, 38.5669, 20.5469 ⬛⛰🔆

15

LOCAL FOOD & DRINK

17 ELENI TAVERNA

A family taverna serving Lefkadian dishes, wines and spirits from a tree-shaded square in the heart of Karya, a mountain village brimming with traditional culture. Wonderful for people-watching, especially with some *riganada* or cod *bianco*.

→ Karya 310 80, +30 69 7886 9630
38.7598, 20.6488 **B**

18 MARIA'S TAVERNA

Home-cooked food at its finest, hidden in Kolyvata hamlet. With no menu, a handful of tables and produce fresh from the garden, Maria's charming taverna is a delight. Ring ahead to check opening times and reserve.

→ Kolivata 310 80, +30 69 8405 6686
38.7492, 20.6911

19 TA LYTRATA

This quaint mountain taverna produces wonderful dishes with Egklouvi's famous lentils. The beetroot and lentil salad and the lentil soup are highly recommended.

→ Egklouvi 310 80, +30 2645 041261
38.7304, 20.6456

20 T'ALONI

Thoughtful, delicious Greek dishes with ingredients from their garden and wine from their vineyard. The terrace gives enormous views over the Ionian, and artefacts indoors preserve the village's history. The slow-cooked lamb is legendary.

→ Chortata 310 82, +30 2645 033240
38.7181, 20.6014

21 TAXIARCHIS TAVERNA

A village taverna from a bygone age, with a delicious grill and even better music. Forget frills, menus and worries as you gaze upon the boat-speckled bay below.

→ Katochori 311 00, +30 2645 095267
38.6668, 20.6912

22 FILIPPA'S TAVERNA

What Ionian tavernas are all about – local food, fabulous views and friendly people – plus live music in the summer and a roaring fire in the winter. The Greek barbecue is superb.

→ Fterno 310 82, +30 2645 095630
38.6561, 20.6861

23 SURFER'S SUITE

A plush loft with a minimalistic surf-hut aesthetic and off-grid energy system. A hammock and terrace gaze above the cypress and olive trees to the Ionian beyond. Sleeps three in one bedroom.

→ Tsoukalades 311 00, airbnb.com/rooms/26696430
38.8297, 20.6538

24 PAVEZZO COUNTRY RETREAT

A hillside country retreat of assorted stone cottages with a swimming pool and spa. Breakfast is included and dinner optional. The site was largely abandoned until the 1980s, when photographer Maria Matsa restored a ramshackle 19th-century cottage.

→ Katouna 311 00, +30 2645 071782
38.7813, 20.7062

25 THE MILL

Perched in Lefkada's mountainous interior, this chic, renovated mill is open from April to November and has space for four. An infinity pool surveys the ocean far below, and an open-air kitchen allows for true alfresco dining.

→ Platistoma 31080, +30 69 7742 7453
38.7434, 20.6703

26 ROUPAKIAS BELL TENT

A furnished bell tent for two hidden in the idyllic groves of abandoned Roupakias where hosts Sylwia and Mariusz are the sole residents. A dry eco toilet, an outdoor shower, running spring water and solar energy exemplify the ecological ethos, and breakfast is served under the fig tree.

→ Roupakias 310 82, airbnb.com/rooms/35955441
38.6768, 20.6107

27 CAMPING VASSILIKI BEACH

A small, welcoming campsite a short walk from the windsurfing and amenities of Vassiliki Beach. Shady plots under trees and clean facilities.

→ Vassiliki 310 82, +30 2645 031308
38.6305, 20.6068

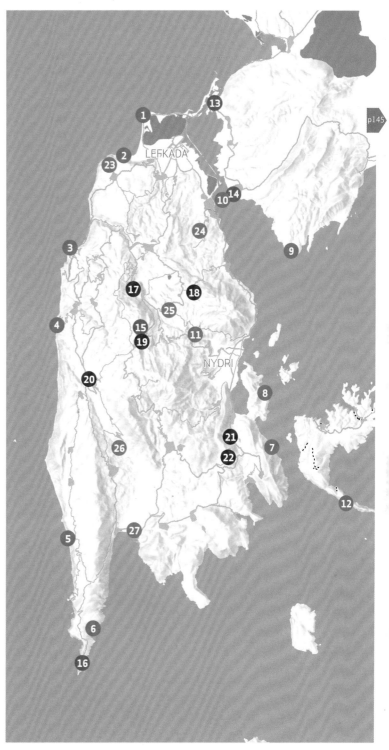

KEFALONIA & ITHACA

Our perfect weekend

→ **Plunge** through the dense foliage and emerge onto Fteri Beach for a day of supreme contentment.

→ **Fill** your belly with delights sweet and savoury from En Kefallinia's organic farm, perhaps as part of a cooking class.

→ **Leap** off Liakas Cape and snorkel through the narrow channel back to land.

→ **Drift** in the translucent waves and shallow waters of St Eleni Beach, beneath the towering white cliffs looking down at you.

→ **Stroll** the overgrown Venetian ruins and aromatic hillside trails of the Assos Peninsula in the golden hour.

→ **Imagine** Saracen pirates raiding the Bay of Vathy from the rusting Venetian cannons set strategically amidst the overlooking pines.

→ **Sink** into history beneath the canopy entangling the open roof of Rizes Cave, imagining a disguised Odysseus talking with Eumaeus, his swineherd.

→ **Simplify** life in the homespun Filiatro Tiny House, gazing at the sea from a wooden terrace without a care in the world.

These Ionian neighbours are an irresistible pair, less developed than Corfu or Zakynthos. Kefalonia is the largest Ionian island, home to Greece's only island national park and a greatest-hits parade of mind-blowing beaches. Ithaca is almost the smallest, and essentially two small islands connected by the vertiginous Isthmus of Aetos. It's the forest-green haven to which Homer's Odysseus struggled to return for 20 years.

In Kefalonia's mountainous south, Ainos National Park was created in 1962 to protect the wildlife and rare Greek fir trees. It is threaded with hiking trails leading to its domineering peak; look out for wild ponies. Descending to the south, don't miss the popular but astonishing Melissani Cave, a giant sinkhole with adjoining caves explorable only by boat. Visit at midday, when the sunbeams pierce the roof, then sample lunch or even a cooking class at the organic farm En Kefallinia. Check in at Bohemian Retreat, a luxurious retreat in the island's heart, before heading north. Savour a sunset stroll around the aromatic Assos Peninsula, riddled with Venetian ruins, or venture through hidden tunnels to swim in the secret cave waters at Foki Beach near fetching Fiskardo.

Talking of beaches, a pin placed blindly into a map of Kefalonia would likely land somewhere sandy and spectacular. Fteri rewards a short walk with a truly paradisal expanse of bright sand and turquoise water, with more heavenly beaches tucked beyond headlands nearby. St Eleni is similarly magnificent, and blissfully quiet despite direct road access. And Platia Ammos is even wilder, requiring a steep, rocky descent. From the shady olive boughs of Chorgota to the nesting loggerhead turtles of Koroni and jumping rocks of Liakas Cape, the list goes on.

A tough act for Ithaca to follow, but this island of consistent beauty holds its own. Afales Beach is one of five in a remote chain as pristine and spectacular as anything on Kefalonia, accessible only by boat, and the south is replete with sandy coves. Gidaki Beach is perhaps the standout, its giant curves and cliffs frequented only by walkers and boaters, but even the walk there passes other contenders.

With a long history that includes rule by Rome, the Byzantine Empire, Venice, the French and the British, both islands are rich in poignant remains of human habitation. But Ithaca holds the advantage here. Venetian Cannons and St Andrews Chapel both overlook the mouth of the Bay of Vathy, for reasons spiritual and strategic. And those seeking mythical associations can visit what may have been the palace of Odysseus, or ascend to where Rizes Cave - supposedly the cave of Odysseus' swineherd, Eumaeus - sinks atmospherically into a hillside. If you don't need luxury, a few nights in the off-grid simplicity of Filiatro Tiny House will only deepen your connection to this landscape.

BEACHES

1 FTERI BEACH

A blissful expanse of bright turquoise shallows framed by elegant white cliffs and a carpet of white pebbles. Absolute gem.

➜ About 3km NW of Katochori on the road to Livadi, take the R fork uphill. Follow it for 2km, forking R twice. Park on the R 1km after the second fork (38.3144, 20.4546) or on either side shortly after this. Go through a gate on the L and follow the path down through the goat farm, marked sporadically with red and green paint. Sturdy shoes required. Also accessible via boat from Zola with Fteri Water Taxi (+30 69 7480 7153). If coming by sea take the opportunity to stop off at Kamari Beach, 1km E of Fteri.

45 mins, 38.3229, 20.4535

2 ATHERAS BEACH

Find a nook, take a dip and relax. You'll feel like you're in a painting, surrounded by bobbing rowing boats beneath deep-green boughs and pastel-blue St Spyridon Church.

➜ Follow the road N from Atheras for 3.3km right to the shore. Park at the main beach and explore the W side of the bay using the path starting at the last bend in the road.

5 mins, 38.3373, 20.4083

3 ST ELENI BEACH

Possibly Kefalonia's most sumptuous secluded beach, its pristine waters and solitary jumping rock sheltered by towering cliffs and promontories. The beach is shaded from late afternoon, and there is another secret, swimmable beach round to the left.

➜ Drive W from the N end of Damoulianata, ignoring turns until you hairpin R and head N after 1km. Fork L at 2.3km, with a low wall on your L (38.2498, 20.3666). Continue 1.6km to the steep, winding descent to the beach, where you can park.

1 min, 38.2603, 20.3674

4 PLATIA AMMOS BEACH

One of Kefalonia's most beautiful beaches, and remarkably quiet due to the tricky access. Its orange sand and scattered boulders are dwarfed by gigantic cliffs, which you must scramble down.

➜ On the coast road 3.2km SW from Kaminarata, take a rough dirt road R by a house and follow 1km to space to turn round and park at the end. A recent earthquake destroyed many steps down to the beach, but you can still descend with sturdy shoes and extreme caution.

25 mins, 38.2164, 20.3546

5 MANIA BEACH

The rich orange hue of the sand, vertical white cliffs and the humped dune formations behind them lend this beach a unique character. To east, Koutala Beach is similar.

➜ Take a signed L off the road heading S into Kounoupetra, about 500m before the village. Continue 400m to park at the shore. For the most beautiful and secluded stretch, head L below the cliffs. For Koutala turn L off the road at 38.1665, 20.4003 to arrive at the clifftop.

1 min, 38.1558, 20.3943

6 LIAKAS CAPE

A tiny footbridge leads onto a rocky plateau surrounded by the sea. Its ledges, steps and tunnel are begging to be explored. There are steps to climb back up from the water.

➜ Signed from the road junction S from Spartia and E from Klismata (38.1030, 20.5648). Follow 2km, twisting steeply between villas down to a parking area at the cape. Walk down to the water.

2 mins, 38.0891, 20.5671

7 PESSADA BEACH

This small, sandy cove of mesmeric shallows is snuggled away behind a

shielding curl of rocks, which helps it feel more secret than its proximity to the port of Pessada suggests.

→ On the road approaching Pessada Harbour, turn R just before the road bends L down to harbour. Park at the end (38.1069, 20.5860) and walk down the narrow, leafy steps for 100m to a pleasant beach. Turn R and pick your way along the shoreline for 250m for the real reward. If this parking is full, park at the harbour and walk to the steps.

1 min, 38.1052, 20.5863 🏊🏖

8 KORONI BEACH

This huge sandy beach is incredibly quiet since a local landowner closed the road to cars and pedestrians. It's an important spring nesting ground for Kefalonia's signature loggerhead sea turtles, so visit with curiosity and caution.

→ Access is now by boat only. You can hire a motorboat in Katelios; Sea Breeze Club (+30 59 4533 5598) provides a good service.

2 mins, 38.0805, 20.6906 🏊🏖⛺

9 LAZARUS BEACH

Part of a string of beaches punctuating a coastline of scrubby meadows dotted with

livestock and rusting farmyard relics, giving a more rustic aesthetic than many of the pristine beaches elsewhere.

→ The coastal track N from Poros becomes very uneven after 4km (around 38.1869, 20.7462), so park in the layby beforehand and continue N on foot for a further 2km, generally keeping R to stay near the sea. The final descent is a bit of a scramble down sloping rocks.

30 mins, 38.1991, 20.7368 🏊🏖🏖

10 CHORGOTA BEACH

A small and magical pebble cove shaded by gnarled olive trees, with views of Ithaca. You may recognise it from the film version of *Captain Corelli's Mandolin*, as the beach where Penélope Cruz tearfully bids farewell to her fiancé.

→ A zigzag road ends abruptly behind the beach with no easy turning point. Pull off at one of the turns on the descent and walk the final stretch.

2 mins, 38.3644, 20.6155 🏊🏖⛺

11 KAMINI BEACH

You are likely to be alone at this remote pebbled cove, with uncertain foot access due to flooding in the gorge. There is sporadic

boat traffic in the high season.

→ Driving SE from Ventourata, turn R after about 250m, and immediately L onto an overgrown dirt track (38.4347, 20.5691). After 200m there is a gate with a grassy clearing to the R. Park here and walk 1.5km downhill; flooding means the gorge is now a scramble in some places. For boat access, rent from Regina's (+30 69 3898 4647) in Fiskardo.

20 mins, 38.4281, 20.5862 🏊🏖⛺🧍🏊

12 AFALES BEACH

One of five breathtakingly wild beaches ensconced below towering white cliffs. Stay the night for an unforgettable sunset and wild camp.

→ Boat access only. Ithaca Boats (+30 6977 280822) in Vathy or Regina's (+30 69 3898 4647) in Fiskardo - in Kefalonia, but closer to the beach - are good options.

1 min, 38.4831, 20.6536 🏊🏖🏊⛺🏊

13 MARMAGKAS BEACH

A tree-lined beach, backed by a lagoon, gazing out towards an islet on which St Nikolaos Church sits. There is a friendly beach bar nearby.

→ Follow a rough but passable track for 3.5km N from Frikes, turning L at the S end of the

12

11

16

beach and forking R at the very end to park at the N end.

1 min, 38.4831, 20.6717 🏊🏖️🚣

14 KIONI BEACH

This photogenic and somewhat hidden micro beach is perfect for a dip after lunch in Kioni, with pebbles and rocks falling away into azure depths.

→ Park in Kioni village and follow the narrow road S along the waterfront. Steps lead down from the road.

5 mins, 38.4485, 20.6901 🏊🏖️🐚

15 MINIMATA BEACH

Trees overhanging a stone wall shade this quiet pebble beach with calm, shallow water. Lovely for children.

→ Driving N with the Bay of Vathy on your L, fork R just before Ithaca Sailing Club (38.3711, 20.7179). Follow 1.4km, to the first beach, and park on the side of the road.

1 min, 38.3806, 20.7178 🏊🏖️🚣

16 SKINOS BEACH

A thin strip of beach beautifully framed by a low stone wall and towering pines.

→ Driving N with the Bay of Vathy on your L, bear R just before Ithaca Sailing Club

(38.3711, 20.7179). Follow for 2km and park in the laybys on either side of the road (38.3839, 20.7213). Walk the final 100m.

2 mins, 38.3846, 20.7234 🏊🏖️🚣🍴🚶

17 MAYA BEACH

A small but immaculate beach in the north-eastern corner of a deep, undulating bay.

→ A quick, shaded walk along the coastline from Skinos Beach, on path to Gidaki Beach.

5 mins, 38.387, 20.7224 🏊🏖️🚶

18 GIDAKI BEACH

This vast picturebook beach, visited only by boats and serious walkers, arcs beneath vertiginous cliffs which block the late-afternoon sun. A rudimentary shack serves food and drink.

→ Follow the path 1km over the headland from the N end of Skinos Beach (see entry). Or take a boat from Vathy: Ithaca Boats (+30 6977 280822) or Odyssey Boats (+30 6949 035670) are good.

20 mins, 38.3855, 20.7306 🏊🏖️⛺🚶

19 FILIATRO BEACH

This is a more developed beach than some of its neighbours, with a food kiosk, kayak rental

and easy vehicle access. Olive trees provide shade and a small ruin surveys from the rear.

→ Follow a lane N from near the Chapel of St Constantine and Helen on the E outskirts of Vathy (38.3626, 20.7347), passing Sarakiniko Beach. Park at the beach.

1 min, 38.3717, 20.7418 🏖️🌊️B

20 PERA PIGADI BEACH

A very remote sandy beach at the bottom of a steep gorge walk with spectacular views. An easier option is to take a boat around from Vathy.

→ The 2km walk starts from the dead-end road to the cape at 38.3324, 20.7329. Ithaca Boats (+30 6977 280822) or Odyssey Boats (+30 6949 035670) are also good options.

45 mins, 38.3273, 20.7454 🌊⛰️⛺🏕️

CAVES

21 FOKI CAVE

Sea cave accessible from both sea and land via an old mining tunnel. Take swimsuits and torch to explore network of rooms and pools.

→ Park on the road at Foki Beach, S of Fiskardo, and take the path S along the shore through the trees and a couple of gates.

15 mins, 38.4515, 20.58 🏖️🌊🚶🏛️☀️🗻

22 MYRTOS BEACH CAVE

The most famous beach on Kefalonia, backed by towering cliffs from which paragliders occasionally swoop down onto the sand. At the left end you can swim through the cliff via a small sea cave.

→ Follow the road signed Mirtos NW from Divarata (38.3315, 20.5464) for 2.5km and park at the beach.

1 min, 38.3408, 20.5329 🌊🏖️🌊B🗻

23 MELISSANI CAVE

This utterly majestic lake cave and cenote (a sinkhole with a collapsed roof) is lit by sunbeams shimmering through its forested mouth past birds whipping above the turquoise pool below. A cinematic boat trip, worth the fee and crowds.

→ At the N end of Karavomylos, past the cemetery, with its own car park. Enter via the gift shop. €7 per person.

5 mins, 38.2569, 20.6236 B🛈🗻

24 RIZES CAVE

An atmospheric, little-known place that some believe is where Eumaeus, Odysseus' swineherd, unknowingly gave shelter to his disguised king. A small entrance leads to a

round cavern, with a twisted canopy growing through a great opening akin to a cathedral window.

→ Follow the road SE from Perachori for 2.5km and park (38.3320, 20.7308). Climb the path 400m from the sign.

10 mins, 38.3314, 20.7276 🚶📷🏞️🚴

ANCIENT SITES

25 ASSOS PENINSULA

An aromatic peninsula scattered with the crumbling remains of a castle of the same name, a Venetian stronghold built in the 1590s. Its shaded footpaths, winding from the postcard bay below with lovely views, promise a magical golden-hour stroll.

→ Park in the car park on the isthmus just W of Assos village. Walk uphill past the bollards to the waterside promenade. Bear immediately L for a direct route, or continue to meander up the broad stone path.

20 mins, 38.3808, 20.5307 📷🏞️🚴🚶

26 ODYSSEUS PALACE

A large Mycenaean complex dating back to 1300 BC, with a funerary enclosure and a sophisticated drainage system. Local archeologists believe this ruin was the

palatial home of Homeric hero Odysseus.

→ About 1.5km NW from Stavros, park by the road (38.4597, 20.6382). Follow the signposted path up a short, steep climb.

2 mins, 38.4606, 20.6378 🚴

27 VENETIAN CANNONS

These twin iron cannons, dating from around 1807, were once a deterrent to Saracen pirates. Now they sit silently among fragrant pines overlooking the entrance to the Bay of Vathy.

→ From Vathy, head N along the NE shore of the bay for 1km to Loutsa Beach, where you can park. The cannons are 50m above the road on the R, just before the beach.

20 mins, 38.3733, 20.7102 🏞️🚴🛶

PEAKS & CHAPELS

28 MOUNT AINOS

Kefalonia's highest point is the crown of Greece's only island national park, founded to protect the island's eponymous *Abies cephalonica* fir trees. The peak is the pinnacle of a ridgeline rising above the trees. If you're lucky you might spot wild ponies.

→ Signed from EO50 where it crosses the high centre of the island (38.1947, 20.5870). Follow SE 13km, past Agios Eleftherios, and

park near the satellite towers. Explore on foot.
30 mins, 38.1365, 20.6713

29 ST ANDREW CHAPEL
This tiny waterside chapel greets seaborne traffic coming and going from Vathy harbour. On 30th November, its name day, pilgrims gather at its blue door.
→ From Vathy, head N along the NE shore of the bay for 1km to Loutsa Beach, where you can park. Continue for 1.5km along the coastal trail.
40 mins, 38.3844, 20.7019

LOCAL FOOD & DRINK

30 GIALOS TAVERNA
The terrace overlooks charming Atheras Beach from beneath a canopy of vines and flowers. A wonderful spot for fresh fish.
→ Paliki 282 00, +30 2671 093819
38.3355, 20.4091

31 LADOKOLLA
This bustling family taverna serves traditional dishes with sunset views. Their signature meat pies come highly recommended.
→ Lixouri 282 00, +30 2671 097493
38.239, 20.3737

32 HARITATOS ESTATE
A charming family vineyard centred around a delightful house and gardens, with farm animals and an events programme beyond excellent tastings.
→ Paliki 282 00, +30 69 7610 8768
38.2248, 20.3937

33 EN KEFALLINIA
From traditional pies to fresh salads and delicious desserts, all dishes here use ingredients from the organic farm. Owners Michael and Georgia (named after St George, the saint of agriculture, whose very name means agriculture in Greek) also offer private cooking classes and eco retreats. Book ahead.
→ Metaxata 281 00, +30 2671 041190
38.1245, 20.536

34 DIMITRIS AND EFTHIMIA'S FISHING TOUR
Let Dimitris and Efthimia take you out on their fishing boat for a day of net fishing, snorkelling and beach-cooked fish with organic vegetables, olive oil and wine - all produced by your hosts. Learn about Kefalonia's marine ecosystem, help empty the nets and enjoy a memorable dining experience. Daily departure from Kateleios harbour at 8am, in groups of around ten;

book in advance to guarantee your spot.
→ Kateleios 280 86, +30 69 4766 7595
38.0625, 20.7485

35 MYRTIA
A newcomer to the Ithaca food scene, bringing with it sensational views and classy interpretations of local recipes.
→ Stavros 283 00, +30 6984 308067
38.4552, 20.6419

36 KANTINA BEACH BAR
A dreamy beachside taverna serving fresh, classic, reasonably priced dishes under dappled shade.
→ Kioni 283 00, +30 6976 593337
38.4444, 20.6975

37 DONA LEFKI
Sunset views over to Kefalonia with modern takes on classic Greek dishes.
Lefki 283 00, +30 2674 031363
38.4184, 20.6478

38 KAMINIA BEACH BAR
Seasonal parasols, beanbags and a relaxed beach bar serving juice, cocktails, snacks and

salads, in a quintessentially sleepy island inlet with a pebble beach and shallow waters.
→ Perachori 283 00. The road is unpaved and rough towards the end.
38.3389, 20.7386 🏖️🏄‍♂️⛺

STAY

39 KARAVOMILOS CAMPING

A pleasant campsite with a shop, restaurant and bar backing onto a shady beach, catering to a whole range of campers.
→ Sami 280 80, +30 2674 022480
38.2507, 20.638 🏕️🏖️

40 LEVENDIS ESTATE

Cottages set in a terraced olive farm with sea views. The tumbling grounds include a summer house, pavilions for yoga and holistic massage and an outdoor cinema. A farm, vegetable garden and orchards provide the chef's organic ingredients.
→ Platrithias 283 00, +30 69 4416 9770
38.4662, 20.6408 🏡🅔

41 VILLA KALOS

This renovated olive-press villa has room for eight and a saltwater infinity pool

surrounded by olive, cypress and almond trees. A luxurious retreat.
→ Platrithias 283 00, villakalos.com
38.4621, 20.6492 🏡🅔

42 FILIATRO TINY HOUSE

A hillside tiny house built by host Rolf from largely upcycled materials. Two rustic floors open onto a wooden balcony with sea views. A charming outpost of off-grid living and ecological awareness over luxury, with a compost toilet and no air conditioning. Usually sleeps three, though an outdoor bed during the drier months increases capacity.
→ Vathy 283 00, airbnb.com/rooms/878335
38.3704, 20.7448 🏡🅟

43 BOHEMIAN RETREAT

With an outdoor cinema, hammocks, swimming pools and two gardens, this recently renovated 19th-century farmhouse has everything you need to unwind in its three two-person cottages.
→ Davgata 281 00, +30 6947 942091
38.2196, 20.4925 🏡🏕️

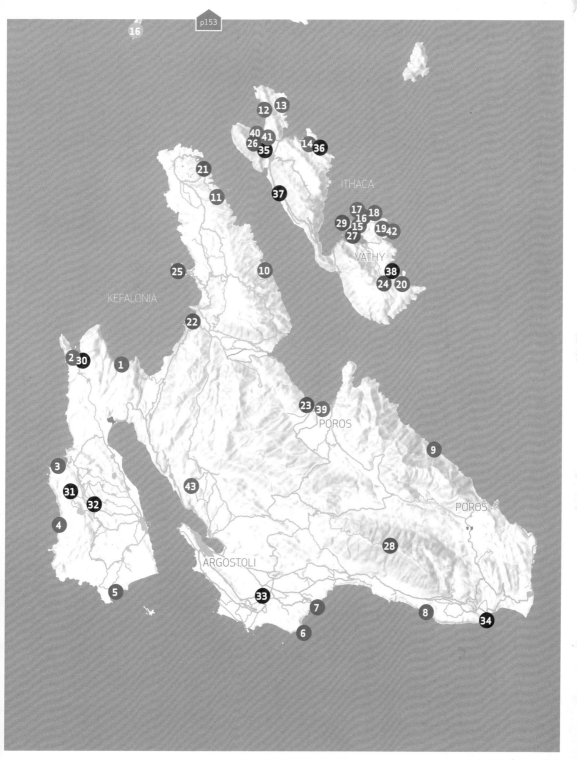

16

12 13

40 41
26 35

14 36

21

11

ITHACA

37

17 18
16
29 15 19 42
27

VATHY

25

KEFALONIA

10

38
24 20

22

2 30
1

23 39
POROS

9

3
31
32

43

POROS

4

28

5

ARGOSTOLI

33
7
8 34

6

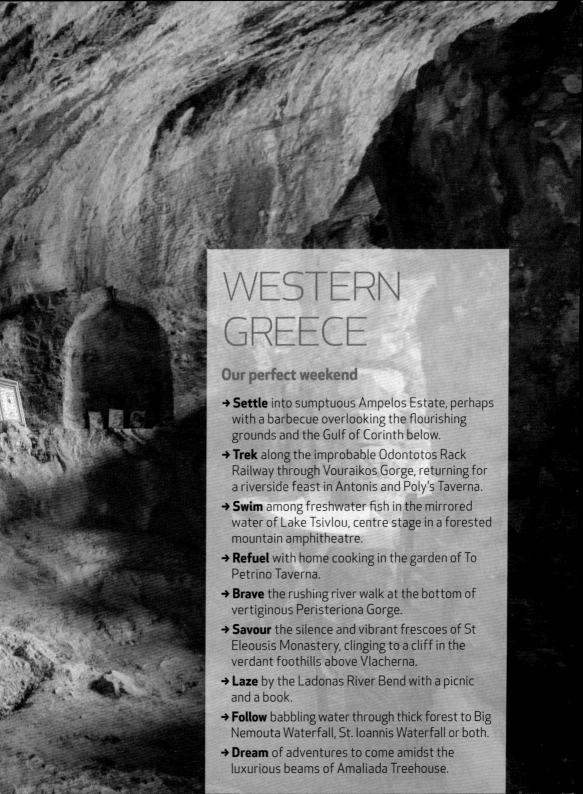

WESTERN GREECE

Our perfect weekend

→ **Settle** into sumptuous Ampelos Estate, perhaps with a barbecue overlooking the flourishing grounds and the Gulf of Corinth below.

→ **Trek** along the improbable Odontotos Rack Railway through Vouraikos Gorge, returning for a riverside feast in Antonis and Poly's Taverna.

→ **Swim** among freshwater fish in the mirrored water of Lake Tsivlou, centre stage in a forested mountain amphitheatre.

→ **Refuel** with home cooking in the garden of To Petrino Taverna.

→ **Brave** the rushing river walk at the bottom of vertiginous Peristeriona Gorge.

→ **Savour** the silence and vibrant frescoes of St Eleousis Monastery, clinging to a cliff in the verdant foothills above Vlacherna.

→ **Laze** by the Ladonas River Bend with a picnic and a book.

→ **Follow** babbling water through thick forest to Big Nemouta Waterfall, St. Ioannis Waterfall or both.

→ **Dream** of adventures to come amidst the luxurious beams of Amaliada Treehouse.

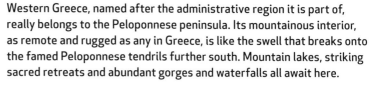

Western Greece, named after the administrative region it is part of, really belongs to the Peloponnese peninsula. Its mountainous interior, as remote and rugged as any in Greece, is like the swell that breaks onto the famed Peloponnese tendrils further south. Mountain lakes, striking sacred retreats and abundant gorges and waterfalls all await here.

If a mirrored mountain lake surrounded by cascading pines isn't the Peloponnese postcard you had in mind, venturing into the Mount Kyllini foothills will convert you. Lake Tsivlou is a haven for freshwater fish, fauna and flora, and a picturesque dip. Nearby Lake Doxa, with St Fanourios Church sitting picture-perfect in its centre, is a similarly fantastic place to swim and picnic. And what Stymphalia Wetland lacks in swimming potential, it makes up for in archeological interest and its rich bird- and wildlife.

Keen walkers, or railway buffs, shouldn't miss the Odontotos Rack Railway. Built at the turn of the 20th century, the plucky line threads through tunnels and narrow clefts in winding Vouraikos Gorge. Walking it, or riding it, is a unique journey, best followed by a selection of seasonal riverside dishes at Antonis and Poly's Taverna in Kato Zachlorou.

Fruit-tree-filled Ampelos Estate, gazing over the Gulf of Corinth, makes a wonderful base when exploring these northern stretches, whatever your group size. Take an evening to sample the organic, naturally fermented wines of nearby Tetramythos Winery, and another to savour the slow-cooked meat at Dimitra's Taverna for a more traditional village-taverna atmosphere, with an extraordinary chapel next door.

There is no more intimate immersion in this landscape of forested foothills than tracing a hurrying creek to a refreshing waterfall plunge pool. For this, head a little further south to Nemouta, surrounded by hidden falls in misty glades. It's within easy reach of Ancient Olympia, and possibly even a night or two in the romantic Amaliada Treehouse, if you want to keep the spirit of adventure alive through the night.

LAKES

1 LAKE PINIOS

Created by a dam in the 1960s, this huge artificial lake is fed by the Pinios River. The shore is undeveloped, much of it forested or grassy, with myriad coves and peninsulas.

→ Quiet roads run close to the water in many places. For this spot, head W for under 1km from Souli village. The road leads close to the shore.

2 mins, 37.9002, 21.4635

2 LAKE TSIVLOU

This deep, mirror-like lake, cradled in the forested foothills of Mount Aroania, was created when a 1913 landslide blocked the Krathis River. A popular spot for swimming, watching wildlife, hiking and mountain biking.

→ A scenic but twisting 25km drive up from Akrata on the coast, looking out for a hairpin turn R around 22km. Parking available at the lake.

1 min, 38.0772, 22.233

3 LAKE DOXA

A beautiful mountain lake created for irrigation, with grassy banks lined with deciduous and conifer forest. The charming St Fanourios Church is perched in the middle of the lake on a narrow, tree-lined spit. Linger for lunch and a swim.

→ A good road leads N out of adjacent Archea Feneos village and circles the lake, with parking midway along the S side.

1 min, 37.9275, 22.2862

4 STYMPHALIA WETLAND

A lake with one of the most important wetlands in the Mediterranean, home to migratory birds, amphibians and weasels. The ruins of ancient Stymphalos lie on the northern shore. An excellent place for a picnic, especially if you have binoculars.

→ On the road S and E from Kastania there is a large separated layby on the R after 10km, just before the museum entrance (37.8575, 22.4537). Park here and follow the signed trail 300m to the ruins.

5 mins, 37.8584, 22.4576

RIVERS & WATERFALLS

5 NEMOUTA WATERFALL TRAIL

A hidden canyon trail passing a series of enchanting waterfalls, including one over a cave mouth, framed by mossy, fern-clad forest. A wonderful walk, approachable from the E or W or doable as a longer loop.

→ From just W of the bridge at Elea (37.7004, 21.8087), walk or drive – depending on how rough you find the track – 1km S to a path L (37.6918, 21.8050). Follow it 500m, passing a building before bending R onto a smaller woodland trail leading to a fall. To walk in from the W, wind just under 3km SE from Nemouta to a sharp R (37.6935, 21.8006). Follow it 650m to 37.6914, 21.7955, then head E across a relatively open field and follow a thin trail into the woods.

10 mins, 37.6917, 21.7988

6 BIG NEMOUTA WATERFALL

Arguably the most impressive of a series of magical waterfalls emptying into a shallow stream above the Erymanthos River.

→ Park to the W of the bridge at Elea as for the Nemouta Waterfall Trail (see entry) and walk 250m S along the track. Turn R onto a trail following a small creek into the forest. The first fall is around 200m, with another 200m beyond. The signage isn't great.

5 mins, 37.6989, 21.8061

7 ST IOANNIS WATERFALL

A series of pristine cascades and swimming pools feed this shallow, steep-sided section of the Erymanthos River. A stunning place that attracts the odd camper.

➔ Park as for the Nemouta Waterfall Trail (see entry), cross to the E side of the river and turn L to walk N for 600m. There is another fall R on the way (37.7054, 21.8103).

10 mins, 37.7074, 21.8082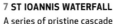

8 LADONAS RIVER BEND

This bucolic bend in the Ladonas River, flanked by grassy fields in a rural valley, is a splendid Greek river dip.

➔ Turn R 9.5km E of Paos on the EO111 (becoming EO33). Continue 4.4km, past a small sports centre on the L, and park on the roadside (37.8026, 22.0735). The river is in sight.

1 min, 37.8022, 22.0743

GORGES & FORESTS

9 STROFYLIA NATIONAL PARK

A divine forest of pines and ancient oaks nestled between protected saltwater lagoons (look out for flamingos) and a sweeping sandy beach. A rejuvenating stroll on a hot day.

➔ Roads surround the park. At the NW corner of the lagoon turn towards the sea (signed for La Mer beach bar) and fork L after 400m on a track to beach parking at the end (38.1522, 21.3689). This gives good beach and forest access.

1 min, 38.1448, 21.3841

10 ODONTOTOS RACK RAILWAY

This memorable railway walk of tunnels, bridges and rickety tracks forges dramatically through Vouraikos Gorge.

➔ The best stretch is N of Kato Zachlorou village. Walk all 13km to Diakopto or just 4km or so out and back to see the canyon. Start walking N from the train station (38.0941, 22.1646).

30 mins, 38.1103, 22.1612

11 PERISTERIONA GORGE

A razor-thin section of Peristeriona Gorge between towering cliffs. Walkable with low water, fearsome with high, and sometimes somewhere in between. A fantastic adventure.

➔ Follow the road SW from Akrata for 3km and fork R. After 1.7km park just before the bridge (38.1460, 22.2843). Walk over the road to a steep 300m trail that switchbacks into the gorge R.

5 mins, 38.1469, 22.2846

10

SACRED SITES

12 PLATANIOTISSA CHURCH

A tiny chapel formed inside the mighty trunk of three plane trees that have grown together. Set in scenic church grounds.

➔ On the N edge of Plataniotissa, just over the river. Plenty of parking right outside.
1 min, 38.1122, 22.087 🔲

13 ST ELEOUSIS MONASTERY

Built dramatically into a cliff overlooking a forested ravine and the village of Vlacherna, the *katholikon* of this faded 15th-century monastery houses splendid frescoes. On the trail up, just above the treeline, steep stairs also lead to a small cave chapel.

➔ Park at the end of the lane on the S end of Vlacherna (37.7148, 22.2512). Follow the forest track up switchbacks about 600m to another track. Turn R here then turn sharp L after 350m, from which it's 300m.
20 mins, 37.7153, 22.2545 🔲🔲🔲🔲

14 VIRGIN OF THE ROCK CHAPEL

A rock chapel burrowed into the base of a huge crack in an imposing red-grey cliff, its cross winking to visitors from afar. Be sure to climb to the roof for the magnificent views and drink from the spring below.

➔ The road winds up 2km from the S edge of Kato Tarsos village. Park at the base of the cliff by the chapel.
1 min, 37.9834, 22.3418 🔲🔲🔲

LOCAL FOOD & DRINK

15 ELIA

Classic Greek cuisine, fresh seafood and creative specials with herbs from their garden – all incredibly tasty, and within walking distance of an azure bay for a post-meal snooze and swim.

➔ Elia, Arkoudi 270 50, +30 2623 096493
37.8462, 21.1108 🔲🔲🔲

16 ALATI & PIPERI

Traditional Greek food served with super-local ingredients in a canopied garden hidden down a narrow lane. Owner Michalis is extraordinarily friendly.

➔ Vartholomio 270 50, +30 2623 041061
37.8611, 21.2064 🔲

17 MAGNA GRECIA

A family estate with an olive mill, vineyard

12

13

and restaurant. The tasting tour ends with a farm lunch and traditional Greek dancing. An enjoyable local experience, even if you are crowded by visiting tour buses.

→ Archaia Olympia 270 65, +30 2624 022739
37.6481, 21.6052 🍴🐎🎠

18 DIMITRA'S TAVERNA

Charming Dimitra serves fabulous traditional meals with local ingredients and homemade wine. The slow-cooked meat is sumptuous. Be sure to visit the tree-chapel over the road (see Plataniotissa Church entry).

→ Plataniotissa 250 01, +30 2692 023101
38.1123, 22.0872 🍴

19 AIGION PELAGOS RESTAURANT

Fresh, reasonably priced seafood and homemade desserts served with a smile on a quiet beach.

→ Aigio 251 00, +30 2691 051890
38.2422, 22.1365 🏊🏕

20 ANTONIS AND POLY'S TAVERNA

A delightful riverside taverna among the trees, serving delicious seasonal dishes with produce from the friendly hosts' garden. A fantastic place to eat before or after walking

the Vouraikos Gorge Railway (see entry).

→ Ano Zachlorou 250 01, +30 2692 022789
38.0936, 22.1647 🍴🚶

21 TETRAMYTHOS WINERY

A small organic winery making naturally fermented wines amid rolling mountain views.

→ Ano Diakopto, 25003, +30 2691 097500
38.1386, 22.2356 🍴🏔

22 TO PETRINO TAVERNA

Tasty, homely Greek cooking in a quiet garden – perfect for a local feast after swimming in Lake Tsivlou (see entry).

→ To Petrino, Zarouchla 250 06, +30 2696 034190
38.0727, 22.2365 🏊

23 CAMPING PALOUKI

A simple, clean campsite set in a shady pine glade next to a sandy beach with a bar and volleyball nets. Space for tents, campers and caravans.

→ Palouki 272 00, +30 2622 024942
37.7536, 21.3060 🏊🏕⛺

24 AMALIADA TREEHOUSE

Enjoy canopy views over pine forests and olive groves from this luxury treehouse. Incredibly romantic, with space for a couple and a child or two. The hosts have a second treehouse nearby.

➜ Amaliada 272 00, +30 6948 503742
37.8304, 21.3972 ▨▨

25 ANCIENT OLYMPIA COUNTRY HOUSE

A stylish, minimalist country house for two in Ancient Olympia, birthplace of the Olympics. A hammock, pool and wood pizza oven adorn a beautiful outdoor dining area.

➜ Archaia Olympia 270 65, airbnb.com/rooms/930681
37.6493, 21.6221 ▨

26 CAMPING TSOLIS WINDMILL

This converted windmill sleeps four, and is one of a few non-tent options on a campsite just a stone's throw from the beach.

➜ Lampiri 250 09, +30 2691 031469
38.321, 21.9721 ▨

27 AMPELOS ESTATE

A gorgeous old farm estate comprising a villa and studio that can be configured to match your group size. Wonderful Corinthian views, characterful furnishing and charming grounds full of olive and fruit trees.

➜ Ampelos 250 06, +30 2696 022910
38.1385, 22.3318 ▨▨

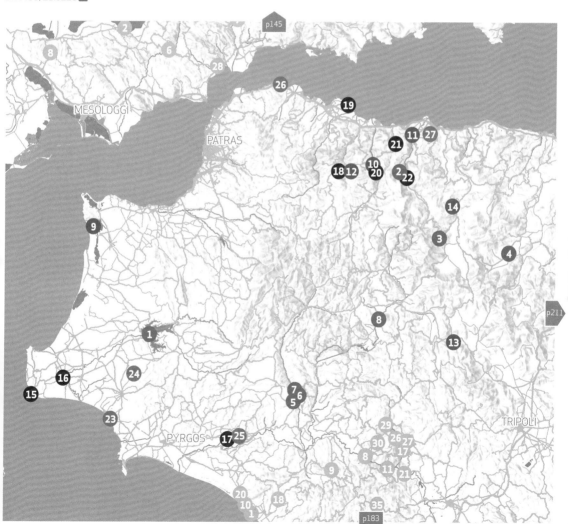

MESSENIA

Our perfect weekend

→ **Laze** deep in the dunes of magnificent Voidokilia Beach, a crescent between a life-giving lagoon, a towering ridgeline and the open sea.

→ **Climb** to the crumbling ramparts of Old Navarino Castle, pausing midway in myth-laden Nestor's Cave.

→ **Walk** the riverside trail through Lousios Gorge to the venerable monasteries of Prodromou and Old Filosofou.

→ **Feast** on local olive production with a tour at The Olive Routes, capped by a local banquet.

→ **Pick** your way down to spectacular Kantouni Beach for sunset and a night of solitude.

→ **Traverse** the via ferrata through paradisal Polylimnio Gorge, before plunging into one of its aquamarine pools.

→ **Craft,** learn and feast in the glamping groves at Skiaxtro Eco Farm.

→ **Plunge** through thick forest into the turquoise swimming hole beneath the powerful cascades of Valtas Waterfall.

Messenia is the westernmost Peloponnese peninsula, unfurling between the Ionian Sea and the Gulf of Messenia. Archeological wonders abound, with ruined castles on strategic promontories above agricultural plains and sheltering bays – the scars of a storied geopolitical history. But visitors here increasingly seek natural wonders: lush rivers with enchanting waterfalls rushing from interior mountains via green valleys and hushed monasteries towards a coastline strung with divine beaches.

As an ancient region variously under Mycenaean, Frankish, Byzantine, Ottoman and Venetian sway, Messenia is replete with archeological riches. Ancient Messene and the Mycenaean Palace of Nestor take the limelight, but wilder ruins await. The derelict city of Ancient Samiko was revived as a fort by the Venetians and Ottomans, its long walls now surveying Kleidi's patchwork coastal plain. Further south, Old Navarino Castle's half-fallen gate and extensive ramparts speak of Frankish influence, and make a memorable escapade across a spectacular coastal ridgeline. And Koroni has some of the region's finest Venetian remnants, scattered across a headland protruding proudly into the Gulf of Messenia.

If forts dominate Messenia's topography, religious sanctuaries take quiet refuge within. St Theodora Church hides beneath the canopy of seventeen holly and maple trees growing from its roof. Old Monastery Filosofou and Prodromou Monastery – the first abandoned, the second a mindful murmur of monastic life punctuated by tolling bells – cling to the walls of verdant Lousios Gorge. Walk between them along the shady riverside path, then celebrate with phenomenal home-cooked boar at Zerzoba and a night in the Arcadian mountain-village retreat of Abeliona.

Messenia's gorges also hide magical water worlds. You can navigate the absurdly picturesque cascade of bright-blue pools and falls in Polylimnio Gorge using via ferrata and stepping stones. Arini Gorge also requires an aquatic expedition: walking, wading or even swimming depending on the season. And Kalamaris and Vrontos falls both offer a simpler dip in pretty plunge pools beneath shady boughs.

These waterfalls flow towards a coastline famed for its signature Peloponnese beaches. Marathi's twin sands await like an open clam shell at the end of a sleepy olive-grove track, while nearby Kantouni Beach, a golden haven cocooned between huge headlands, is blissfully overlooked. And the duned crescent of Voidokilia Beach by Navarino Bay – site of the 1827 Battle of Navarino, which helped secure Greek independence – is a magnificent must, with plenty of hideaway nooks even when busy. Follow it with an evening of fine beachside dining at Deroko, and a morning or two of creativity and wellness at Skiaxtro Eco Farm.

10

BEACHES

1 ZACHARO BEACH

One of the longest beaches in Greece, its endless sands facing the sunset and backed by a labyrinthine pine forest with private pockets aplenty.

→ Head W from Zaharo for 3km to the little seaside enclave of Agios Nikolaos. Park at the N end of the houses, at Fratzata Beach Bar. Walk N for seclusion.

3 mins, 37.4888, 21.615 🏖️🏞️⛺

2 AMIROLAKA BEACH

This open, sandy beach isn't as striking as its neighbour Voidokilia (see entry), but this makes it a peaceful place to while away an afternoon.

→ Head SW out of Petrochori for 350m then turn R onto a track just after a stone church (36.9767, 21.6596). Park at the chapel at the end and walk 100m S via the coast or field edge.

2 mins, 36.9729, 21.6593 🏖️✝️

3 GLOSSA BEACH

A funnel-shaped cove with a narrow entrance, creating still waters lapping onto a little yellow beach where visitors build rock pools with clay stones. Popular with naturists and wild campers.

→ Park as if for Voidokilia Beach (see entry) and follow a footpath around 150m W from its N end.

3 mins, 36.9665, 21.6587 🏖️🏖️⊗☀️⚡

4 VOIDOKILIA BEACH

This magnificent duned crescent connects the mainland to a magical ridge that is home to Nestor's Cave and Navarino Castle (see entries). The open Ionian lies before it, the wildlife of Gialova Lagoon behind. A divine basecamp; if busy, its southern end will be quieter.

→ Drive about 2km S from Petrochori, turn R when you get to the edge of the lagoon (signed for archeological sites) and park in the large sandy area at the N end of the beach.

2 mins, 36.9631, 21.6624 🏖️🏖️🏖️⛺🚶B

5 DIVARI BEACH

An arc of sand stretching along an isthmus between Gialova Lagoon and Navarino Bay. Head for the farthest end, with vertiginous Sphaktiria Beach a short swim across a shallow channel. An excellent stopping point on a circular walk around the lagoon from Voidokilia Beach via Navarino Castle (see entries).

→ Follow the coastal road around 5km W from Gialova and park anywhere on the dirt road set back from the beach.

1 min, 36.9518, 21.6626 🏖️🏖️☀️

6 KANTOUNI BEACH

A sumptuous sandy beach hidden between towering green headlands, with a Venetian watchtower guarding from above. A rough track keeps it quieter than its beauty might suggest.

→ Drive NW from Akritochori, and about 270m after joining the coastal road heading N for Finikounta, take a dirt track L (36.8035, 21.8313). Bend L, then park after 900m where the track peters out just past the house. Follow the trail, bending R and descending to the coast (passing the tower on your L at 36.7963, 21.8248) before turning L to the beach.

10 mins, 36.7954, 21.8241 🏖️🏖️🏖️⛺☀️⚡

7 MARATHI BEACH

Two secret sand-shingle beaches with shallow waters, connected by a short footpath. The rough approach road keeps this inviting nook quiet save for the odd boat or camper.

→ Take the track (R fork) that leaves the paved road 2.3km N from the beach at Tsapi (36.7686,

21.8507). A rough 1km drive, only advisable in a 4x4, ends at the first beach. Follow a short footpath from its N end to the second.

1 min, 36.7719, 21.838 🏊🏖⛰❓🚶

WATERFALLS & WILD SWIMS

8 ALFEIOS RIVER

An overgrown track, passable in a normal car, snakes down to the secluded bank of this tumbling mountain river. Particularly scenic amidst the early autumnal hues.

➜ From the church on the E edge of the small village of Paleokastro, follow the downhill road E. After 1.3km take the track on the first major R hairpin (37.5417, 21.9701). Turn L at the T junction after 500m, take the first R fork at 1.6km and wind 600m down to the grass by the river.

2 mins, 37.5394, 21.9498 🏊🌿🐚

9 TRITON WATERFALL

This secret waterfall plunges 40m down a mossy rockface into a tiny, inaccessible pool, almost out of sight entirely. A steep, overgrown chute spills onto a tiny viewing platform, giving the feeling of discovering the falls for the first time.

➜ Drive N on the primary road from Kato Amigdalies to Alifeira for 1km and turn L onto

a track (37.5266, 21.8542). Park on the L at the R bend and continue on foot for 300m to a tiny, steep path descending between the trees on the L to a private perch.

5 mins, 37.5307, 21.852 ⛰◀🚶

10 KAIAFAS LAKE

Jump from the small swimming and fishing jetty that extends into the vast blueness of Lake Kaiafa from a verdant, elongated island strewn with mostly abandoned buildings. Keep an eye out for turtles.

➜ Turn off the EO9 about 5km N of Zaharo and park just before the bridge. Continue onto the island and turn R at the water.

15 mins, 37.5096, 21.605 🏊

11 VRONTOS WATERFALL

This shaded waterfall feeds a pretty stream that rushes past picnic benches and down a series of cascades into the Alfeios River below.

➜ Heading S from Vlachoraptis, cross the Alfeios River heading S via the striking Cuckoo Bridge (37.5041, 21.9964) and bear L at the hairpin just after. Park at the next bend and follow the slippy, wet track R along the creek 100m to the falls.

5 mins, 37.5021, 21.9989 🏊🍴🔽

12 NEDA WATERFALLS

A bright round swimming hole lying at the bottom of a thunderous cascade and emptying into a series of rapids and chutes. The interior mountain valleys of the Peloponnese at their finest.

➜ Cataracts and the archeological site are signed L from the road heading W of Figaleia (37.3990, 21.8389). Take the first R and park at the bend after 3.2km (37.3940, 21.8265). Walk on down, turn R just before the bridge and follow the creek trail 300m to the main fall.

10 mins, 37.397, 21.8207 🏊↩🚶🅱

13 VALTAS WATERFALL

This picturesque double waterfall, heavy in winter, sometimes dry in summer, fills a wide pool ensconced by small cliffs and lush forest.

➜ Take the main track W from Valta for about 1.7km and bear L on a R hairpin (37.1010, 21.6140). Bend R to arrive at a large olive grove. Park and follow red arrows on trees to the SW corner (37.0954, 21.6103). Continue W into the forest and 200m along a steep path to the falls.

10 mins, 37.0954, 21.6087 🏊🌿🐚

14 DEBRIZ BRIDGE

Originally built to connect Venetian castles in the 16th century, this elegant and lofty stone bridge is now a lovely picnic spot, especially in the spring. It crosses a cooling river meandering through olive groves.

→ Head W from Strefi, crossing the main road at a crossroads (37.0536, 21.8845), and continue 1km W on a dirt track.

1 min, 37.0554, 21.8749 🚶‍♂️🌲🐟🍃🗿🌼

15 POLYLIMNIO GORGE

This luscious gorge is a string of bright-blue cascades and pools, linked by stepping stones, via ferrata and ropes. It gets busy in the summer, but it's an essential visit.

→ Head around 1.2km S from Charavgi to a cobbled parking area right by the river (36.9819, 21.8507). Follow the riverside path winding NE along the series of falls.

5 mins, 36.9837, 21.8538 🍴🌲🏊🚶‍♂️🅱

16 KALAMARIS WATERFALL

Sliding over a smooth rockface, this waterfall feeds an enchanting pool and a series of shaded rivulets running beneath crooked boughs. The waterfall may dry in late summer, but the pool should last.

→ Head S from Gianouleika and turn L 180m after the petrol stations. Branch R on a R bend after 900m (36.9582, 21.7113). Follow the main track E for 1.7km, ignoring all turnings, to a parking area and a 200m forest walk to the falls.

5 mins, 36.9579, 21.7305 🌲🏊🐟🗿

GORGE WALKS & CAVES

17 LOUSIOS GORGE

Follow this lush, forested gorge walk across the scurrying Lousios River by some old monastic baths, before climbing to beautiful Prodromou Monastery and Old Monastery Filosofou (see entries).

→ To hike in from the S, follow twisting roads 6km NW from Elliniko to parking at the end of the road by a bridge (37.5394, 22.0464). Alternatively, enter the gorge in the N at Old Monastery Filosofou or middle at Prodromou Monastery (see entries).

5 mins, 37.5439, 22.0506 ✝🚵🚶‍♂️

18 ARINI GORGE

Depending on the water levels, this enticing river canyon is explorable by paddling, wading or swimming expedition. Especially at the start, the riverbed is always slick and occasionally stagnant.

→ Take a track E into the olive groves just N of the bridge on the road N out of Kato Arini (37.5020, 21.6939). Follow it for 200m to arrive at the gorge proper and begin walking, paddling or wading. Bring good shoes and prepare to get wet.

5 mins, 37.5022, 21.6948

19 NESTOR'S CAVE

A clean cave with a high, triangular mouth with views over grassy dunes to sweeping Voidokilia Beach - a fine spot for a contemplative break on the walk up to Old Navarino Castle (see entries). It is reputed to be the mythical cave of Nestor, the elderly warrior in Homer's Iliad and Odyssey, where the god Hermes hid 50 cattle he stole from Apollo.

→ Hike along the ridgeline for 10 minutes S from Voidokilia Beach (see entry) or 30 minutes NW from Divari Beach (see entry).

10 mins, 36.9597, 21.6577

HILLTOP CASTLES

20 ANCIENT SAMIKO

In a commanding position overlooking the patchwork plain of Kleidi and the Ionian coastline beyond, this ancient city was revived as a fort in the Middle Ages. Today there are walkable walls and the remains of tombs.

→ Turn E off the E09 just S of Fragokklisia and park where a path leaves the winding track R after 900m (37.5364, 21.6005). Follow the path S for 400m past a number of small ruins up to a clearing in the trees where the castle sits.

15 mins, 37.5338, 21.5987

21 KARYTAINA CASTLE

Rising from the pretty mountain village of Karytaina, this 13th-century Frankish castle surveys the surrounding valleys above the remnants of a Byzantine tower house.

→ Park in the large layby across the road from Zoodochos Pigi Church in Karytaina and take the signed, cobbled alley S from the road bend (37.4850, 22.0410). Bend R then L up the stairs, following the signs, passing the tower house on the R (37.4841, 22.0408).

5 mins, 37.483, 22.0403

22 SAFLAOURO CASTLE

Crumbling 13th-century castle walls atop a hill looking down a green valley alive with smoke tendrils and wolf calls.

→ Climb W out of Paleokastro for about 3km and branch R onto a track with the castle visible ahead (37.1725, 21.8149). Continue about 300m to below the castle and walk up the slope. Proper footwear recommended.

1 min, 37.1758, 21.8162

23 OLD NAVARINO CASTLE

The overgrown ramparts and imposing gate of this 13th-century Frankish castle are arrayed across a wonderful ridgeline overlooking the Ionian Sea and splendid Voidokilia Beach (see entry).

→ Park as for Voidokilia Beach and hike for 30 minutes S via Nestor's Cave (see entry). Alternatively, park as for Divari Beach (see entry) and hike 10 minutes NW. It's also just under a 5km coast walk W from Gialova.

10 mins, 36.9585, 21.6568

24 METHONI CASTLE

A vast 13th-century Venetian castle complex extending over a long peninsula beside a boatyard, featuring an arched-bridge entrance and old prison. Entrance is €3 to €6.

→ Use the castle parking at the S end of Methoni (36.8180, 21.7052).

2 mins, 36.8166, 21.7043

25 KORONI CASTLE

Homes and olive groves are scattered within the protective walls of this 7th-century fortress, sprawled across a coastal peninsula above Koroni. A fantastic sunrise stroll.

→ Walk the lane that climbs E from Koroni to the fortress gates. Explore the complex S and E from here, and loop back to the harbour along the N coastal path.

5 mins, 36.7956, 21.9624 🏔🚵🚶

SACRED SITES

26 OLD FILOSOFOU MONASTERY

The original Filosofou (Philosopher) Monastery, clinging to a narrow ledge along the red walls of Lousios Gorge. From the crumbling *katholikon*, with its faded frescoes, you can see all the way south to Prodromou Monastery (see entry).

→ Descend E from Markos about 5km and take a hairpin turn R to park at the new monastery after 450m (37.5565, 22.0458). A short trail heads 250m S before turning uphill to the old ruins. You can also hike N from Prodromou Monastery.

5 mins, 37.5538, 22.047 🏔✝🚵🚶🏵

27 PRODROMOU MONASTERY

A 16th-century monastery hanging from the cliff walls of verdant Lousios Gorge (see entry), its wood-beam balconies festooned with plants and signs of life. The friendly monks will welcome you with refreshments.

→ The road snaking down the E side of Lousios Gorge is signed 1km SW of Stemnitsa village. Continue 7.5km down and park at the end (37.5462, 22.0533). Descend a short trail to the monastery. You can also hike S from the Old Monastery Filosofou (see entry) or N along Lousios Gorge.

5 mins, 37.5486, 22.0532 ✝🚶

28 ST THEODORA CHURCH

Seventeen holly and maple trees grow from the roof of this peculiar Byzantine church, irrigated by a stream running beneath. Remarkably, the trees aren't visible from within. A delightful rest, especially with a sprawling taverna garden over the road.

→ Fairly prominent on a bend in the road 3km N from Dasochori village. Park in the large shaded car park by the taverna, 50m E of the church.

1 min, 37.3538, 21.9786 ✝B

LOCAL FOOD & DRINK

29 MPLEXEIS

A traditional mountain taverna with an incredibly warm welcome, serving tasty Greek dishes made with fresh, local ingredients.

→ Zatouna 220 07, +30 697 3306226 37.5904, 22.0237 🏖

30 ZERZOBA

Phenomenal home cooking in an enchanting village overlooking Louisos Gorge, with salads fresh from the garden and meats from the farm. Try the Greek pasta and wild boar, followed by *galaktoboureko*. Worth booking ahead.

→ Gortynia 220 07, +30 693 2847358 37.559, 21.9904 🍴🏖

31 THE OLIVE ROUTES

A range of thoroughly enjoyable tours, tastings and cooking classes exploring the cultural significance and preparation of olives, led by wonderful guide Dimitra. The tours include a fantastic, locally sourced lunch.

→ Androusa 240 13, +30 693 7101215 37.1086, 21.9429 🍴🏖🐾

32 DEROKO

Fine beachside dining at a reasonable price. The creative, beautifully presented international dishes are made with local ingredients and paired with excellent wines.

→ Gialova 240 01, +30 2723 022301 36.9499, 21.7027 🏖€

33 SOCRATES

Fabulously fresh seafood dishes served with surprising touches and sea views. If you can, order a few dishes to share.

→ Chrani 240 10, +30 2725 031944 36.9034, 21.9239 🏖

34 METHEXIS

You might find this restaurant just by the name of the friendly owner, Fotis, who serves generous portions of tasty traditional dishes in a charming village square, often accompanied by live music.

→ Evangelismos 240 06, +30 2723 081282 36.8332, 21.7691 🐾

35 ABELIONA RETREAT

An Arcadian mountain-village retreat with a programme of yurt-based yoga, meditation and therapeutic workshops and outdoor activities including trekking, rafting and rappelling. A vegetable garden, a greenhouse and free-range chickens contribute restaurant ingredients. Double rooms and family suites available.

➜ Ampeliona 270 61, +30 69 4837 5905
37.4373, 21.9494

36 HOME OF SILENCE

Wooden lodges and tents set on a forested plateau near the Neda River are home to this yoga community, with retreats throughout the year. You can also enjoy a small pool and massage therapies.

➜ Avlona 240 03, homeofsilence.com
37.3864, 21.7563

37 AGRIKIES COUNTRY RETREAT

An oasis of stone maisonettes and safari tents set in a manicured olive grove, with a pool and an abundance of food and wellness activities.

➜ Marathopoli 244 00, +30 2763 061226
37.0707, 21.5858

38 SKIAXTRO ECO FARM

A utopian farmstay with luxurious tents and a revolving circus of creative workshops, agricultural activities, thoughtful seminars and wellness sessions, all amidst hammocked olive groves by the beach.

➜ Marathopoli 244 00, +30 6937 840077
37.0549, 21.5839

39 SEE YOU SOON, CHRANI

Shower beneath the olive tree and savour your coffee in the morning sun on the patio of this idyllic cottage with green shutters, a stone's throw from a semi-private pebble beach. Sleeps up to four, with two on a sofa bed.

➜ Aipeia 240 10, +30 69 3771 3842
36.8945, 21.9235

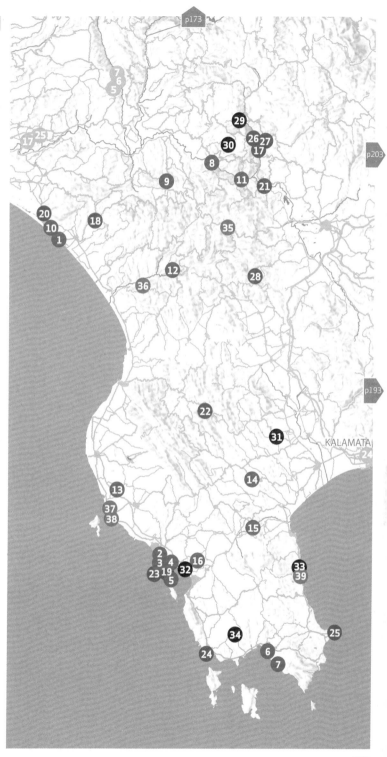

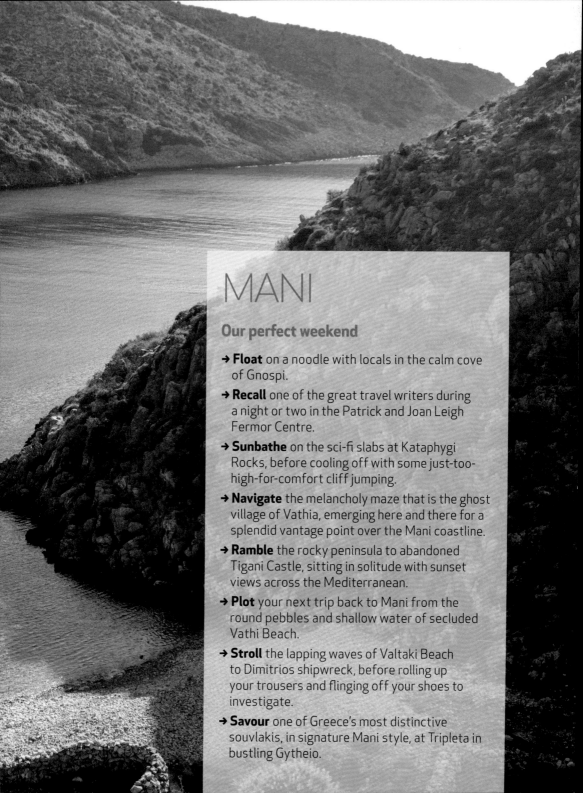

MANI

Our perfect weekend

→ **Float** on a noodle with locals in the calm cove of Gnospi.

→ **Recall** one of the great travel writers during a night or two in the Patrick and Joan Leigh Fermor Centre.

→ **Sunbathe** on the sci-fi slabs at Kataphygi Rocks, before cooling off with some just-too-high-for-comfort cliff jumping.

→ **Navigate** the melancholy maze that is the ghost village of Vathia, emerging here and there for a splendid vantage point over the Mani coastline.

→ **Ramble** the rocky peninsula to abandoned Tigani Castle, sitting in solitude with sunset views across the Mediterranean.

→ **Plot** your next trip back to Mani from the round pebbles and shallow water of secluded Vathi Beach.

→ **Stroll** the lapping waves of Valtaki Beach to Dimitrios shipwreck, before rolling up your trousers and flinging off your shoes to investigate.

→ **Savour** one of Greece's most distinctive souvlakis, in signature Mani style, at Tripleta in bustling Gytheio.

Mani is a proud, guarded prong splitting the Laconian and Messenian gulfs. The towering Taygetos mountains in the north descend via twinkling coves to the signature fortified villages of 'Deep Mani', a scorched yellow peninsula that ends in mainland Greece's most southerly point. Said to be descended from the Spartans, the Maniots were the last Greeks converted to Christianity, and maintained a degree of autonomy through Greece's long history of occupation. Mani remained inaccessible to most visitors until roads arrived in the 1970s; celebrated travel writer Patrick Leigh Fermor researched his classic *Mani* on foot with a mule. To this day travel here is rugged and rewarding.

The mighty Taygetos range, named after the nymph Taygete, dominates 'Outer Mani' in the north-west. The breathtaking trails along Lagadiotissa Gorge, hewn in places from the gorge wall, and Ridomo Gorge, with old stone bridges spanning its ravine-like narrows, are stirring portals into this landscape. Spartis Mountain Refuge, by the Mount Taygetos trailhead, is a wonderfully rustic base for exploring, or simply marvelling at, the grandeur. Alternatively, Art Farm is a hive of creative activity amidst cosy huts and treehouses in the coastal foothills.

Mani's west coast is a string of sapphires, often underrated because they lack soft sands. The rock ledges and crystal waters of Gnospi present a fine place to cool off and chat with locals. The sci-fi marble formations of Kataphygi Rocks, once the outfall of an underground river that has left an eerie cave to the rear, are sumptuous for lounging and leaping. Spend an afternoon at each, punctuated with a night at the Patrick and Joan Leigh Fermor Centre, once home to the writer; his book Mani is a poetic ode to the region's history and culture. While there, enjoy the creative beachside cuisine at nearby Elies or Lela's Taverna, owned by the sons of the house's old housekeeper.

Mani grows scrubbier and more watchful as you travel south. Stay at Citta dei Nicliani, a chic hotel in a converted tower house, and venture to the corner of coastline west of Mezapos Bay. The ruined foundations of Byzantine Tigani Castle, laying low and lonesome at the tip of a sparse rocky peninsula, exude wild guardedness. And nearby Odigitria Church, hidden behind a bluff cascading into the sea, is one of Greece's most aesthetic, ascetic churches.

Tenaro Lighthouse, at the end of a dusty trail, marks mainland Greece's most southerly point. It was thought in antiquity that Cape Tenaro hid an entrance to Hades, guarded by the three-headed-dog beast Cerberus that Hercules kidnapped with his bare hands. Mark the fire of this place before retreating to calmer pockets. Vathi Beach, just north, is an overlooked sliver of solitude. And the ghost village of Vathia, an eerie knot of crumbling alleyways and dark doorways, is slowly resurrecting to the renovating clink of tools.

BEACHES & WILD SWIMMING

1 KALAMITSI BEACH

A long strip of pebbles bookended by rock pools, cypress-clad slopes and the Patrick and Joan Leigh Fermor Centre (see entry), where you can stay in summer.

→ Follow the coast road S from Kardamylia for 1.5km, turning R 600m after passing Hotel Kalamitsi on your R. Park on the side of this road, which runs 500m to the beach S of the Leigh Fermor Centre.

2 mins, 36.8775, 22.2400 🏊🛶📷🐚

2 FONEAS BEACH

Cradled by cliffs below a bend in the road, this popular beach has a cantina, tree shade and a hulking rock for varied jumping.

→ Heading S on the coastal road, turn sharp R just under 3km S of Kalamitsi, in the middle of the hairpin bend, and park in the shade behind the beach.

1 min, 36.8674, 22.2482 🍴🛶📷B

3 GNOSPI

A concealed gathering place for local villagers to lounge on paved stone ledges above pristine water, with a small chapel built into the rock.

→ Park in a layby on the coastal lane on the N edge of Agios Nikolaos (36.8266, 22.2799). Walk 20m back towards the village, then turn R down an alley to the hidden cove.

5 mins, 36.8259, 22.2793 🍴🛶📷✝🐚⊙

4 KATAPHYGI ROCKS

A higgledy-piggledy amphitheatre of marble-limestone blocks and platforms descending into deep, clear water, formed by the outfall of an underground river that once flowed through Kataphygi Cave (see entry). A wonderful arena for sunbathing and swimming.

→ Follow the coastal road 3km S from Agios Dimitrios and park carefully in a layby on the R (36.8031, 22.2975). Walk down, in good shoes for some light scrambling at the end.

5 mins, 36.8027, 22.2972 🍴🛶📷🐚⛰

5 DEXAMENI BEACH

The charming village of Limeni sits in a shallow bay, boasting perfect waters, classic Mani architecture and this concrete platform with steps and jetties into the water.

→ Head W along the coastal lane from Limeni and park in the wide layby at 36.6802, 22.3741, just above the platform on the S side of the bay, around 200m before the lane ends.

1 min, 36.6801, 22.3751 🍴🛶📷🐚

6 MEZAPOS BAY

A near-circular bay doubling as a colourful fishing marina and natural swimming pool. A postcard scene, with views across to remote Tigani Castle (see entry).

→ Mezapos is signed W from the main road 800m W of Mina. Park anywhere in the tiny village and wind your way to its W tip, where there are steps into the water.

2 mins, 36.5424, 22.3903 🛶📷⛰

7 ALMIROS BEACH

Busy with locals in high summer, this beach has a shady cave and popular jumping rocks. The low ruins of a 2,000-year-old city with a temple to Aphrodite lie above.

→ Park alongside the coastal road on the NW edge of Kiparissos (36.4647, 22.4373) and walk a track 300m SW to the beach, signed for the beach and Ancient Kenopolis (which is L about halfway to the beach).

5 mins, 36.4627, 22.435 🍴🛶📷

8 KAPI BEACH

A tranquil pebble beach between rolling headlands, with a protective rocky claw on the south side.

➔ Park at the first hairpin just W of Kapi on the coastal road. Follow a clear 100m path down.
3 mins, 36.4552, 22.4503 🏊‍♀️🏖️🖼️

9 TAINARO BEACH

The middle of three exposed coves that offer a cooling dip after the hike to Tenaro Lighthouse (see entry). It lies between the remnants of Roman baths to the right and a temple to Poseidon on the headland left, beyond which is a cove with a cave once reputed to be the entrance to Hades.

➔ Follow the road S through Kokkinogia to the parking area at the very end. Follow the path SW for 75m.
5 mins, 36.4019, 22.4854 🏊‍♀️🏖️🚴‍♂️🥾

10 VATHI BEACH

A drop-dead gorgeous beach of large smooth pebbles secluded at the end of a deep, angled cove between the signature yellow-grass hillocks of Mani's Tigani peninsula.

➔ Follow the road S from Paliros for 900m and park by the cluster of buildings at the end. Walk S past the buildings.
10 mins, 36.4126, 22.4889 🏊‍♀️🏖️🐚🌅

11 SKOPA BEACH

Twin coves meet in a picturesque isthmus at the end of a narrow lane, forming a single beach among squat olive trees and the fishing bric-a-brac of nearby houses. Explore the eastern coast of the peninsula for a second, more secluded beach.

➔ Follow a narrowing lane 500m SW from the playground in Kotronas (36.6211, 22.4865). At the very latest, park where it briefly widens at a fork (36.6181, 22.4879).
5 mins, 36.6168, 22.4874 🏊‍♀️🏖️

12 TOURKOPIGADO BEACH

A charming cove harbouring a tiny stone beach backed by tall grass, plus a platform for jumping midway out.

➔ Follow the main road SE from Kalyvia for 1.3km to a five-road skewed crossroads. Go straight over, L of the building, and park where the tarmac ends by a house. Take a path L to the beach.
5 mins, 36.6624, 22.5448 🍴🏊‍♀️🏖️🚶‍♂️

17

13 VALTAKI BEACH

The dramatic rusting hulk of the cargo ship Dimitrios dominates this sandy beach. An arresting sight from the road above, and well worth a short walk for closer inspection.

→ Head NE from Selinitsa on the coast road and about 500m after it pulls away from the coast hairpin R to the W end of the beach. Park in the clearing at the end.

3 mins, 36.7893, 22.5857 🏊🏖🦆

CASTLES & RUINS

14 BARDOUNIA CASTLE

A 9th-century castle, finally abandoned in the 1820s, poking through the undergrowth on a valley hillock. A fun outing, though watch out for snakes, per the advice of a local farmer.

→ Follow the R fork downhill NE out of Agios Nikolaos for 100m to a L bend with steps leading up to a cemetery chapel. Turn R onto the lane immediately L of the steps and follow it 500m round the hill to the R. Park and follow a footpath E skirting anticlockwise up the R side of the hill.

5 mins, 36.8340, 22.4469 ⛰🦆

15 KELEFA CASTLE

You can circle the overgrown grounds of this 17th-century Ottoman castle by walking its crumbling but still substantial walls and turrets, all overlooking the deep-blue bay far below.

→ Climb NE from Neo Itilo to Kelefa and you can't miss it on the L; there is a layby at the corner of the wall.

2 mins, 36.7012, 22.3957 📷⛰🦆

16 TIGANI CASTLE

This Byzantine settlement is likely the oldest in the region and a place of supreme solitude, resting at the end of a barren peninsula protecting Mezapos Bay (see entry).

→ Follow a bumpy track just under 1km N from Agia Kiriaki (N of Stavri) to a small space to park and turn at the end. Walk 1km N along the peninsula path to the castle.

25 mins, 36.5458, 22.3659 📷⛰🦆⛰🚶🦆🐚

17 VATHIA

Perhaps Greece's most famous ghost village, offering an atmospheric snoop through a melancholy maze of beige tower houses, crumbling alleyways and demolished timber.

11

13

The odd tink of a renovating hammer now floats above.

→ Follow the road about 2km SE from Kapi, park anywhere along the E edge of the village and explore on foot.

2 mins, 36.4535, 22.4655 ▲🚶

18 TENARO LIGHTHOUSE

An exposed, undulating walk leading to a 19th-century lighthouse at the southern tip not just of Mani's Tigani peninsula, but mainland Greece. Check out the Roman mosaic en route, and stop for a refreshing dip at Tainaro Beach (see entry) on the way back.

→ Park as for Tainaro Beach and follow the path S along the peninsula for 2km. There is no shade, so take plenty of water.

40 mins, 36.3861, 22.4829 ▲🚶

GORGES & CAVES

19 LAGADIOTISSA GORGE

The hiking path along this breathtaking gorge is at times hewn into its sheer wall. The dramatic cave temple with 15th-century frescoes is an added bonus.

→ Park in Parorio and walk to the SW corner. Just over the bridge take the path

S (37.0619, 22.3826). After 300m you will reach the temple.

15 mins, 37.0586, 22.3795 ▲✝🚶☀

20 RIDOMO GORGE

A fabulous gorge hike with tiny twin stone bridges crossing the narrowest, ravine-like section.

→ Park on the E edge of Pigadia hamlet (best reached from Agios Vasilios to the N) by the hairpin bend (36.9962, 22.2589). Follow the track heading S for 1km into the gorge to the bridge.

30 mins, 36.9844, 22.2612 ▲🚶

21 KATAPHYGI CAVE

Opening onto the slabs of Kataphygi Rocks (see entry), this labyrinthine cave descends 3.5km underground. Ducking and crawling through its slick passages as the darkness descends and the (harmless) spider crickets appear is thrilling, with appropriate clothing and ample lighting. Stick to the main passage, follow the arrows, ensure you can retrace your steps and don't explore beyond 100m.

→ Park as for Kataphygi Rocks. The cave is at the back (road side) of the first flat slab area.

5 mins, 36.8029, 22.2975 🔦🔦▽☀

SACRED PLACES

22 TSIGOU MONASTERY

This 16th-century monastery, now in ruins, became a private home in the 19th century. It was abandoned during the Greek Civil War when seven family members were killed there. It stands as a solemn monument in a sleepy valley.

→ Drive N from Oitylo for 2.5km and take a hairpin turn L onto a track (36.7222, 22.4003). Continue N for just under 3km and walk the final 50m up the hill.

5 mins, 36.7401, 22.3921 △ ✝ ⌖

23 ODIGITRIA CHURCH

An exquisite Byzantine church decorated with ancient paintings and carvings, built precipitously into a hidden bluff giving way to a steep slope rolling to the sea. A wild, ascetic place, along a gem of a coastal path. Celebrations occur here on 23rd August.

→ Follow the track for Tigani Castle (see entry) but take the first track L just N of Agia Kiriaki and continue 600m to parking at the end. Walk the final 400m L along the path.

20 mins, 36.5300, 22.3639 △ ✝ ⬆ ⌖ ⌖

LOCAL FOOD & DRINK

24 OINOPANTOPOLEION

Known for its beautiful courtyard setting and focus on seasonal local ingredients. The signature Mani pasta dish, *tsouhti*, is a fine choice, and the eight-hour beef ribs aren't too shabby either.

→ Kalamata 241 00, +30 2721 082759 37.0437, 22.1151 ⌖

25 ELIES

Mani through and through. You'll be hard-pushed to find a prettier table than those in its shady olive grove, accented with bougainvillea, gazing over a gorgeous beach. The food is fabulous too, a modern approach to local classics. Run by a friendly couple; the husband, Stavros, is the son of Lela, whose taverna (see entry) is also highly recommended.

→ Kardamili 240 22, +30 2721 073140 36.8955, 22.2236 ⌖

26 YIORYITSA'S BACKYARD

A magical hidden garden with a small menu of exquisite local delicacies. Call ahead to align your trip with live music or a film event.

→ Kardamili 240 22, +30 69 4284 9549 36.8895, 22.2323 ⌖

27 LELA'S TAVERNA

The place to go for gourmet Greek and Mediterranean cuisine in Kardamili, famed for its beautiful waterside setting and its founder Lela, a renowned local and former cook to writer Patrick Leigh Fermor (see entry). It's now run by her son Giorgos.

→ Kardamili 240 22, +30 69 7771 6017 36.8860, 22.2318 ⌖ ⌖ ⌖

28 TAVERNA TO LIMPERDON

Charming courtyard dining with a menu of daily dishes read by the chef, many made with family-farm ingredients. A locals' favourite.

→ Platanos 232 00, +30 2733 091356 36.7765, 22.4918 ⌖

29 BIOHOF KARABABAS

An organic farm and shop selling farm-produced olive oils, capers, unusual jams and marmalades and more. Run by a friendly Greek-German couple.

→ Passavas 232 00, +30 2733 022381 36.7506, 22.5316 ⌖

30 TRIPLETA

Owner and host Anestis and his sons have one thing on the menu at this quaint alleyway joint: souvlaki. But not like you've had it before. This is Mani style, with pork and a hunk of matured kasseri cheese in a signature pitta made from Mani flour.

➜ Yithion 232 00, +30 2733 025147
36.7604, 22.5644 🐚

31 TRATA

A bustling seafront seafood taverna that does everything well. Wonderful sea views, fresh food and reasonable prices – check, check and check. Don't miss the fish soup!

➜ Githio 232 00, +30 2733 024429
36.7567, 22.5696 🅱

32 TO MICRO ALGERI

A quiet seaside taverna offering superb seafood platters and quaint vibes for all.

➜ Néon Oítilon 230 62, +30 2733 059401
36.6962, 22.3787 🏖🐚

33 MAZARAKI GUESTHOUSE

A plush stone guesthouse with suites for between two and five amidst pine and cypress trees beneath the towering Taygetos mountain range. The small cafe serves choice local wines and delicacies.

➜ Pikoulianika 231 00, +30 2731 020414
37.0807, 22.3567 ▨

34 SPARTIS MOUNTAIN REFUGE

Scenic refuge with bunks and tent space at the trailhead to Mount Taygetos. Friendly hosts and supreme mountain views. Call ahead to confirm openings and food availability. Follow the rough road from Manganiari Springs.

➜ Sparta 230 54, +30 69 4583 2701
36.9504, 22.3678 ▨▨

35 ART FARM

Crafty activities abound at this wonderful multi-functional farm and artistic hub. Bamboo treehouses overlook stone huts, organic gardens, traditional wood ovens and a stone amphitheatre.

➜ Megali Mantineia 241 00, +30 69 365 13421
36.9655, 22.1749 ▨▨

36 DIANE'S YURT

A large yurt for two overlooking a colourful, terraced garden of banana and olive trees and a sweeping valley leading to the sea.

➜ Megali Mantineia 241 00, +30 2721 058260, airbnb.com/rooms/128861
36.9554, 22.1686 ▦

37 PATRICK AND JOAN LEIGH FERMOR CENTRE

Patrick Leigh Fermor was one of the greatest travel writers of the 20th century. He and his partner Joan lived in this house, which is now a museum, retreat centre and, from June to September, a holiday home. It sleeps ten – six in the main house and two each in two smaller guesthouses – all overlooking a delightful stretch of coastline.

➜ Kardamyli 240 22, +30 2103 671090
36.8785, 22.2403 ▦▦

38 CAMPING MELTEMI

A campsite set in a beachside olive grove with a restaurant, shop (with fresh bread), pool and sport facilities. A comfortable basecamp.

➜ Gythio 232 00, +30 2733 022833
36.7303, 22.5535 ▦▦▦

39 PIRGOS MAVROMICHALI

Converted tower-house hotels are a feature of Mani, and this one is supremely located overlooking picturesque Limeni Bay. The exceptional restaurant makes the most of these views, and there are steps directly down to a private deck and a protected mini cove.

➜ Limeni 230 62, +30 2733 051042
36.6797, 22.3770 ▦▦

40 CITTA DEI NICLIANI

A small rustic-chic hotel in a converted 18th-century tower house. Stunning Mani views and an equally romantic courtyard for alfresco dining.

➜ Areopoli 230 71, +30 2733 051827
36.5144, 22.4034 ▦

41 TAINARON BLUE RETREAT

Idyllically sited where the Taygetos foothills meet the sea, this 19th-century defence tower has been beautifully converted into bare-stone suites connected by narrow passages. An infinity pool and gourmet restaurant round out the offering.

➜ Vathia 230 62, +30 2733 300461
36.4367, 22.4656 ▦

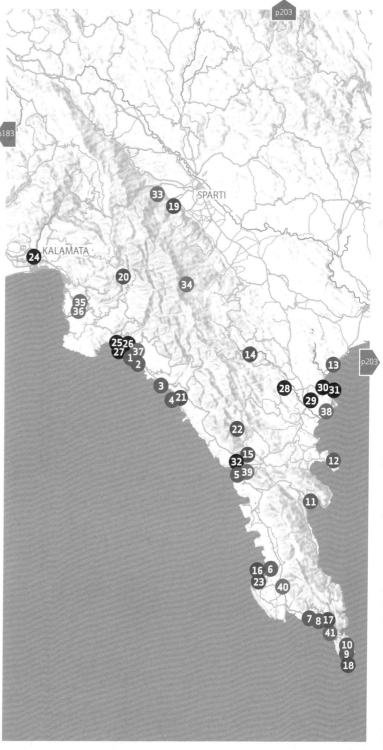

EAST LACONIA & KYTHIRA

Our perfect weekend

- → **Walk** the walls of Ancient Zarax, arrayed above Greece's only fjord.
- → **Bask** in the dancing glow of a campfire on utopian Damos Beach, where a remote gorge kisses the open sea.
- → **Survey** the Laconian Gulf from crumbling Asopos Paleokastro on its striking plateau pedestal.
- → **Feast** on simple, succulent Greek cooking from the terrace at Epidilion, gazing across to Monemvasia below.
- → **Snorkel** above the ruins of the ancient city of Pavlopetri, Europe's oldest drowned settlement.
- → **Find** silence at St Irini Monastery, the closing note of a gorgeous coastal trail.
- → **Ramble** through an overgrown ravine to the alluring dipping pool near Philippi's Watermill.
- → **Dare** to swim through a towering mouth into the dark waters of Hytra Sea Cave.
- → **Retreat** to the rustic isolation of Shepherd's Croft, sharing the astonishing vista with the neighbouring sheep.

Shaped by the mighty Parnon range as it plunges south between the Myrtoan Sea and Laconian Gulf, Eastern Laconia is a staggering landscape of verdant mountains crashing into deep blue water. Remarkable coastal ruins, cloistered fishing villages and dreamlike beaches abound. And off its southern coast comes the encore: the island of Kythira, mythical home of Aphrodite and replete with sparkling swimming havens.

The Laconian symphony rises near the climbing mecca of Kyparissi, where the hulking Parnon mountains meet the sea. Stay at Eumelia, a sumptuous regenerative farmstay of slow culinary experiences and farm-to-table cuisine, before crossing the mountains east. Don't miss sublime Damos Beach, unfurling from the mouth of a remote coastal gorge cloaked in deep green - arguably the region's finest beach, although neighbouring Vlychada runs it close and is more accessible.

Moving south you enter the land of marvellous Laconian ruins. Monemvasia is the most famous, a jumbled terracotta castle town of twisting cobbleways beneath a looming acropolis, all huddled on an islet that was cleft from the mainland by an earthquake 2,000 years ago. Visit even if it's busy, and consider staying in Almi Guesthouse, sitting audaciously by the water above a private swimming terrace.

Ancient Zarax, just north, is more ruinous, but its stone walls and crumbling foundations cover a headland of total solitude above Greece's only fjord, Gerakas. The delightful fishing village of Limin Leraka shelters within, featuring the excellent waterside fish taverna, Remetzo. Asopos Paleokastro is even humbler, but enjoys a striking position atop a plateau protruding abruptly above the plains by Plitra, west of Monemvasia. A superb spot for sunset or stargazing.

Southern Laconia grows yet more rugged and surprising. St Irini Monastery awaits deep in the southeast, alone and contemplative at the end of a terrific coastal trail. Near the trailhead lies the Petrified Forest of St Marina Beach, a geological wonderland of petrified trees and sea creatures, all millions of years old. Surprise also lurks southwest, at Pouda Beach, where you can snorkel Europe's oldest submerged settlement. Simos Beach, just across the water on the islet of Elafonisos, is a simpler sandy paradise.

Kythria, administratively in Attica, also lies across the water. Base yourself in the rustic elegance of the Shepherd's Croft Retreat, with only sheep and island vistas for company, and get exploring. The crooked rock cove at Kiriakoulou Beach, the canyon-mouth beach at Kakia Lagada lake and the crystal shallows and lounging ledges at the Baths of Venus are just some of Kythira's watery delights. The most memorable though, even when full of boat trippers, is the enormous mouth of Hytra Sea Cave, biting into the southerly islet of the same name.

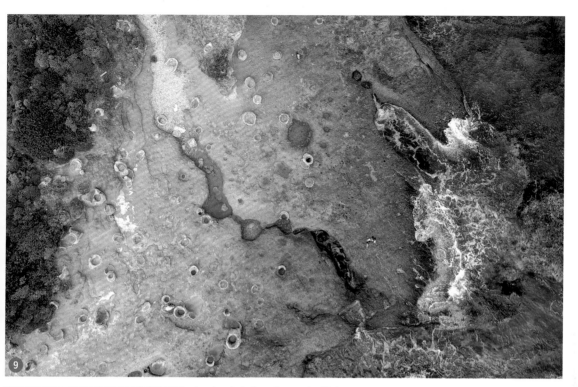

BEACHES

1 TYROS BEACH

A pebble beach backed by a steep, verdant cliff, lending a more remote feel than the proximity of the road suggests. A delightful stop, with ancient walls atop the hill behind and traditional windmills looking down from the headland.

➔ Follow the road E from Tyros around the headland for about 800m and park in a layby on a sharp R (37.2434, 22.8738). A steep trail switchbacks R of the windmills, 300m or so down to the beach.

5 mins, 37.2421, 22.8745 🏊🚣⛺🐚🥾

2 VLYCHADA BEACH

Sheltered sands set in an otherworldly landscape of forested mountain faces plunging into deep blue. The sun sets early, but the light lingers.

➔ Follow the road E from Richea via a series of switchbacks, keeping L after the fifth sharp turn, where a track goes off R. Park at the beach.

1 min, 36.8587, 23.0382 🏊🚣🐾🐚

3 DAMOS BEACH

The less accessible neighbour of Vlychada Beach (see entry), this spectacular, remote beach unfurls from the mouth of Balogeri Gorge flanked by sheer forested bluffs. An epic wild camp.

➔ Drive as for Vlychada but take the dirt track R after the five switchback hairpins. Follow 2km to the end; you'll need to go slow and possibly move a few pesky rocks if not in a 4x4. Park at the end and walk a footpath starting 100m back up the track; proper shoes needed.

4 mins, 36.8374, 23.0522 🏊🚣⛺🐚

4 KOCHYLA BEACH

This pretty pebble beach, with a little lagoon and Swiss-cheese rocks, is relatively humble in the context of this region's riches, but that keeps it quiet. Be careful of the underwater rocks.

➔ Turn SE off the coastal road 6.7km S from Ierakas, by a bend almost opposite the turning into Ariana hamlet (36.7627, 23.0761). Continue 850m to park at the beach.

1 min, 36.7586, 23.0838 🏊🚣🐟

5 KASTRAKI BEACH

A tree-lined beach popular with the odd campervan, quiet but within sight of iconic Monemvasia (see entry).

➔ Drive 3km SE from Agios Ioannis to the coast, forking L at 1km, and park in the shade of the trees behind the beach.

1 min, 36.7298, 23.0276 🏊🚣⛺

6 POUDA BEACH

Vast sands backed by dunes and wetland gaze across to Elafonisos island, with the submerged ruins of Pavlopetri (see entry) awaiting curious snorkelers not far offshore.

➔ Drive S from Vigklafia, fork L after 400m, then make a quick R-L after 300m to park in a sandy area behind the beach.

2 mins, 36.5187, 22.9833 🏊🚣🐾⛺🥾

7 SIMOS BEACH

This stunning sandy beach is the jewel of Elafonisos. Its shallow, crystalline waters are very popular, but the outer reaches away from the campsite offer quieter pockets when busy.

➔ Heading S down the island's E coast, fork L just before Lefki towards the SE headland. Park in the large area E of the beach, by Asimos Beach Bar.

1 min, 36.4701, 22.9781 🏊🚣🐾B

8 TSOUMALA BEACH

A weatherbeaten pebble cove with a footpath leading up onto its S headland. You will likely be alone here.

→ Head SW from Agios Nikolaos past the round-towered church. Continue 3.4km and fork L just before Tsoumala (36.4526, 23.0823). Follow the track 1km along the coast to a R turn to the beach.

1 min, 36.4478, 23.0855

9 PETRIFIED FOREST OF ST MARINA BEACH

Petrified palms, logs and fossils of small sea creatures strewn across a series of rock ledges. An otherworldly, geologically fascinating place, unmatched in Europe.

→ Follow a good track that heads S from Valtaki, leading S and E around the hill (climbing area) for around 3km. Park on the main track by the two buildings (36.4409, 23.1411) and walk the final short, rough stretch.

2 mins, 36.4408, 23.1437

10 KAKIA LAGADA BEACH

A bar of shingle has created a lake between this wild, scenic cove and the towering gorge behind, which is fun to venture into when dry enough. At the other end lies Palaiochora Castle (see entry).

→ Drive 2.3km SE from Agia Pelagia on the coast road, which becomes a dirt track, right to the end. A short path leads down to the beach.

1 min, 36.3076, 23.0037

11 LIKODIMOU BEACH

A narrow, ear-shaped pebble beach beneath crumbling cliffs, with a breakwater extending into the clear shadows.

→ Take the paved road W from Katsoulianika for 5km, zigzagging down through a valley to the beach.

1 min, 36.2874, 22.9227

12 KALAMI COVE

A tiny beach at the mouth of a snaking gorge spilling into a delightfully curved inlet. The glassy water is guarded by rock walls with a tricky descent and occasional goats.

→ Drive NW from Milopotamos and park after 4km by a church. Follow the dirt track from here for 500m through the trees, finishing with a tricky, rope-assisted scramble.

10 mins, 36.2545, 22.9231

13 BATHS OF HELEN BEACH

Together with Limni Beach to the south (beyond a headland featuring a mighty sea-carved arch),

these long sands are associated with Aphrodite and the ill-fated Helen and Paris of the Trojan story. Enjoy the blissful quiet.

→ Drive W from Avlemonas and turn L after 2km (36.2244, 23.0595). Park at the end of the lane by the beach.

1 min, 36.2233, 23.0597

14 KALADI BEACH

Two dramatic, picturesque bays separated by a squat sea stack, with tall cliffs tumbling behind and an arch looking out to sea at the far end.

→ Follow the coast road SW from Avlemonas for about 3km, turn L after the riverbed then fork L to Kaladi Rock Resort. Park in the big parking area just to the S and walk around 150 stairs down to the first beach.

10 mins, 36.2101, 23.0526

15 VLICHADA BEACH

The wild, remote neighbour to popular Kaladi (see entry). The tough access is rewarded with isolation.

→ Follow the coast road 1.8km SW from the L fork to Kaladi Rock Resort and Kaladi Beach, and take a rough track L (36.2134, 23.0356). You will need a 4x4 to drive much of the 2km to the beach.

30 mins, 36.2072, 23.0500

16 SPARAGARIO BEACH

A little cove tucked around the corner from Kapsali Beach, popular with visiting loggerhead turtles and pedal boats.

→ Drive W from Kapsali and turn L 60m before the road forks (36.1464, 22.9962). Park at the chapel and follow the path down.

2 mins, 36.1442, 22.9953

17 KIRIAKOULOU BEACH

Snuggled between overhanging rockfaces in a deep, crooked inlet, this tiny pebble cove is a hidden swimming haven.

→ Only accessible by boat. Captain Spiros (+30 69 7402 2079) in Kapsali is a good port of call.

2 mins, 36.1413, 23.0182

MEMORABLE SWIMS

18 LEPIDA WATERFALL

A tall double waterfall followed by a series of small cascades in a rugged valley. Spring is the time to visit, when the falls are rushing and the plunge pools full.

→ Take the road S from opposite the school in Agios Ioannis for 1.3km and turn R shortly after the road becomes a track (37.3503,

22.6432). Turn L after 900m, just past the building, then R after another 1km to the parking area and a 100m path to the falls.

3 mins, 37.3423, 22.627

19 SUNKEN CITY OF PAVLOPETRI

Remnants of a Minoan settlement, one of the oldest submerged sites in the world, scattered just 4m beneath the crystal waters of Pouda Beach (see entry). A weaving centre and thriving port 5,000 years ago, it was drowned by an earthquake 3,000 years ago.

→ Park for Pouda Beach. The submerged ruins are midway between the beach and the tiny islet.

5 mins, 36.5165, 22.9879

20 PHILIPPI'S WATERMILL

Pretty walking trails and streams thread through a verdant ravine studded with the remnants of past cereal milling. Walk up from this restored working watermill, now with a café near an enticing pool at the bottom of a small waterfall.

→ Head 600m N out of Milopotamos, forking R at the end, and park by the mill.

2 mins, 36.2470, 22.9444

21 BATHS OF VENUS

This scenic inlet, furnished with rock perches for lounging and jumping into the azure water, feels designed for a summer afternoon.

➔ In the heart of Avlemonas, W of the inlet used as a marina. Park in the surrounding lanes.

1 min, 36.2268, 23.0814 🍴🚤🏖️🅱️

22 HYTRA SEA CAVE

A wondrous sea cave on an islet of the same name, with a spectacular domed roof sheltering dark swimming water and protruding rocks for sitting and marvelling.

➔ Only accessible by boat. Captain Spiros (+30 69 7402 2079) runs an excellent tour – €20 for adults and €10 for children aged three to ten.

2 mins, 36.095, 22.9957 🚤🏊🏖️🚶

MONASTERIES & CHURCHES

23 ST NIKOLAOS OF SINTZA MONASTERY

Deep in the Leonidio valley is this white monastery wedged into a cavernous hollow in a hermitage-pocked cliff. A solitary nun opens the monastery during the summer months; she may not be there in winter, but the monastery and views are still impressive.

➔ Follow a paved road about 5km SW from Leonidio, S of the riverbed. There are two openable gates.

1 min, 37.1475, 22.8192 ✝️❓

24 KYPARISSI CRAG CHURCHES

Two tiny churches cling to a steep gorge near the famed climbing crags above Kyparissi.

➔ Park at the first L hairpin after leaving Kyparissi heading S. A short trail leads to the first church and continues sharply up to the second.

5 mins, 36.9578, 22.985 ✝️🧗

25 ST IRINI MONASTERY

A monastery near the end of a wonderfully wild coastal trail to a ruined church. A solitary nun was living there when we visited.

➔ Drive E from the Petrified Forest of Agia Marina (see entry) for about 3km and park where the track ends. Continue on a 2km trail to the monastery.

20 mins, 36.4366, 23.1952 🏔️✝️🚶🏊🌿

SCENIC RUINS

26 GERAKI CASTLE

For some 300 years this well-preserved estate, arrayed on a grassy hill and

plateau, was one of the main cities of the region. The views over Geraki from the ramparts of the 13th-century Frankish castle are fantastic, and don't miss the wall paintings in the churches.

➔ Drive E from Gerkaki for 900m and turn L (36.9894, 22.7176) towards the hills, with the castle visible on one. Continue 2.5km, winding up to the entry booth (free entry).

1 min, 36.9939, 22.7256 🏔️🐾🚶

27 PROPHET ELIAS CHURCH

A church and ruined Byzantine lookout on a peak between the mountains and sea. Climb up for a special sunrise over this spectacular stretch of coastline.

➔ Drive E from Charakas for about 500m and fork R onto a track after passing a church on your L (36.9146, 23.0028). Park at the lower church and walk back to climb a rough track 300m to the lookout.

5 mins, 36.9151, 23.0047 🏔️✝️🐾🚶

28 ANCIENT ZARAX

The thick walls of this ancient city, still inhabited through the Roman and Byzantine periods, overlook the spectacular Gerakas Fjord - the only fjord in Greece. A delightful place for lunch and a swim.

→ Park in the harbour at the E end of Limin Leraka. Walk back about 50m and take a narrow staircase on your R that resembles a broken wall, to the L of a white and blue house (36.7858, 23.0859). This joins an easy path.
5 mins, 36.7865, 23.0888 ⚡🏔🐾🚶

29 ASOPOS PALEOKASTRO
Humble Byzantine ruins sit atop this majestic plateau rising from olive groves to give panoramic views across the Laconian Gulf. It was probably never a castle, but a place of refuge during raids. On a calm night this would be a stunning place to camp.
→ Drive around 1km S from Papadianika and park in a layby-cum-track on the L (36.6994, 22.8620). Follow a trail E, curving quickly S, then bend anticlockwise around the plateau to steps at its E base. If you lose the markers the scramble is easy enough.
20 mins, 36.6964, 22.8641 📷🏔🐾🏔🚶🐚

30 MONEMVASIA
There are two tiers to this castle town, the bottom a picturesque terracotta labyrinth, the top a plateau of ruins. It crouches dramatically on an islet separated from the mainland by an earthquake in 375 AD. Famous but stunning.

→ Cross the isthmus extending E from Gefira and park in the large car park. If it's not busy, you can even park along the road near the city gates.
1 min, 36.6879, 23.0557 🏔🐾🚶🅱

31 ST PARASKEVI CASTLE
A conserved castle in the foothills overlooking Neapoli Voion and the island of Elafonisos beyond.
→ Head around 2.4km NE from Neapoli Voion and fork L at a house just before a bend. Continue 600m to a parking area right by the castle.
2 mins, 36.5300, 23.0721 🏔🐾

32 PALAIOCHORA CASTLE
The medieval capital of Kythira, built in the 12th century but destroyed by raiding Turkish pirate Barbarossa in 1537. The ruins look down the barrel of a narrow canyon, with Kakia Legada Beach (see entry) at the other end of an adventurous hike.
→ Drive SE from Kampos for about 3.5km, initially on a track and then bending L past a chapel, to end in a small parking area. Continue 200m on foot past St Barbara Church.
5 mins, 36.2986, 22.9979 🏔🐾

30

39

43

33 KATO CHORA CASTLE

A Venetian castle complex of fortifications, churches and houses – many inhabited until the 1950s – extending from the lanes of Kato Chora onto a promontory with sea views along the valley. A fine wander.

→ On the W edge of tiny Kato Chora, itself NW of Milopotamos. Park right by it.

2 mins, 36.2455, 22.9347 ⛰️†♿❄️🚶

LOCAL FOOD & DRINK

34 EN LEONIDIO

A Greek-Italian pizzeria serving wood-oven pizzas with a local twist and traditional Greek dishes in a relaxed, eclectic environment.

→ Leonidio 223 00, +30 2757 022068
37.1675, 22.8593 🅱️

35 MYRTOON

Consistently excellent Greek dishes with local ingredients and beach views. Try at least one aubergine (*melitzána*) dish.

→ Poulithra 223 00, +30 2757 051339
37.1189, 22.8975 ❄️🅱️

36 DIMOTSIS TAVERNA

A classic taverna spilling into a neat garden amid almond and olive trees with distant mountain views. Order a bit of everything for the table – it's all delicious.

→ Molai 230 52, +30 2732 023814
36.8064, 22.9079 ❄️

37 TO REMETZO

Fresh seafood in a waterside taverna in a sleepy village on Greece's only fjord. The grilled sardines are divine.

→ Limin Leraka 230 52, +30 2732 023933
36.7863, 23.0845 ❄️

38 EPIDILION

Simple, authentic, delectable food on a terrace with magnificent views over the sea to Monemvasia (see entry).

→ Foutia 230 70, +30 2732 066252
36.6181, 23.0087 ❄️⛰️

STAY

39 THE CLIFF RETREAT

The large terrace of this seafront villa overlooks the Argolic Gulf and a small beach, accessible by private steps. Two inflatable kayaks and some homegrown produce are cherries on top. Sleeps six in one bedroom and a spacious living room.

→ Xiropigado 220 01, airbnb.com/rooms/42595185
37.4963, 22.7286 ⬛

40 CAMPING ZARITSI

A clean, relaxed campsite in a long crystal bay backed by olive groves. The friendly owner serves delicious homemade dishes in the neighbouring taverna.

→ Agios Christoforos 220 29, +30 2757 041429
37.2757, 22.8405 ⬛

41 THE DONKEY HOUSE

A stone cottage in a hillside village, built on a spur with a majestic sea-and-mountain vista from the cocooned patio garden. Laze in a hammock to the sound of roosters, goats and bees. Sleeps two (twin beds) in a rustic studio.

→ Pragmateftis 223 00, airbnb.com/rooms/36943601
37.1881, 22.8953 ⬛

42 EUMELIA

At this upmarket regenerative farmstay you can participate in olive picking, grape harvesting and other farm activities, and indulge in slow experiences like wine tasting, farm-to-table cooking and wellness workshops.

→ Gouves 230 55, +30 6947 151400
36.9216, 22.7321 ⬛⬛

43 ALMI GUESTHOUSE

A teeny studio-space guesthouse for two right on the southern shoreline of remarkable Monemvasia (see entry). Enjoy a terrace sunrise, swim in your private sea pool, amble into the Monemvasia alleyways and smile at the exclamations of passers-by astounded at your abode.

→ Monemvasia 230 70, +30 69 7411 4585, airbnb.com/rooms/42801908
36.6859, 23.0481 ⬛

44 SHEPHERD'S CROFT RETREAT

An artful croft of exposed stone walls and wood beams, with solar energy, enormous sea-sunset views from a double terrace and only sheep for neighbours. A sublime place, with room for two.

→ Kythira 802 00, airbnb.com/rooms/638152041770514513
36.3243, 22.9201 ⬛⬛

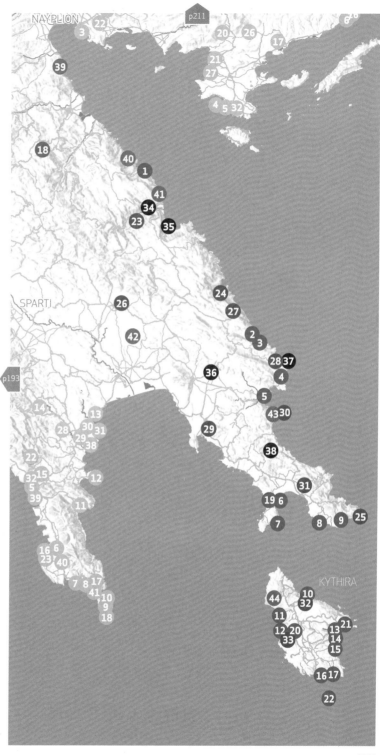

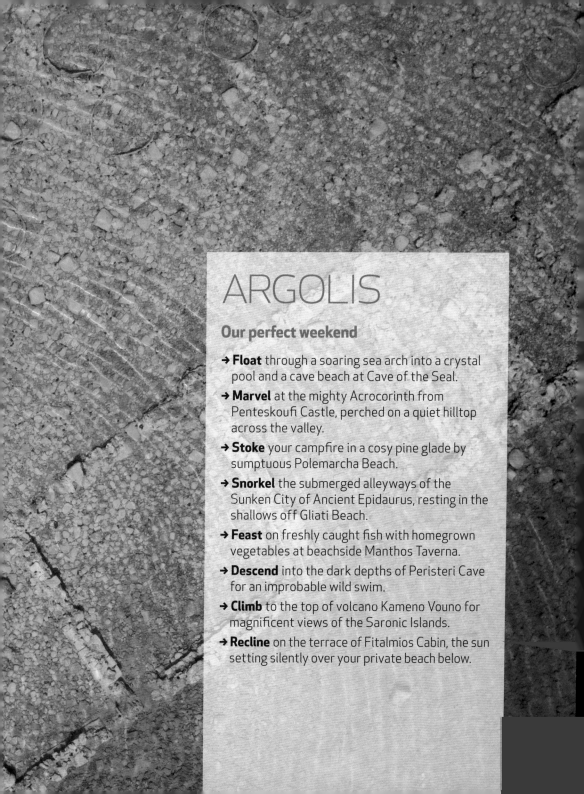

ARGOLIS

Our perfect weekend

→ **Float** through a soaring sea arch into a crystal pool and a cave beach at Cave of the Seal.

→ **Marvel** at the mighty Acrocorinth from Penteskoufi Castle, perched on a quiet hilltop across the valley.

→ **Stoke** your campfire in a cosy pine glade by sumptuous Polemarcha Beach.

→ **Snorkel** the submerged alleyways of the Sunken City of Ancient Epidaurus, resting in the shallows off Gliati Beach.

→ **Feast** on freshly caught fish with homegrown vegetables at beachside Manthos Taverna.

→ **Descend** into the dark depths of Peristeri Cave for an improbable wild swim.

→ **Climb** to the top of volcano Kameno Vouno for magnificent views of the Saronic Islands.

→ **Recline** on the terrace of Fitalmios Cabin, the sun setting silently over your private beach below.

International travellers often overlook Argolis, overshadowed as it is between Athens and the Peloponnese. But the region is no mere corridor. Spectacular archeological sites and hilltop ruins rule the north, and wild beaches, remarkable caves and surprising swims dot a shoreline that meets the Corinth, Saronic, Hydra and Argolis gulfs. Along the coast, settlements like Porto Cheli and Nafplion – the first capital of modern Greece – ooze cosmopolitan charm.

Northern Argolis narrows at the Isthmus of Corinth, the land bridge connecting the Peloponnese with mainland Greece. The ancient fortifications of Acrocorinth standing above it are one of Greece's finest hilltop citadels, and an archeological adventure to rival nearby Mycenae, the great city of the Mycenaean civilisation that previously dominated this region. Penteskoufi Castle, sitting dwarfed and forgotten across the valley, surveys the sublime panorama from afar. Whichever perspective you choose, follow it with a detour to the Cave of the Seal: towering arch, swimming cove, sea cave and secret beach all in one delicious package.

Argolis' eastern seaboard is punctuated with delights. Floating above the Roman walls and amphoras of the Sunken City of Ancient Epidaurus is a memorable archeological snorkel. Swim too at idyllic Polemarcha Beach, before settling down by a campfire among the pine glades. Continuing south, descend into a shaded ravine to a cleansing waterfall pool at the Devil's Bridge, or continue to the string of small, secluded beaches near Poros, Pergani being the pick.

Another isthmus extends northeast of Poros to the volcanic Methana peninsula. Kameno Vouno is one of 30 volcanoes here, with a short, steep trail leading to a peak promising astounding views – and some striking climbing routes for those inclined. You may even spy Fitalmios Cabin from here: a charming hut, rustic and remote, overlooking a private beach, altogether an ideal Argolis retreat. Before returning to the mainland, visit the underworld in Peristeri Cave, its hidden roadside mouth sinking to an unlikely pool in its dark depths.

Southwest Argolis revolves around the sailing-chic town of Porto Cheli, a leafy Athenian holiday outpost. Picnic at Thermisia Castle on your way in, with dramatic views of the Saronic Gulf framed through windows from its overgrown innards. Stay for a while in delightful Porto Cheli Summerhouse, which distils the town's essence, and venture out for a day (or a night) to Triantafyllou Beach, an oasis of lime-green pines tucked in a deep, calm cove on an unassuming headland. When it's time to depart, do so via fresh fish and homegrown vegetables at charming Doroufi, walked off with a visit to the fascinating Paleolithic dig site in Franchthi Cave.

9

BEACHES

1 KALAMAKI BEACH

A pretty cove with wonderfully placid
swimming backed by shady glades. Popular
with local picnickers at weekends.

→ Park at Vagionia Beach just N of Palaia
Epidavros. Walk the paved path from its N end
for 200m.

3 mins, 37.6417, 23.1619 ⊠◁❦⦆B

2 POLEMARCHA BEACH

Campfire rings dot this stunning, forested
bay backed by pine glades. Bring a tent, a
hammock and food for a couple of nights.

→ On the coastal road 650m N past the Palaia
Epidavros turning, turn R on a track shortly
after the petrol station on the L (37.6539,
23.1548). The track leads 800m to the beach.
Ignore the first R but take the second, as you
arrive at the water.

1 min, 37.6555, 23.1638 ⊠◁▲⦆

3 NERAKI BEACH

A pair of pleasant pebble beaches set
below an enjoyable gravel trail, with
climbing routes snaking up the rocks
above.

→ Head S out of Nafplion and after around
3km turn R, then R again and continue to a
fishing marina at the N end of Karathonas
Beach (37.5464, 22.8163). Take the coastal
trail 1.25km N.

15 mins, 37.5525, 22.8083 ⊠⦆⦅

4 TRIANTAFYLLOU BEACH

An enchanting, pine-covered beach
enveloped by an undulating bay with
placid water and signs of slow, makeshift
camping.

→ Follow the winding road from Porto Cheli
NW up the middle of the peninsula for 2km,
then fork L (37.3289, 23.1208) and after
300m fork R. Park after 200m, NW of a
cluster of large houses (37.3269, 23.1170).
A narrow trail descends 50m through the
shrubs.

2 mins, 37.3276, 23.1166 ⊠◁❦⦆▲⦆⦅

5 PORTO CHELI BEACH

Cocooned by an aromatic lime-green pine
glade, this deep, shallow cove is a calming,
seemingly unknown nook.

→ Leave Porto Cheli to the SW and follow the
network of tracks to the W coast, curving SW
away from Edem Resort and aiming for the
track to the SW tip. Park at a turnoff 700m

before the end of this (37.3203, 23.1266) or
descend the rougher remaining 150m R to
the beach.

3 mins, 37.3202, 23.1248 ⊠◁❦⦆▲⦆⦅

6 ST ATHANASIOS MONASTERY BEACH

A beach protected by a rocky spit and shady
boughs, popular with campervans. The
ruined St Athanasios Monastery sits on the
hill above.

→ Head SW from the coastal hamlet of
Pergari and turn L at the T junction to reach
the top (37.4254, 23.4986) of the zigzag
down to the beach.

1 min, 37.4236, 23.4961 ⊠◁❦⦅

7 PERGANI BEACH

With arching trees for shade and a seasonal
café run by a sweet elderly couple, this small
cove is an oasis amidst the arid hills.

→ Head NE from the coastal hamlet of Pergari
and turn sharply R (37.4314, 23.4982). Keep L
and continue 850m to the beach.

1 min, 37.4288, 23.5068 ⊠◁⦅

8 GALATAS ISTHMUS

A twin-beached isthmus with a natural rock
arch and a shaded knoll for a hammock or

chair, hidden on the far side of a tiny island from the crowds of Aliki Beach.

→ Park on the SE shore of the lagoon S of Aliki Beach (37.48267, 23.4768). Head N past the building, where a footpath runs 400m clockwise around the island to the beach at the other end.

5 mins, 37.4853, 23.4769

MAGICAL SWIMS

9 CAVE OF THE SEAL

An arresting rock arch guards a rocky pool that flows into a sea cave with a swimmable beach; this is what wild coastal swimming is all about.

→ Take a dirt track N from the road at a fork just NW of Alkiona (38.0681, 22.9811), fork L after 200m and park after another 300m when it opens up on the L. Follow steep switchbacks down to the cave from the N side of this area.

10 mins, 38.0741, 22.9845

10 SUNKEN CITY OF ANCIENT EPIDAURUS

The ruins of an ancient settlement lie above and below the water here. You can walk around public buildings like the theatre and baths, while others, including a Roman villa and semi-preserved amphoras, lie just beneath the glistening surface at Gliati Beach. A wonderful snorkel, but beware the sea urchins.

→ The beach and ruins are signed on the coastal road heading S from Palaia Epidavros; turn S after the signs and park at Athina Ecofarm Shop at the end. Follow the water 100m L, and the ruins are 40m out.

5 mins, 37.6257, 23.1577

11 DEVIL'S BRIDGE

Approach through remnants of ancient Trizina, including a defensive tower, to a footbridge overlooking a steep descent to a sequence of pools and waterfalls at the bottom of a wooded canyon. A magical place, especially in the wetter shoulder seasons, but mind your footing.

→ Drive W from Troezen for about 800m to a signed fork L (37.4991, 23.3566). Park at the end of the 750m lane, or as far along as you feel comfortable, and walk. Cross the footbridge, turn R and wind down the steep hillside to the pools.

3 mins, 37.4973, 23.3511

13

CASTLES & ANCIENT RUINS

12 MALAGAVI CAPE

Lying like a cluster of jewels at the end of this west-facing cape are the ruins of an ancient temple to the goddess Hera, a 19th-century lighthouse and a glorious swimming bay with jumping rocks.

→ Follow the road W from Limni Vouliagmenis 1.7km to a parking area just before the ruins.
2 mins, 38.028, 22.8532 🍴🏊🌊🏖️📷🚴

13 ACROCORINTH

The acropolis of the ancient city-state of Corinth, commanding enormous views across the isthmus it defended from ancient times until the 19th century. Well worth the crowds in the busier months.

→ Take a signed turning S (37.9006, 22.8779) from the road along the S edge of Archaia Korinthos (Ancient Corinth). Continue 3km to a parking area at the first gate.
1 min, 37.8911, 22.8702 📷⛰️🚴🅱️

14 PENTESKOUFI CASTLE

The hilltop remnants of a small Frankish castle, built in 1205 to support the siege of imposing Acrocorinth (see entry), which is arrayed across the valley. The David to a famous

Goliath, it seems to have fallen from use almost as soon as this purpose was served.

→ Drive as for Acrocorinth but take the last R fork before the parking, bend L at 400m, then immediately fork R and park after 300m by the abandoned buildings (37.8863, 22.8601). Continue on the path and turn L after 250m up the hill.
15 mins, 37.8837, 22.8572 📷⛰️🚴🌊🐚

15 FAVIEROS CASTLE

Built on ancient foundations on the isthmus connecting the volcanic Methana peninsula to the mainland, this fort dates back to the Greek War of Independence in the 1820s, and is named for the French general instrumental in creating the tactical army. Sea views and an easy trail make this a pleasant stroll.

→ Follow the road from Taktikoupoli N for 2km to the N end of the isthmus and turn L. Park 200m up the hill at the track turning L and follow a footpath 550m S past the church to the castle.
5 mins, 37.5567, 23.3655 🚴🚶🌊

16 TSELEVINIA CASTLE

Modest and obscure ruins, probably of a Venetian watch tower, and a small church sit on a headland between two tiny, secluded

beaches, looking out on a small archipelago.

→ Head NE from the coastal hamlet of Pergari and turn R after 850m (37.4340, 23.5024). Follow the track for 1.5km and park at the end.
2 mins, 37.4308, 23.5165 🌊🚴⛰️🚶

17 THERMISIA CASTLE

The rarely visited ruins of a 12th-century Byzantine castle arrayed across a grassy bluff, with arrowslit views to the southern Saronic Islands. A wonderful sunset outing.

→ Head E from Achladitsa towards Thermisia and turn L 350m past Lake Thermisia. Follow L fork after 500m (37.4114, 23.3179). Ignoring turns and minor forks, follow this good track 3.2km, bending W and ascending. Park at a hairpin at the highest point (37.4223, 23.3020). Follow a path clockwise around the ridgeline above.
5 mins, 37.4209, 23.3040 📷⛰️🚴🌊🐚

CAVES & VOLCANOES

18 KAMENO VOUNO

The youngest of over 30 volcanoes on the Methana peninsula. A steep trail leads to a cascade of volcanic rocks with small caves, panoramic views of the northern Saronic Islands and even some bolted climbs.

→ Follow the road NE from Kaimeni Chora about 1km and take the steep trail by the parking layby on the L (37.6186, 23.3360).
15 mins, 37.6184, 23.3330 🏞🚷🏊🏖🏊

19 PERISTERI CAVE

A secret roadside cave with a clear pool in its dark depths. With a light and good shoes you can descend the slick rocks for a memorable plunge.

→ On the W coastal road about 1km N from the fork at the N end of the isthmus, pull aside carefully onto the gravel shoulder on the coastal side (37.5731, 23.3598). The short path opposite turns into a rocky scramble; be careful and wear good shoes.
2 mins, 37.5734, 23.3601 🏊🚷🏞🔺🐚🏊

20 DIDIMA CAVES

One of two striking dolines or sinkholes incongruously set amidst fields, one a vast rugged amphitheatre and the other this lost world, alive with roosting birds and vegetation. A tunnel entrance among the trees leads down into a church built into the wall.

→ Signed from the main road just NW of Didima down a dirt track heading NW (37.4652, 23.1689). Continue 500m NW to the tree-ringed edge; stairs are to the R. For the larger cave follow the L fork another 500m to the end.
1 min, 37.4702, 23.1679 🚹🏃🐕🏊

21 FRANCHTHI CAVE

This domed cave, half collapsed, is the site of an important archeological dig documenting the communities that have lived in Kiladha Bay since the Upper Paleolithic period, around 38,000 BC.

→ Park on the beach 300m W of Paralia Fournon. From the S end, follow a 700m coastal trail to the cave.
10 mins, 37.4225, 23.1311 🏊🏃🏊

22 PSALIDAS TAVERNA

A charming taverna in a quiet village, the patio almost entirely enclosed by grapevines. Hearty, succulent dishes served by a family with big smiles and kind hearts. Definitely try the moussaka.

→ Lefkakia 211 00, +30 2752 061814
37.5595, 22.8603 🏔

23 KOSTAS

This unassuming restaurant and shop is brimming with delicious local recipes and homemade pasta, preserves and other products. Stop by for a bite and a browse.

→ Trachia 210 52, +30 2753 071252
37.5618, 23.1528 🍴🐚

24 ANDREOU WINERY

A wonderful family winery offering tastings, tours and excellent accompanying food.

→ Trizinia 180 20, +30 69 7356 3731
37.5197, 23.3605 🍴🍷

25 APAGIO TAVERNA

This bay-view taverna isn't the wildest, and certainly isn't hidden. But its family recipes are relentlessly exceptional. The best restaurant in Poros, though reasonably priced, so book ahead.

→ Poros 180 20, +30 2298 026219
37.4977, 23.4583 🅑

26 BOUKOURIS TAVERNA

This village taverna, run by a friendly couple, specialises in tender meat dishes paired with home-produced vegetables and cheeses. Humble but exceptional.

→ Loukaiti 210 51, +30 2754 091358
37.4560, 23.2367 🍴

27 DOROUFI

An idyllic, seasonal seaside taverna serving scrumptious, creative Greek cuisine, with fish fresh from the sleepy bay and vegetables picked from their garden.

→ Doroufi Kilados 213 00, +30 69 4881 2063
37.3979, 23.1102 🍴🏔

STAY

28 FITALMIOS CABIN

A remote wooden cabin overlooking a private beach, with space for four. Simple, slow living deep in nature, with hospitable Theodoros happy to show you his patch.

→ Kamini Chora 180 30, +30 69 7771 5676,
airbnb.com/rooms/51284568
37.6170, 23.3082 🏕

29 CAMPING NICOLAS II

Clean, shady beachfront camping and studios set in orange, mulberry and banana trees. There is a taverna, cafe and small shop, and a second site a little further N.

→ Palaia Epidavros 210 59, +30 2753 041445
37.616, 23.1594 🏕

30 OPORA COUNTRY LIVING

A sumptuous farm estate of rustic stone houses and rooms sleeping up to four, built with traditional techniques and materials. Enjoy wellness activities, food workshops, a shared pool and excellent local cuisine.

→ Pyrgiotika 211 00, +30 2752 022259
37.5818, 22.8887 🐐🏕

31 ODYSSEY ECO FARM GLAMPING

Luxurious bell tents, stone chalets and wooden cottages snuggled in a grassy citrus and olive grove on a small beachside farm. All enjoy private hammocks and outdoor areas, plus access to a shared alfresco kitchen and pool. A rejuvenating retreat.

→ Galatas 180 20, +30 69 4970 7053
37.5027, 23.4371 🏕

32 PORTO CHELI SUMMERHOUSE

A vintage two-bedroom summerhouse on a peninsula by Porto Cheli, with a dock for sunbathing and swimming. Sleeps five.

→ Porto Cheli 213 00, airbnb.com/
rooms/12695299
37.3150, 23.1449 🏕

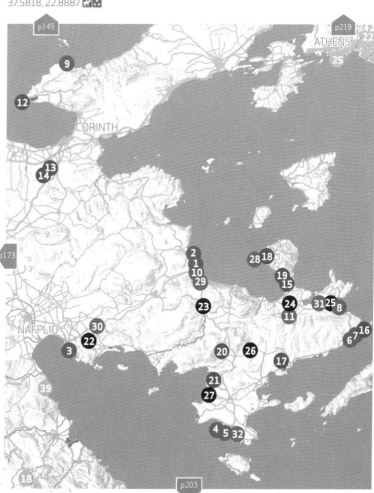

ATTICA

Our perfect weekend

→ **Scramble** into dramatic, open-topped Trypia Cave, hiding on a wooded mountainside less than an hour from Athens.

→ **Survey** a different side to Athens from the Quarry Meadows overlooking its northeastern suburbs.

→ **Sample** classic Greek *kourou* pies from Ariston Bakery, run by the welcoming Lobotesis family for over 100 years.

→ **Hike** through forested valleys in Parnitha National Park to secret St Marina Church.

→ **Frolic** in the cool waters of Liminaki Cove, a cult Athens Riviera swim spot.

→ **Drift** for an afternoon in the shaded pools at Valanari Waterfall.

→ **Gasp** from the sidelines as local daredevils cross heart-shaped Chaos Crater on a highline.

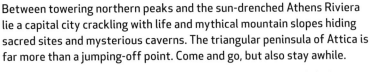

Between towering northern peaks and the sun-drenched Athens Riviera lie a capital city crackling with life and mythical mountain slopes hiding sacred sites and mysterious caverns. The triangular peninsula of Attica is far more than a jumping-off point. Come and go, but also stay awhile.

Athens is wilder than many cities. Its canopied streets twist and climb between ancient ruins and secret squares, festooned with kaleidoscopic murals, street art and polemical graffiti. Rambling is an adventure here, different every time, with plenty to enjoy beyond the hotspots of the Acropolis and Mount Lycabettus. Wander far enough for a hillside walk in Quarry Meadows, or simply stroll to sample warm treats at Ariston Bakery or honey-drenched *loukoumades* from Loukoumades Ktistakis.

Mountains guard the Athenian plain. To the west, above the Gulf of Elefsina, stands Mount Aigaleo, with the sprawling Diomidous Botanical Garden in its verdant foothills. The Hymettus range looms in the southeast, a wooded spine of monasteries and caves. Aromatic Taxiarchis Hill, where Kaisariani Monastery stands, makes a splendid outing here. And Trypia Cave's magnificent open roof encourages a different reverence, awaiting at the end of a hike that feels miles from any metropolis.

Beyond Athens to the north are larger mountains. Mount Pentelicus' famous marble gleams in the Acropolis, extracted through quarrying that created explorable Davelis Cave, with a chapel at its mouth and enormous views over the city. The wild trails of Mount Parnitha, Attica's apex, lead to forested shrines like St Marina Church and Pan's Cave. And in the north-west, where Attica gives way to Central Greece, mythical Mount Kithairon gazes for miles over the Gulf of Corinth.

To the south lies Attica's coastal peninsula, including the so-called Athens Riviera lining its western seaboard. This chain of glitzy enclaves hides swimming spots far from the tourist track. Kavouri Deck, Vouliagmeni Rock and locals' hangout Limanaki Beach are some of the jewels. Swing by while journeying further south, and sample the sumptuous farm-to-table dining at The Margi Farm on your way back up.

RIVIERA SWIM SPOTS

1 KAVOURI DECK

A small, inconspicuous platform with a ladder into the sea, with views across to the city in the distance.

→ In Vouliagmeni head W towards the headland and park behind Kavouri Beach. Walk to its very SW edge, skirting over some small rocks and through shallow water to the platform.

5 mins, 37.8172, 23.7648

2 VOULIAGMENI ROCK

Protruding into the sea in the Athens Riviera, this flat rockface is ideal for a cooling city dip. Head over the rocks to the south for a couple of smaller secluded spots, or to the north for a beach.

→ At the S edge of Vouliagmeni park on Litous Road. Heading N from The Margi hotel, take the first L (37.8145, 23.7735), continue SW for 250m, fork R and follow the path ahead to the shore.

10 mins, 37.8118, 23.771

3 VOULIAGMENI LAKE

A beautiful, natural saltwater lake on the Athens outskirts. It's organised, with smart decking, a restaurant, manicured gardens and lifeguards, but surrounded by towering cliffs. €15 per person.

→ At the SE edge of the town and bay. Heading S on EO91, turn L just after Vouliagmeni Park on the R. Parking available right by the lake and by the seashore.

2 mins, 37.8071, 23.7858

4 LIMANAKI BEACH

A cult swim spot for young Athenians looking to spend a day frolicking, this deep blue cove is lined with wooden seating on rock ledges and has a small canteen serving simple refreshments. There are more coves to the east; clothing and inhibitions both diminish the further you go.

→ Follow EO91 for 1km S from Vouliagmeni Lake (see entry) and park on the R on the second major L bend, just W of the cove.

3 mins, 37.8004, 23.7888

BEACHES & WATERFALLS

5 SCHINIAS BEACH

Lined with shady pine groves harbouring private picnic nooks, this seemingly endless beach is part of Schinias National Park, and an excellent place to watch windsurfers.

Parts are organised, but there are plenty of wilder stretches.

→ Follow the coast road S of Schinias E for 4.5km, curving R to the car park at the E end of the beach, S of Dikastika.

2 mins, 38.1425, 24.0383

6 VALANARI WATERFALL

A waterfall, which becomes two falls with high water, filling a soft turquoise pool is the main event at this charming string of pools and cascades in a lush wooded valley, popular with young locals.

→ The short, steep path down to the falls starts on a residential road at the E edge of Drafi suburb (38.0365, 23.9051).

5 mins, 38.0369, 23.9062

7 KAPE BEACH

Tucked below the coastal road and reached by a long stone staircase, this lovely little beach has an even tinier neighbouring cove over the headland to the west. Popular with locals.

→ The turning S off the EO91 is just W of Legrena village, and signed if approaching from the W. Park by Kape Beach Bar overlooking the beach, or further back along the road.

3 mins, 37.6595, 23.979

8 DUNI ISLAND BEACH

A great sweep of sand just south of Athens, punctuated with a small island accessible by wading over a sandbar. Head to the south end for shade and seclusion.

→ Follow the EO91 S along the coast from Vari for 8.4km. Just after passing a church on the L, fork R signed 'Prehistoric Settlement (Islet)' and park in a small area at the end. It's an awkward L turn on a busy road if heading N.

5 mins, 37.8078, 23.8464

SACRED PLACES & RUINS

9 ST MARINA CHURCH

A small, ornate white church hidden in a mountainside in Parnitha National Park, reached along an easy path through pine-covered peaks and ravines.

→ On the track S of Antliostasio village, turn S up into the hills at the W end of the canal running alongside (38.2575, 23.6307). Continue 2km, turning R after 650m, then forking L 650m later, to park at the trailhead (38.2441, 23.6378). Follow the path S for 2.5km.

45 mins, 38.2293, 23.6373

10 DAVELIS CAVE

A Byzantine chapel is built directly into the rock at the entrance to this deep, quarried cave. Bring sturdy shoes and a torch to explore the cave, taking care as it can be very slippery. The huge views over Athens alone are worth the trip.

→ A 1km dirt track leaves the road from the bottom of a set of switchbacks to the NW (38.0756, 23.8698). Keep R at the fork, and park on the side 200m before the cave.

10 mins, 38.0707, 23.8773

11 ANAVYSSOS TOWER

A ruined watchtower on a small knoll in a peaceful valley, with a rope to assist the short climb.

→ Head SE from Palaia Fokaia and turn L into the scrub at about 1km or 1.4km. Park anywhere along the track when you see the knoll and scramble up from any side.

10 mins, 37.7111, 23.9697

12 TAXIARCHIS HILL

A lush, forested hill, home to ornate Kaisariani Monastery and a botanical garden nursery at the bottom. Make sure you explore the churches and viewpoints hidden around the peak, all shrouded in perfumed foliage.

10

→ From near the university in SE Athens, follow the road from Kaisariani Municipal Stadium E past the cemetery for 2km, under the bypass. Park by the road outside the monastery.

3 mins, 37.9608, 23.798 🏕️⛪🚶

VIEWPOINTS & PARKS

13 MOUNT KITHAIRON

The Kithairon range features in many myths. It is associated with Dionysus, and this peak is where Hercules killed the Lion of Kithairon before starting his twelve labours. This summit offers sensational views in all directions.

→ Head W 1km out of Vilia and take the fork R up into the hills. After 2.4km fork R again and continue 9km to the summit.

1 min, 38.184, 23.2493 📷🏞️

14 DIOMIDES BOTANICAL GARDEN

This vast garden has shady paths through an arboretum, and the walled garden is a beautifully kept, sprawling oasis with a cafe and areas for picnics. Secure a free ticket online in advance (+30 2105 811557).

→ At the W edge of Athens, S of the EO8. Easiest by bus, with several services; get off at Diomideios, Daphni or Psychiatreion. If driving E, turn R at traffic lights roughly 3km from Scaramagas and park on the R; heading W, turn L at the lights just after the bushes on the central strip end, with filling stations on your R, then turn R and park by the playground. Walk to the main gates. Parking may be tricky.

2 mins, 38.0109, 23.6429 🅱️🚶

15 QUARRY MEADOWS

Abandoned and overgrown, this curious hilltop quarry provides a unique place for a stroll with great city views.

→ In Menidiatika, NE Athens, park at the bend in the road around the NW side of the quarry, where Iras becomes Lato Idiotiki (38.0127, 23.7597). Follow the path E up the hill.

10 mins, 38.0138, 23.7622 📷🏞️📷

16 CHAOS CRATER

A dramatic heart-shaped crater created by a collapsed cave (although local legend blames a meteor), popular with climbers, highliners and picnickers.

→ Head SE from Agios Konstantinos, on the road signed 'Ancient Mine Workshop', for about 500m. You can park right by the crater, which is fenced; climbers duck under on the S side.

1 min, 37.7204, 24.0217 🏕️❓📹📷

CAVES

17 PAN'S CAVE

You can explore the stalagmites and stalactites in this small cave for 50m or so with a flashlight, but the real treat here is the beautiful hike deep inside Goura Canyon.

→ A challenging, but well-signed, 12km round trip starts at St Cyprian Monastery just NE of Fyli. The final descent is very steep, with rough steps hewn into a sheer rockface and a metal rope for support.

90 mins, 38.1467, 23.6685 🏕️🚶⛰️🔦📹📷

18 DUCAS TUNNEL

This abandoned mining tunnel, burrowing for a thrilling 130m into pitch darkness, ends in small rooms with pretty stalagmites and stalactites. You can stand after the low entrance, but beware the bats and bones along the way…

→ Driving the main road W from Sphettus, fork L 700m after passing San Siro Sports Center on the R (37.9068, 23.8294) and continue 2km to the tunnel.

1 min, 37.9079, 23.8082 🔦📹📷

19 TRYPIA CAVE

An epic open-top cave that punches an arch right through a ridge on the edge of a wooded mountain. Reached by a lovely, if sweaty and shadeless, hike an hour from Athens.

→ The trail starts in the car park behind the football field at the E edge of Glyfada; park in the street and walk around the gate (37.9003, 23.7748). After the initial climb the path is very well marked with red paint on the rocky floor, and the cave appears on the R. Bring water.

90 mins, 37.9043, 23.7984

20 VARI CAVE

Also called Nympholyptos Cave or the Cave of Pan, this small cave was occupied before and during the Roman period, and is a shrine dedicated to Apollo, Pan and the nymphs. Carvings inside depict the builder, who claimed he was directed by nymphs.

→ Follow the road from Voula NE for 2.5km, past Voula Cemetery, and park on the roadside (37.8599, 23.7972). Follow the track E past the barrier for 500m. There is a rope and small steps into the cave.

10 mins, 37.8582, 23.8017

LOCAL FOOD & DRINK

21 MANI MANI

Classic Mani grandmother dishes with modern flair. Beautifully presented and reasonably priced.

→ Athina 117 42, +30 2109 218180
37.9667, 23.7284 B

22 ARISTON BAKERY

Greece is known for its traditional pies, and these are the best in Athens. The welcoming Lobotesis family have managed this place for over a century, and know how to bake!

→ Athina 105 62, +30 2103 227626
37.9767, 23.7328

23 LOUKOUMADES KTISTAKIS

Loukoumades are little deep-fried balls, like doughnuts, doused in syrup or honey and sprinkled with cinnamon or sugar. They taste every bit good as they sound, especially at this unassuming cafe in a neighbourhood neglected by tourists.

→ Athina 104 31, +30 2105 240891
37.9839, 23.7267

24 THISION OPEN AIR CINEMA

Built in 1935, and operated by a family through spring and summer, this quaint open-air cinema with Areopagus views plays a mix of classics and new releases, accompanied by homemade nibbles.

➜ Athina 118 51, +30 2103 420864
37.9727, 23.7205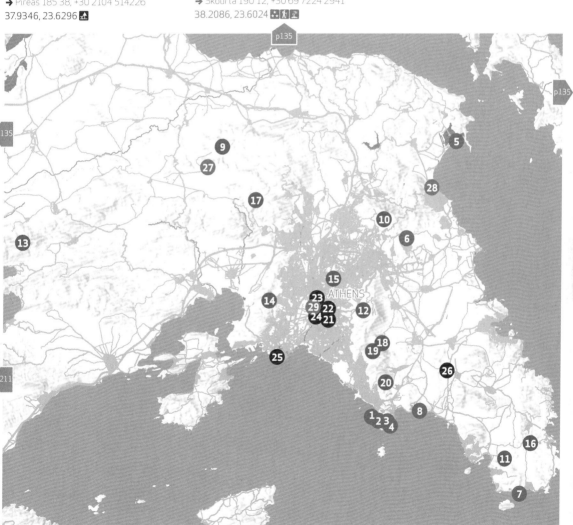

25 MARGARO

An incredibly understated taverna serving the best fresh fish in Piraeus. Sometimes the menu only features a couple of dishes: whatever has been caught that day, served with lemon, and a greek salad. Joining the locals here is a pre-ferry must.

➜ Pireas 185 38, +30 2104 514226
37.9346, 23.6296

26 THE MARGI FARM

A true farm-to-table dining experience, with your ingredients picked from the 20-acre farm surrounding the alfresco dining table and cooked in front of you. Book ahead.

➜ Saronikos 190 10, +30 2109 670924
37.8489, 23.9126

STAY

27 SKOURTA WOOD CABIN

This fairytale forest retreat is just an hour from Athens. Woodland walks from your doorstep, dinners grilled on the BBQ and even a standalone sauna with forest views. Sleeps five.

➜ Skourta 190 12, +30 69 7224 2941
38.2086, 23.6024

28 NEA MAKRI CAMPING

A particularly useful location for Rafina port, if you're heading to the nearby islands, this very friendly campsite is near the beach and has a café and mini market.

➜ Nea Makri 190 05, +30 2294 097277
38.0922, 23.9742

29 SELINA THEATROU ATHENS

A stylish yet affordable hostel in central Athens with private rooms and dorms, all with private balconies. Rooftop bar overlooking the Acropolis and Athens!

➜ Athina 105 52, +30 2160 010891
37.9808, 23.7252

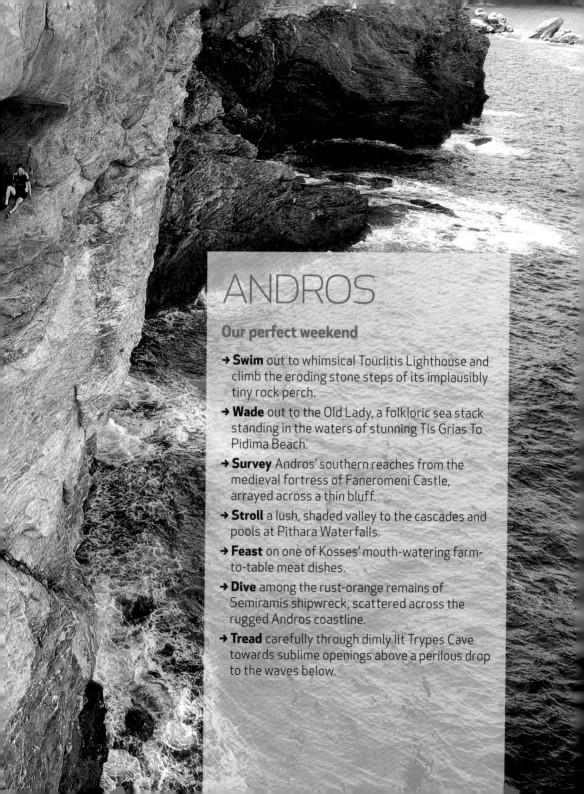

ANDROS

Our perfect weekend

→ **Swim** out to whimsical Tourlitis Lighthouse and climb the eroding stone steps of its implausibly tiny rock perch.

→ **Wade** out to the Old Lady, a folkloric sea stack standing in the waters of stunning Tis Grias To Pidima Beach.

→ **Survey** Andros' southern reaches from the medieval fortress of Faneromeni Castle, arrayed across a thin bluff.

→ **Stroll** a lush, shaded valley to the cascades and pools at Pithara Waterfalls.

→ **Feast** on one of Kosses' mouth-watering farm-to-table meat dishes.

→ **Dive** among the rust-orange remains of Semiramis shipwreck, scattered across the rugged Andros coastline.

→ **Tread** carefully through dimly lit Trypes Cave towards sublime openings above a perilous drop to the waves below.

The tranquil Aegean island of Andros is unusually verdant, thanks to a schist subsoil riddled with springs that feed bountiful trees and explosions of flowers. The recent development of a network of walking trails tracing trade and pilgrimage paths makes it a wonderful choice for slow meandering through storied countryside, with no shortage of dramatic beaches and coastal surprises thrown in.

Since 2010, the commendable Andros Research Centre has established over 100km of 'Andros Routes' along island paths of old, and taken steps to record an oral history of the island, protect the environment and promote sustainable tourism in the process. Fantastic walks abound. Route 9a circles through bucolic farmland above Ancient Paleopolis, Andros' one-time capital, and a forgotten harbour faintly visible beneath the waves of Paleopolis Beach. Route 7 brings you to the Iron Age settlement of Zagora at the island's southwestern tip, its ruins overlooking the sea from a peaceful coastal plateau. And Dipotamata Bridge is one of many charming checkpoints along the flowering Dipotamata River, which babbles beside Route 3 via crumbling watermills to Andros town.

Also called Chora, Andros town is a coastal mishmash of Cycladic, Venetian and neoclassical architecture, and a fine basecamp for outings. Stroll down the main promenade, pausing at Paradosiako Pantopoleio Andros for local delicacies, and through the twisting back streets to Andros Castle, standing forlorn but symbolic beyond a cute arched bridge. From here you can spy curious Tourlitis Lighthouse, and fling yourself from a small cliff into the waters of the bay. For dinner, consider winding up into the foothills for Asemoleuka's delectable daily menu and views.

The capital is also the place to rent a boat to explore the island's eastern coastline, which is one of its wildest regions – particularly heading north. You could spend days travelling slowly from empty beach to empty beach here, by either boat or car. Semiramis Shipwreck, a rusting hulk and its flotsam scattered across rocks by remote Vori beach, is a snorkeller's dream. On wilder beaches, like Rozos or Platanisto, forage some firewood and sleep in the sand beneath the stars for an unforgettable experience.

The natural jewel here, though, is Trypes Cave. Following Route 20 over a barren headland, the trail suddenly burrows beneath ground. Clamber down, turn on your torch and proceed through the darkness to two magnificent arched vantage points beholding the crashing seascape below. It's a magical place that will linger with you long after you leave – perhaps indulging in a final feast of mouth-watering farm-to-table meat at Kosses en route to the ferry at Gavrio.

BEACHES

1 ZORKOS BEACH

A somewhat organised beach with rentable deck chairs, but a stunning cove nonetheless.

→ Follow the road E from Varidi for 3.5km, passing Aegea Blue Cycladic Resort on your R, and park at the back of the beach.

2 mins, 37.9699, 24.7915 🏊🤿🛶🏐 **B**

2 PIRGOS BEACH

A small beach beyond the last houses of northwestern Andros, protected by an old watchtower standing guard on a sheer, sheltering peninsula. Scramble up its western flank for the sunset or its rockier eastern flank to leap into the waters below.

→ Follow the main track W from Kalamos for 3.2km, eventually winding down to park at the back of the beach.

1 min, 37.9450, 24.6872 🍴🏊🤿🛶🚲🏕🚶

3 GIDES BEACH

Quieter than organised Vitali Beach over the headland, this golden pebble beach has clear waters and jumping rocks to the L (as does its neighbour).

→ The dirt track to Vitali Beach is informally signed on a hairpin about 2km S of Vitali (37.9277, 24.8017). Follow it 2.5km, to just above Vitali Beach, then turn sharp R and zigzag up to park by the houses on the headland. Walk on down to the beach.

5 mins, 37.936, 24.8255 🍴🏊🛶

4 MIKRO ATENI BEACH

Tucked away to one side of the larger Megalo Ateni Beach, with protected waters and tranquil sand dunes receding into a notch between shrubbed hillsides.

→ Follow the dirt road NE from Ateni Katakilou and park at the church on the headland between the beaches. Follow a 50m path L down to the dunes.

3 mins, 37.9122, 24.8369 🏊🤿⛪

5 VORI BEACH

A fantastic base for exploring Semiramis Shipwreck (see entry), this wild beach is very quiet but relatively accessible.

→ From the main road just N of Arni village, turn N at St Constantine Church and then fork L before the next bend (37.8650, 24.8462). Continue 7km, forking R at 3.2km to park right at the beach.

1 min, 37.9023, 24.8733 🏊🤿🏕🚶

6 ROZOS BEACH

Another wonderfully remote beach, barely 100m wide, set in a deep cove along this rugged stretch of coastline.

→ Boat access only; try Karaoulanis Riva rentals from Andros (+30 69 7446 0330).

2 mins, 37.9003, 24.8929 🏊🤿🛶🏊

7 PLATANISTO BEACH

You will probably be alone at this remote crescent of sand, cradled in a huge bay surrounded by steep green hills.

→ Follow the same road as for Achla Beach (see entry) but fork L at 2.7km; again, a 4x4 is needed. Boat access with Karaoulanis Riva rentals from Andros is better (+30 69 7446 0330).

2 mins, 37.9012, 24.9062 🏊🤿🛶🏕🚶

8 ACHLA BEACH

A sweeping sandy beach backed by a wetland oasis of plane trees, dragonflies and migratory birds where the Achla River finishes its journey from Mount Vourtoki.

→ A twisting mountain road leaves the main road on a hairpin about 600m N of Vourkoti and heads NE for 8.7km; only attempt in a 4x4. Hiring a boat is popular and more pleasant; try

Karaoulanis Riva rentals from Andros (+30 69 7446 0330).

2 mins, 37.8934, 24.9511 🏊🚶🧗🏕️🏃

9 LYDI BEACH

With calmer waters and fewer crowds than its larger neighbour, Paraporti Beach, this deep cobble cove is a delightful short excursion from Andros.

→ Turn off the coast road SE of Andros onto the peninsula on a hairpin (37.8300, 24.9409). Pass a church on the L and park 280m later on the R (37.8336, 24.9456). Follow the winding path 150m SE down to the cove. Alternatively you can walk from Andros (30 mins), on a signed path starting at the SW corner of the athletics track behind Paraporti Beach (37.8324, 24.9404).

3 mins, 37.8327, 24.9473 🏊🚶

10 ANCIENT PALEOPOLIS

The remains of the ancient capital of Andros, sunk by an earthquake in antiquity, lie scattered across a bucolic hillside of crumbling outbuildings and tiered fields, with a ruined harbour scarcely visible beneath the waves.

→ Fork downhill off the main coastal road at the NW end of Palaiopoli village and park at end

(37.8193, 24.8299). Follow the path SW between houses for 1km to the W end of the beach.

15 mins, 37.8147, 24.8254 🏊🚶🏕️🚴🏃

11 TIS GRIAS TO PIDIMA BEACH

A divine, though popular, sandy beach dominated by the striking Old Lady sea stack, named after an old woman who, according to legend, leapt to her death in remorse after aiding the Ottomans in their attack on Faneromeni Castle (see entry).

→ Follow the coastal lane signed 'Grias Pidima Beach' NE from Ormos Korthiou for 1.6km and park in the layby on the L or along the road. A path heads towards the sea then curves L and descends to the beach.

5 mins, 37.7828, 24.958 🏊🚶🏕️🐚B

WILD SWIMS

12 SEMIRAMIS SHIPWRECK

Lying forsaken by a remote beach since 1996 - above and below the surface, and more scattered with every year - this rust-orange wreck is a fantastic snorkelling adventure.

→ Follow the directions to Vori Beach (see entry) and walk 700m E along a coastal track to the wreck. Alternatively, combine with other

12

beaches on a boat trip from Andros marina. Try Karaoulanis Riva rentals (+30 69 7446 0330).
1 min, 37.9011, 24.8825 🪧🏊🐚🌀

13 PITHARA WATERFALLS

A small waterfall filling a series of refreshing pools along the side of a canyon humming with life. A pleasant family walk.

→ On the SW edge of Apikia follow the cul-de-sac L of the church, if coming from the village, and park at the end (37.8470, 24.9056). Head SW along the shaded footpath for 300m.
10 mins, 37.8447, 24.9029 🏊🚶

14 TOURLITIS LIGHTHOUSE

This whimsical lighthouse, on a tiny rock perch beyond Andros Castle (see entry), is not the 19th-century original; that was destroyed in the Second World War. In the 1990s a Greek shipping tycoon paid to build this replica, Greece's first automated lighthouse, in memory of his daughter.

→ The best views are from Andros Castle. For a closer look, strong swimmers can set off from the painted white fish just S of the footbridge, or by leaping from the 6m cliff N of the bridge (37.8403, 24.9428). Both avoid swimming too near to the submerged rock spit.
10 mins, 37.8431, 24.9465 🍴🏊🏖📷

CAVES & RIVER BRIDGES

15 TRYPES CAVE

A jewel in the Andros crown. Follow the trail underground and through the dark cave to two magnificent arched windows overlooking the open Aegean, pummelling the cliffs beneath. A wondrous place to ponder.

→ Follow the route to Zorkos Beach (see entry) but park in the small layby 200m before the beach. Walking Route 20 starts here; follow it NE for 500m up and over the headland. The markings stop at the cave entrance. Descend carefully and walk another dark 30m to the windows.
25 mins, 37.9769, 24.7928 ⛺🚶🏊🌊🐚📷

16 DIPOTAMATA BRIDGE

The Dipotamata River babbles through a flourishing gorge of mulberry, fig and wild oak, winding beneath quaint stone bridges and old watermills in various states of disrepair. A charming bridge and walk.

→ Fork off the tarmac road about 760m S of Syneti (37.8082, 24.9415). Continue 200m and park at the well. There is a well-marked 800m path from here, part of the longer walking Route 3.
15 mins, 37.8014, 24.9372 🚶

14

15

CASTLES & RUINS

17 ANDROS CASTLE

Once a strategically important Venetian castle, bombs reduced the 'lower castle' to ruins in 1943. The remainder stands on an islet connected to the seaward tip of whitewashed Andros town by a seemingly precarious but perfectly walkable stone bridge. It's a popular local swimming spot, with small cliffs just NW of the bridge.

→ Park further W in Andros or at one of the beach car parks and walk to the NE tip of town.
10 mins, 37.8406, 24.9433 🅟🚣♿⛱♥️🅥

18 FANEROMENI CASTLE

Arrayed magnificently along a narrow bluff, Andros' largest medieval city fortress dominates the centre of the island and surveys the Aegean with magnificent views to the east. It was abandoned in the 17th century, but the church still celebrates the Feast of the Assumption.

→ The road winds N up from Kochilos for 2km to parking at the base of the bluff. You can also park along the road. 150 stairs take you to the top. Alternatively, hike 2.5km along walking Route 3 from Korthio Bay.
10 mins, 37.7993, 24.9486 🅐✝♿🚶

19 ZAGORA

The sprawling, remarkably intact archeological excavation of an Early Iron Age settlement sitting on a vertical-sided plateau overlooking the ocean.

→ Head S from Peleopoli for about 6km and turn R to a small roadside church (37.7876, 24.8673). Park and follow the walled path S for 1.5km. This is the SW end of walking Route 7.
30 mins, 37.7741, 24.8648 🅐♿🚶🏊

LOCAL FOOD & DRINK

20 O KOSSES

A farm and grill house tangled in vines in the hills above Gavrios. Their meat dishes are roundly celebrated, so omnivores can't go far wrong, and kids will love the animals. Book ahead.

→ Kato Fellos 845 01, +30 6972 002975
37.9205, 24.7243 🍴⛰♥️🅑

21 TO STEKI TOU ANDREA

A welcoming family taverna spilling into a shaded courtyard with a playground for children. In the summer they even deliver their fresh fish and excellent desserts to Fellos Beach, a short stroll away.

→ Gavrio 845 00, +30 2282 072070
37.9005, 24.7115

22 ASEMOLEUKA

A homely taverna serving delicious traditional dishes from a terrace with wonderful views – often from a daily menu delivered verbally by a waiter championing local specialities. The salads are excellent.
→ Ypsila 845 00, +30 2282 022227
37.8395, 24.9169

23 PARADOSIAKO PANTOPOLEIO ANDROS

A convenience store brimming with local and boutique produce in the centre of Andros town. A lovely place for gifts and treats.
→ Andros 845 00, +30 2282 023462
37.8376, 24.9386 B

24 SEA SATIN NINO

Elegant Greek classics presented with full flavour and creative twists in a shaded square. A top spot for a celebration.
→ Ormos Korthiou 845 02, +30 2282 061196
37.7733, 24.9507

STAY

25 ARNI STONE HOUSE

An old stone olive press built into a grassy hillside above Arni village. A terrace overlooks the forested valley beyond, and there is a log burner for the colder months. The owner runs an animal sanctuary in the vicinity, meaning cats as curious neighbours! Sleeps three in one bedroom and the common area.
→ Arni 845 01, +30 69 7201 4121
37.8524, 24.8386

26 THE BLUE GETAWAY

Enjoy slow village life tucked away in this cosy blue house in Apikia, surrounded by a garden of olive, lemon and pomegranate trees. Sleeps two.
→ Apikia 845 00, +30 6940 961934
37.8473, 24.9069

27 LEMONIES ESTATE

A restored farmhouse estate producing organic vegetables, olive oil, fruit and wine, and named after the lemon trees encircling its outdoor dining area. It sleeps ten across four independent rooms and lodgings, rentable independently (without self-catering) or as a self-catered estate. You can also organise yoga, pilates and massage sessions.

→ Andros 845 00, +30 2282 023677
37.8306, 24.9176

28 MELISSES

Melisses means 'bees' in Greek, and ecological harmony is the guiding mantra at this stunning sanctuary. Homemade dishes come with fresh garden ingredients, and you can participate in culinary workshops or retreats year round. Two saltwater infinity pools top things off.
→ Kalamaki 845 01, melissesandros.com
37.8236, 24.8055

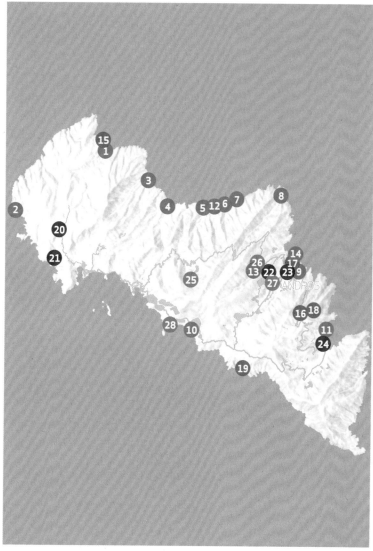

NORTHWEST CYCLADES

Our perfect weekend

→ **Pitch** a parasol and recline for the day after a short, sweaty hike to secluded and wild Varvousa Beach.

→ **Roam** the hilltop ruins of ancient Kastri, dating back to 2300 BC, and survey the neighbouring Cycladic islands in the distance.

→ **Descend** sheer steps to St Stefanos Chapel, wedged into a groove at the back of a magnificent sea cave.

→ **Join** locals and pilgrims to celebrate and reflect at the magnificent Virgin Kastriani Monastery.

→ **Indulge** yourself with dappled shade and splendid isolation at the perfectly formed St Ioannis Beach.

→ **Feel** Serifos' long and troubled mining history amidst the rusted remains of the Old Mines overlooking Megalo Livadi.

→ **Settle** in charming Pano Piazza in Chora, Serifos, among the whitewashed buildings tumbling down the mountainside, with a morning coffee from Stou Stratou.

→ **Wake** to sea views and fragrant fruit trees in a rustic stone cottage on Ktima Pomogna farm.

Kea, Kythnos, Serifos and Syros, all within tantalising reach of Athens and each other, lack the instant name recognition of other Cycladic islands. But all four have spectacular beaches, ruins ancient and recent, breathtaking churches and distinctive cultures. Enjoy them individually or together, if you have time to island hop.

Northerly Kea is closest to Athens, meaning Greek weekenders reliably outnumber international tourists. It's also greener than its neighbours, with oak forests, aromatic shrubs and colourful orchids, all criss-crossed by 40km of hiking trails. Follow Route 6 to the well-preserved ruins of ancient Karthea, the most important of Kea's four ancient cities, overlooking a remote beach accessible only by foot, hoof or boat. Nearby Kaliskia Beach is also one of Kea's finest. And Sikamia Beach, to the north, is a more accessible deep cove with calm waters and shady tamarisk trees.

Below Kea sits Kythnos, a sleepy island of sporadic hamlets, scattered chapels and endless stone walls. The most renowned beach here is the golden isthmus of Kolona Beach, threaded between two idyllic coves leading to an empty island. Our pick though, for walking and solitude, is sweeping St Ioannis Beach in the east. You can also enjoy reflection of a different nature beneath the lonesome bell of St Eleousa Church, surveying bare hills and a glistening ocean from a northwestern cliff edge.

Serifos is the southernmost island of this quartet, its jagged mountains a dramatic background for traditional windmills and whitewashed cubes draped in bougainvillea. From antiquity to the 1960s it was also a land of iron and copper mining, as evidenced by the abandoned tunnels and rusty tracks, wagons and loading bridge scattered above the sea by Megalo Livadi. But it also has untouched spots, like remote Kalo Ampeli Beach, riddled with snorkelling nooks. When it's time to replenish, climb to Chora's delightful square, Pano Piatsa, for mezze, *rakomelo* and dessert at Stou Stratou.

Syros is the most developed of these islands, its sprawling capital a combination of neoclassical Orthodox (Ermoupoli) and medieval Catholic (Ano Syros). But the best historical adventures await further out. St Stefanos Chapel, hidden in a magnificent sea cave below a steep tumble of steps, evokes smugglers and saints alike. High on a dramatic, sloping plateau, the ancient ruins of the 5000-year-old settlement Kastri gaze across to Tinos. And Grammata is the pick of the wild beaches in the north-west, named for the ancient prayers of sailors giving thanks for its shelter etched into its rocks.

15

BEACHES

1 PLATIA AMMOS BEACH, KEA

A deep, peaceful cove with two trees for shade. A fine place for a final swim before hopping on a ferry from the port nearby.

➔ Follow the lane W from Coressia just over 1km to a track R on the inside of a hairpin (37.6560, 24.2995). Follow it 250m to park just behind the beach.

2 mins, 37.6584, 24.3000 🏊‍♀️🤿

2 SIKAMIA BEACH, KEA

An easily accessible sandy beach with diamond-sparkling waters and a handful of lush, shady trees.

➔ Follow a track downhill E, then curving S, from Agios Theodoros for about 4km, keeping R at the two main forks; drivable in an ordinary car if you stay slow. Park in a small space behind the beach.

2 mins, 37.6266, 24.3944 🏊‍♀️🤿

3 TELEGRAFOS BEACH, KEA

Bookended by steep, rugged hills, this long, shallow cove is well worth the hike if you seek seclusion.

➔ On the road between Astras and Ellinika turn SE onto a track at the apex of a big bend (37.6062, 24.3512). Continue 300m, keeping R, and park at the switchback bend L by a house (37.5971, 24.3565). Descend steep switchbacks for 2.5km to the beach on foot, unless you have a 4x4.

60 mins, 37.593, 24.3703 🏊‍♀️🤿⛺🚶

4 ANCIENT KARTHEA BEACH, KEA

One of the most unspoiled ancient cities in Greece, partly because it can be reached only by boat, foot or donkey. The ruins sit above a stunning, remote and equally unspoiled beach.

➔ Take walking Route 6, which starts at the end of the first R turn heading N from Chavouna (37.5702, 24.3165). Park at the main road and walk to the trailhead, as the track becomes very narrow.

60 mins, 37.5604, 24.3323 🏊‍♀️🤿🚴🚶

5 KALISKIA BEACH, KEA

A remote, idyllic cove with deep sands, shallow waters and a few trees for shade.

➔ Follow a path SW over the headland from Ancient Karthea Beach (see entry). Or, with a 4x4 and good nerves, you can drive in on the track heading 5.8km S from Stavroudaki, keeping L at forks and turning L at the T junction to continue NE to the coast.

75 mins, 37.5556, 24.3256 🏊‍♀️🤿⛺🐚

6 KOLONA BEACH, KYTHNOS

Probably the most famous beach on Kythnos, and you can see why. One thin, golden isthmus to the church-topped island serves as a beach for calm coves on both sides. Come early to avoid the crowds.

➔ Head 2.2km W from Apokrisi, park at the back of adjacent Fikiadas Beach and walk the final 100m.

5 mins, 37.4144, 24.379 🏊‍♀️🤿🐾🅱

7 ST IOANNIS BEACH, KYTHNOS

A remote, gently curving bay with soft sand shaded by a row of obliging trees. A special, quiet place.

➔ Hike in along the coast from the W, parking on the headland SE of Agios Stefanos (37.3935, 24.4607). The path fades on the headland E of Lagoussi Beach (see entry); if you lose it, descend to the small beach ahead and hug the coast. It's also drivable with a 4x4 in a long arc E then S from E of Kithnos.

40 mins, 37.3996, 24.4699 🏊‍♀️🤿⛺🐚🌊

8 LAGOUSSI BEACH, KYTHNOS

Tucked away from the world, this calm, shallow cove has a thin strip of rocky beach.

→ Park as for St Ioannis Beach (see entry). Head N up the path for 100m, then turn R over a dip in the stone wall. Scramble down to the beach.

10 mins, 37.3955, 24.4633 🏊🏖️⛺🚶

9 GAIDOUROMANTRA BEACH, KYTHNOS

A wide bay sheltering a lovely expanse of beach, with no crowds and just a few houses around. There is no shade.

→ Driving S along the road from Dryopida and Agios Dimitros, turn L about 8km S of Dryopida (37.3374, 24.3959) past solar panels on the L. The road turns into a track. Keep R at major turns for 3km; once you see the beach, park in one of the laybys and continue on foot past driveways to a path down to the sand.

10 mins, 37.3186, 24.4017 🏊🏖️

10 ALIKI BEACH, KYTHNOS

Despite the easy access, this quiet triangle of sand has a wild character. Sheltered from the north winds, but be aware there is no shade.

→ Leave Agios Dimitrios NE, fork L at the first R hairpin (37.3178, 24.3782) and take the next L after 700m. Park just after turning and walk the final 300m.

5 mins, 37.3185, 24.374 🏊🏖️

11 SKALA BEACH, SERIFOS

A lonely beach well protected from the waves and adorned with a cluster of trees and a small white church. You are likely to be alone here.

→ Hike 1km along the coastal path close to the water from the N end of Sikamia Beach (see entry).

20 mins, 37.2044, 24.4779 🏊🏖️⛺🚶🐚

12 SIKAMIA BEACH, SERIFOS

Remote but easily accessible, this sweeping pebble beach offers plenty of natural shade and a classic mountain backdrop. There is a friendly taverna nearby.

→ There is easy car access via either of the two tracks from Sikamia village. Simply park as you approach the beach.

2 mins, 37.1963, 24.4748 🏊🏖️

13 LIA BEACH, SERIFOS

A quiet, nudist-friendly beach with pebbles. There is a distinct lack of shade, so brollies are advised, and the water can be choppy with a northerly wind.

→ Driving NE from Livadi town and beach, fork R from the tarmac after 1km, just before passing Hotel Rizes (37.1529, 24.5246), then R again

immediately. Park on the L by the track after 300m and walk the final 500m to the beach.
15 mins, 37.1498, 24.5315 🏊⛱

14 MALLIADIKO BEACH, SERIFOS
An outstanding beach tucked deep between steep, protective peninsulas, with an abundance of tree shade. As such it is very popular with wild campers.
→ Follow the coastal track 2km W from Koutalas to a L fork. Park here, before the final 800m of zigzagging descent.
15 mins, 37.1354, 24.441 🏊⛱△⛱

15 KALO AMPELI BEACH, SERIFOS
White sand, clear waters and smooth rocky peninsulas for snorkelling and jumping. A small beach that punches well above its weight; bring your own shade.
→ There is parking on a bend about 200m NW of Sotiras hamlet (37.1277, 24.4967). The path heads 600m down the hill via Sotiros Church.
10 mins, 37.1235, 24.4956 🏊🐚

16 GRAMMATA BEACH, SYROS
A tiny beach overlooking a vast three-pronged bay at the remote tip of the island, with rock inscriptions from sailors of yore.

→ The path hugs the water for about 800m W from Americanou Beach (see entry).
50 mins, 37.4994, 24.8879 🏊⛱△⛱

17 AMERICANOU BEACH
Lazy waves travel along this deep inlet and break before a glade of pines and palms planted by an American economist in the 1960s. The canopy shades an off-beat wild campsite.
→ Park at the NW of Kampos where the road ends (37.4946, 24.9150). Hike NW for 2.5km, forking L away from the wall after passing through a gap at about 700m, descending gradually through scrubland to the beach.
40 mins, 37.499, 24.8955 🏊⛱⛱

18 LIA BEACH, SYROS
A long pebble beach with trees for shade at the mouth of a steep valley. A lovely spot for sunset.
→ Park as for Americanou Beach (see entry) and walk back 160m to a path R (37.4938, 24.9164). Follow this 1.5km SW. The path is uneven and can be hard to find in places, but enters a gorge about halfway there.
25 mins, 37.4895, 24.9016 🏊⛱🏖△❓⛱

19 VARVAROUSA BEACH, SYROS

This wide beach, sprinkled with trees and guarded by an islet in the bay, yawns a quiet, sleepy welcome as you crest the ridge above.

→ Park at Delfini Beach, 2km N of Kini, and follow the path heading 1km N up and over the headland.

30 mins, 37.4681, 24.8964

SACRED PLACES

20 VIRGIN KASTRIANI MONASTERY, KEA

The views are spectacular, the blue and white towers serene, the courtyards tree-shaded. And on 15th August Orthodox locals and pilgrims gather at this sprawling hilltop monastery to celebrate the Virgin Mary.

→ Heading SE through Kastriani, fork L (37.6729, 24.3818) and continue just over 2km to park at the monastery.

1 min, 37.6658, 24.3962

21 ST ELEOUSA CHURCH, KYTHNOS

This church sits precariously at the edge of a cliff on the end of the island, frozen in time. A lovely shaded square and solitary bell overlook the rugged hills tumbling down to the sea below. On the summit above are the medieval ruins of Orya Castle, abandoned in the 16th century.

→ Head N from Loutra for about 1.5km, fork L (37.4534, 24.4232) and park in a clearing by a small church after 1km (37.4599, 24.4161). Take a path between two stone walls, passing a small building with white crosses painted on the wall. The path is easy to follow from here.

20 mins, 37.463, 24.4105

22 ST JOHN CHURCH, KYTHNOS

Impossibly picturesque, this beautiful church sits on a rocky islet accessible only via a thin causeway.

→ There is a small parking area 100m behind Zogkaki Beach in Aosa. From the L end of the beach join a path that skirts the headland and crosses to the church.

10 mins, 37.3883, 24.4579

23 ST STEFANOS CHAPEL, SYROS

This remarkable chapel, poised in the jaws of a looming sea cave that lights up in the evening sun, was supposedly an offering of thanks by a fisherman saved by St Stefanos from a mighty octopus. Pilgrims descend the sheer trail on 19th August and 26th December.

25

→ Head 1.5km SW from Galissas, fork R and park at the end (37.4117, 24.8667). Continue NW on foot for 400m, with the stone wall to your R at first, to the stepped descent to the church.
30 mins, 37.4136, 24.8606 🏊🏕✝🏃🖼🏖

RUINS

24 OLD MINES OF SERIFOS
Iron ore mines are central to the history of Serifos, dating back to before the Romans, and operated sporadically down the centuries before finally closing in 1965. The rusted remains are now strewn across the hillside, fascinating for poking about.
→ Park in Megalo Livadi and explore on foot from the SE end of the beach.
10 mins, 37.1386, 24.4300 🏊🚲🏃🔺

25 KASTRI, SYROS
The dramatic ruins of Kastri cling to a steep slope, flanking a gorge to the south and falling away north towards the sea and distant Tinos. They date to around 2300 BC, making this one of the island's earliest settlements, probably associated with metalwork.
→ Park on the N edge of Chalandriani (37.4848, 24.9335) and follow the path here

1km NE along and then down into the gorge, turning L along the floor to the base of a climb. Steeply ascend the rugged path - noting where you cross the stone wall, as it's easy to miss the gap on the return - and head L to the ruins.
40 mins, 37.4907, 24.9340 🚲🐚🏖

LOCAL FOOD & DRINK

26 STOU STRATOU, SERIFOS
Pano Piazza is centred around the 17th-century church and neoclassical town hall, and scattered with colourful tables and chairs – some of which belong to charming Stou Stratou café, open morning and evening. You'll do well to find a prettier town square in all of Greece.
→ Serifos 840 05, +30 2281 052566
37.1556, 24.5058 🍽

27 MAZI, SYROS
Fairytale courtyard dining amidst vines and ceramics in a converted Venetian mansion in central Syros. The prices belie the creative, upscale dishes and excellent cocktails.
→ Ermoupoli 841 00, +30 2281 088811
37.4443, 24.9417 🍽

28 SEMINARIO, SYROS
A friendly alleyway restaurant spread beneath a canopy of bougainvillea, with great vegan (and meat) dishes on offer.
→ Ermoupoli 841 00, +30 2281 301339
37.4443, 24.9441 🍽

STAY

29 ELLINIKA LOVE NEST, KEA
A tiny one-bedroom stone house for two perched on the east side of the island surrounded by nothing but peaceful valleys. This will be an unforgettable stay.
→ Ellinika 840 02, airbnb.com/rooms/12513797
37.6029, 24.3474 🏠🏨

30 KEA CAMPING
This remote campsite, with cabins and pods, is close to stunning Pisses Beach – and not much else! Don't fear, there is a mini-market and café on the amply shaded site.
→ Pisses 840 02, +30 2288 031302
37.5994, 24.2786 🏕

31 NATURE ECO LIVING SERIFOS

A laid-back collection of rooms with private access to Lia Beach (see entry), shaded gardens and sun-drenched terraces. Embrace the barefoot luxury, or book a vineyard visit or pottery workshop.

➔ Serifos 840 05, +30 2108 010688
37.1500, 24.5305 🏖️💶🏊

32 KTIMA POMOGNA FARMSTAY, SYROS

There are splendid sunset views from this back-to-basics traditional house engulfed by aromas of fig, pear and sage. Almost self-sufficient, the house is powered by two solar panels. There are also two wood ovens, the smaller one especially for pizza. Accommodates two.

➔ Papouri 841 00, airbnb.com/
rooms/49898812
37.4691, 24.9225 🏔️🎿

33 ANEMOMYLOS WINDMILL, SYROS

A converted windmill for two with truly exceptional views of the town and the sea beyond, from gazebo and bedroom alike.

➔ Ano Siros 841 00, +30 69 5166 0451
37.4527, 24.9346 🏔️

34 ARISTIDE HOTEL, SYROS

A unique and opulent hideaway in historic Ermoupoli, with no under 12s. There is a superb roof terrace, a separate garden bar and an art gallery. If you book the right room, you can even get a private plunge pool.

➔ Ermoupoli 841 00, +30 69 8662 4881
37.4478, 24.9472 💶

35 PLOES HOTEL, SYROS

A listed 19th-century neoclassical mansion in the centre of Ermoupoli, with a romantic dining terrace and a private area for sea swimming.

➔ Ermoupoli 841 00, +30 2281 079360
37.4449, 24.945 🏖️🏔️💶

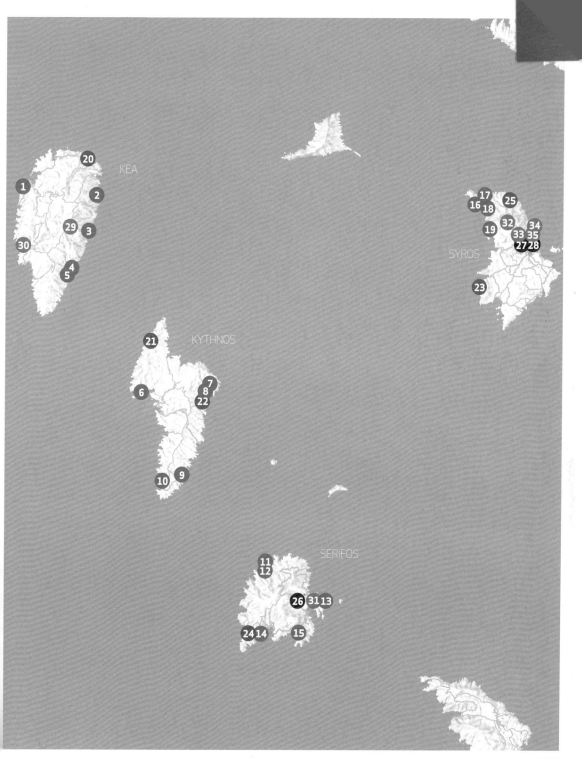

KEA

SYROS

KYTHNOS

SERIFOS

MILOS

Our perfect weekend

→ **Marvel** at the lunar rocks of Sarakiniko Beach and ensure you're not dreaming by jumping from their windswept forms into the enticing waters.

→ **Flow** to the slow rhythm of a Milos fishing village, your toes dangling in the water, from your private patio at Fisherman's Syrma House.

→ **Explore** the abandoned sulphur mine at Thiorichia Beach, then wash off the dust in the gleaming sea.

→ **Sneak** away to idyllic St Ioannis Beach on Milos' quiet western coast, and find even deeper seclusion by hopping over the far headland to your own little patch of paradise.

→ **Relax** your shoulders and take a deep breath as you soak up the setting Greek sun from Plaka Castle.

→ **Throw** caution to the wind as you charge down Gerakas Beach's volcanic sand dunes, accessible by boat.

→ **Wrestle** with the dilemma of whether to laze on the sand or explore Papafragas Caves by sea – there's no wrong answer.

→ **Groan** with delight at O! Hamos! Taverna, where all ingredients are sourced within a literal stone's throw on the family farm.

The best-known volcanic Aegean islands after Santorini, Milos is half as busy and just as beautiful. Ancient volcanism has created a curved island of mineral-rich, otherworldly geological colours and contours, peppered with breathtaking swimming holes, quarrying operations and white fishing villages of traditional boathouse homes adorned with colourful woodwork, called *syrmata*. The largely uninhabited western region, often overlooked, is also a Natura 2000 site.

Milos' volcanic coastal formations are the face of the island and sites of much adventure. Famous Sarakiniko Beach, a lunar landscape of volcanic rock and sandstone riddled with old mining tunnels, jumping nooks and even a rapidly vanishing shipwreck, is popular but unmissable. The tiny golden carpet of Tsigrado Beach and its surrounding cave-pocked cliffs makes another fine option, accessible by wooden ladder. And, if you arrange some boat time, the cascading volcanic dunes of distant Gerakas Beach and the Glaronisia Islets' mind-bending columnar basalt feel like interplanetary visits. Back on earth, it would be remiss not to relive the adventure over local wine from vines grown in volcanic soil at Kostantakis Winery.

Volcanic geology is also conducive to caves, creating some memorable wild-swimming arenas. The sparkling sea caves at Kleftiko are one of Greece's finest wild swims, especially if you avoid the crowds. The name derives from the ancient Greek word for 'thief', and legend has it one of the caves is a lair for piratical treasure. Papafragas Caves provide a similar symphony of arches, caves and pools amidst white volcanic rock, and Sikia Cave, in the barren west, feels even wilder, its huge roof collapsed into a divine pool with a small beach.

Minerals have been quarried and mined here for almost 15,000 years, starting with obsidian. The best place to experience this industrial imprint is the abandoned sulphur mine at Thiorichia Beach, where buildings and shafts littered with rusting machinery climb the hillside from a coastal valley mouth. More ancient remnants of civilisation include hilltop ruins and churches, and the Ancient Theatre of Milos, gloriously sited near where the Venus de Milo was found.

Fishing is Milos' other signature industry. The wonky geometry and colourful syrmatas of its coastal villages ooze charm – nowhere more so than miniature Mandrakia, ringed by bobbing boats in bright water. Medusa serves some of the island's best seafood from the shoreline here, although the garden of homegrown delights at O! Hamos!, southeast of Adamantas, is arguably the island's most memorable dining experience. Equally memorable is staying in your own *syrma*, like Fisherman's Syrma House in Pachena, with the sea lapping below your balcony.

9

BEACHES

1 ALOGOMANDRA BEACH

A small, enchanting cove with a dramatic domed cliff providing shade. Visit on calm days, as the shallow beach is overcome by waves when the northerly wind picks up.

→ Follow the road 200m SW along the coast from Agio Konstantinos port and park in the clearing behind the sandy beach. Walk 50m NE to the hidden cove.

5 mins, 36.7488, 24.488 🏖️🏊

2 SARAKINIKO BEACH

This moonscape stretch of coast is one of the most beautiful and photographed in Greece. The blinding white formations are carved by nature from volcanic rock and sandstone, and are riddled with old mining tunnels that are fun to explore with a torch. Arrive early to avoid the crowds, and be sure to snoop along the coastline, looking out for any remaining trace of the 2003 shipwreck to the east.

→ Turn N off the main road 1km E of Katifora (36.7355, 24.4565). There is a parking area after 750m and a further 200m walk downhill. At busy times you may have to park back along the approach. The shipwreck is at 36.7434, 24.4628.

5 mins, 36.7428, 24.4582 🍴🏊🅱️

3 ACHIVADOLIMNI BEACH

One of the island's largest beaches, at 1km, this stretch of pristine, accessible sand has shallow water and trees for shade. In the middle of the beach, away from the beach bar, you will probably be alone; the north-east end is nudist.

→ Follow the coastal road S from Adamantas, via Kanava, and turn R 2.5km after passing the airport on the L. Park in the tree shade set back from the W end of the beach.

5 mins, 36.6907, 24.4509 🏖️🏊

4 AGATHIA BEACH

An estuary meandering through a soft-sand beach and into warm, shallow water, with a smattering of trees for shade. A stunning pocket of this quiet end of Milos.

→ Follow the road N from Psathadika about 2.3km, bending L with the river and forking L at the very end, to park at the N end of the beach.

2 mins, 36.7266, 24.3418 🏖️🏊⛺🚶

5 TRIADES BEACH

One of a chain of three isolated bays, separated by wind-carved outcrops, on Milos' secluded western coastline.

→ Heading W on the track just S of Ralaki, fork R just after the village and continue for 3.5km,

keeping R at 1.3km and 2.5km. Park at the last bend and walk down 100m.

5 mins, 36.7066, 24.3372 🏖️🏊⛺🚶☀️

6 ST IOANNIS BEACH

A true hidden gem. For total isolation, walk to the northern end and over the headland to a second, smaller beach. Spend the afternoon and stay for sunset.

→ Follow the road from Xilokeratia 3.5km W then N to St John Siderianos Monastery. Park and walk the final 700m down the L fork behind the monastery (36.6762, 24.3377) to the beach.

10 mins, 36.6782, 24.3319 🏖️🏊⛺🚶🐚

7 FIRIPLAKA BEACH

Something for everyone. Popular for swimming and snorkelling, this beach has shallow waters, colourful volcanic cliffs, a snack bar and watercraft rental. Head to the far end if you want solitude.

→ Follow the coast road as for Achivadolimni Beach (see entry) but keep L at the big junction just after that beach to cross the island S, bending E and finally S again between quarries to park above the SE end of the beach.

2 mins, 36.6655, 24.4657 🏖️🏊🏄🐚🅱️

10

8 TSIGRADO BEACH

The waters of this small beach are surrounded by a horseshoe of cliffs pocked with swimmable caves, uniquely accessed via rope and wooden ladders. Come early, before it's cast into shade.

➔ Drive as for Firiplaka Beach (see entry), but fork L as you hit the coast after the quarries and park at the end, above the beach.

5 mins, 36.6619, 24.4692 🏊⛱️🅱️🏖️🤿

9 GERAKAS BEACH

Run down the imposing dunes, formed by nearby Kalamos volcano, straight into crystal waters. If you take a boat trip around the island, make this beach a priority.

➔ Only accessible by boat; there are many options in Adamantas, including Blue Mile (+30 69 4429 6892).

1 min, 36.6665, 24.4815 🏊⛱️🏖️🚶

10 THIORICHIA BEACH

Milos is famous for minerals and beaches, and this is a fantastic place to experience both. The abandoned machinery and infrastructure of a 19th-century sulphur mine, operational until the 1950s, stand directly behind a golden beach.

➔ 6km E from Zefiria. The difficult dirt road is best tackled with a quad bike or 4x4. Otherwise park before the final descent, around 36.6946, 24.5396.

20 mins, 36.6942, 24.5445 🏊⛱️📷🔺

11 KASTANAS BEACH

A secluded pebble nudist beach surrounded by rugged rock formations, including a sea arch. Well worth the trip.

➔ A slightly complicated 7km drive S from Pollonia. Plug it into your satnav, but beware that it will likely direct you L down a marked private road. Ignore this, continue straight and look for 'Kastana' signs, which will direct you safely. A 4x4 is best.

1 min, 36.7349, 24.5381 🏊⛱️⚠️🤿

SEA CAVES & ISLETS

12 GLARONISIA ISLETS

A tiny archipelago of striking formations made from igneous rock, including rare columnar basalt.

➔ Visible from Papafragas Caves (see entry) but only accessible by boat. There are many hiring options in Adamantas, including Blue Mile (+30 69 4429 6892).

1 min, 36.7637, 24.4865 🏊🔺🤿

13 PAPAFRAGAS CAVES

Volcanic cliffs, arches, swimmable caves and a dramatic enclosed pool reached through a sea arch, all surrounding a micro beach. A stunning place.

➔ Park on the side of the main road as you leave Pachena heading E. Be careful following the narrow path L down the rocks to the beach. Swim right around the headland to the caves and pool; do not try to jump into the enclosed pool, it's not deep.

2 mins, 36.754, 24.5035 🍴🏊⛱️🅱️📷🤿

14 SIKIA CAVE

Swimming from the small beach-like area in this stunning roofless sea cave - huge and round, its waters winking in the sun above - is a thrill.

➔ You can hike to the rim on a winding 3km path S from St Ioannis Beach (see entry). The water is only accessible by boat. There are many hiring options in Adamantas, including Blue Mile (+30 69 4429 6892).

1 min, 36.6677, 24.3204 🏊⛱️🅱️🤿

15 KLEFTIKO

Legend has it that one Kleftiko cave was a pirate hideaway and is home to lost treasure. Even without pirates, this bay of astounding

rock formations hides treasure aplenty in the form of twinkling sea caves crying out for snorkel exploration. They are a highlight of all organised boat trips, so you will not be alone.

➔ Only practically accessible by boat. There are many hiring options in Adamantas, including Blue Mile (+30 69 4429 6892).

2 mins, 36.6506, 24.3324 🍴🏖️🚤♨️🅱️🛶

CULTURAL VIEWPOINTS

16 PLAKA CASTLE

There may be little left of this Venetian castle, just cobbles and the outlines of walls, but its location commands tremendous sunset views over the island, and is topped by a little white church.

➔ There are a number of dedicated parking places dotted around Plaka village. Follow signs to the NW edge of the village (36.7448, 24.4218) and continue along the path as it zigzags up the hill.

15 mins, 36.7457, 24.423 📷⛰️♨️

17 ANCIENT THEATRE OF MILOS

Below the famous and more developed Catacombs of Milos near Trypiti lies this amphitheatre, often overlooked, staged on a hillside with a dramatic sea backdrop.

It was built around the 3rd century BC, then rebuilt in the Roman era from Parian marble after Athenians destroyed it. Keep an eye out for the occasional musical or theatrical performance.

➔ Follow road SW out of Trypiti towards the coast. Park in the car park for the catacombs, at the end. Walk back to the final bend and take the path L downhill to the theatre.

10 mins, 36.7377, 24.421 ⛰️♨️🅱️

18 PROPHET ELIAS CHURCH

Stunning views from a white church on the highest peak on the island.

➔ The road twists 8km up from the monastery above St Ioannis Beach (see entry), and is tricky in places, best tackled with 4x4 or quad bike. Otherwise there is a steep, 2km zigzag hike (60 mins) from a junction of tracks on the NE side (36.6808, 24.3923).

1 min, 36.6762, 24.3829 📷⛰️✝️❓

FISHING VILLAGES

19 FIROPOTAMOS

A fishing port, church and beach combine to create a quintessential Milos dip. A delightful scene.

→ Head N from Pera Triovasalos for about 1.3km and make a hairpin turn L to park in the shade of the trees just behind the beach. There is some parking further along the road too.
2 mins, 36.7583, 24.4284 🏊🏖️⛺️B

20 MANDRAKIA

This minute fishing village is a living postcard of whitewashed homes, colourful doors and staircases down to boats bobbing in bright blue water.
→ Head NE from Pera Triovasalos for about 850m and fork L. Park in the seafront parking area on the L after 200m.
2 mins, 36.7509, 24.4458 🏊🏖️⛺️

21 KLIMA

A vibrant string of traditional fishermen's houses, known as *syrmata*, stretch along the shore. They were originally painted different colours so owners could identify them. A fine sunset spot.
→ A narrow road winds W from a fork between Trypiti and Klimatovouni. Park 1km after the fork, at the final sharp bend with the stairs to the cave church (36.7364, 24.4227).
10 mins, 36.7353, 24.4197 🏖️🏊⛺️B🚲

22 KIVOTOS TON GEFSEON BAKERY & DELI

Sample Milos' classic *karpouzopita*, or watermelon pie. Oven-baked watermelon with honey, cinnamon, flour and sesame. Fresh batches every half hour, and a lush tree-filled courtyard to enjoy them in!
→ Pollonia 848 00, +30 2287 041121
36.7619, 24.5251 🏊

23 CHARALAMBAKIS

Charalambos "Babis" Mallis has produced traditional goat-milk cheeses for over a century, but has only sold them outside the island since 2013. This is the friendly farm shop on the family property, selling a range of dairy products.
→ Agios Gerasimos 848 00, +30 2287 041397
36.7495, 24.4965 🍴

24 MEDUSA

Perched on the water's edge in pretty Mandrakia village (see entry), adorned with drying octopus. Classic but refined seafood. Follow it with a crisp white wine. Life is good.
→ Mandrakia 846 000, +30 2287 023670
36.7511, 24.4466 ⛺️🏊

25 O! HAMOS!

Hand-written menus and heart-warming grandmother vibes in an overgrown garden. If the Psatha family can't grow it, breed it or produce it on their farm, it's got no business being on their hand-thrown plates. They supply all the taverna's meats and vegetables and make their own cheeses.

→ Plaka 846 000, +30 2287 021672
36.7222, 24.4584

26 EMBOURIOS TAVERNA

A waterfront locals' hangout with a goat farm out back, at the end of a bumpy ride. The slow-cooked goat is their specialty.

→ Embourios 848 000, +30 2287 021389
36.7100, 24.3925

STAY

27 MELIAN BOUTIQUE HOTEL & SPA

A spa, cocktails and direct access to your own private portion of the gleaming Aegean, surrounded by Cycladic luxury. Perfect.

→ Pollonia 848 00, +30 2287 041150
36.7658, 24.5223

28 KOSTANTAKIS WINERY

Milos' only winery, run by the Kostantakis family with typical island hospitality. Finish your tasting with a sunset over the volcanic vineyards, and even a night or two in one of the sea-view suites.

→ Pollonia 848 00, +30 6982 594859
36.7576, 24.5269

29 FISHERMAN'S SYRMA HOUSE

The sea is your front garden at this charming studio for two. Dip your toes in the water with your morning coffee and watch the sunset from your balcony. A slice of Milos heaven.

→ Pachena 848 00, +30 2287 041479
36.7533, 24.4975

30 MILOS BY THE SEA

A no-fuss fisherman's house directly on the west-facing water, away from the hustle and bustle. Traditional but new, and powered by solar. Sleeps two.

→ Areti 848 00, airbnb.com/rooms/47839369
36.7428, 24.4144

31 DROUGAS WINDMILL

Enjoy panoramic island views from the patio pagoda outside this converted stone windmill. It sleeps four; be sure to claim the master bedroom in the conical roof!

→ Tripiti 848 00, +30 6944 999332
36.7382, 24.4300

32 SKINOPI LODGE

Three sleek villas perched on a cliff with spectacular sunset views over the sea, inspired by the local fishing-house aesthetic but oozing contemporary minimalist style.

→ Skinopi 848 00, +30 69 4695 4415
36.7278, 24.4265

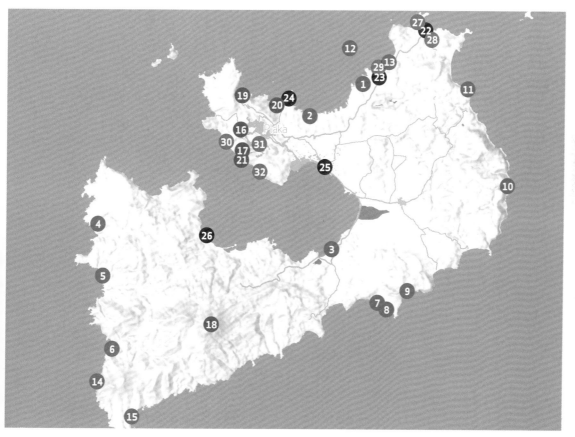

245

PAROS &
ANTIPAROS

Our perfect weekend

→ **Glide** through the waters of Faneromeni Beach, a calm cove so perfect for swimming that it feels more like a salty pool.

→ **Sip** coffee from the wooden balcony at House in the Kastro, overlooking a 15th-century Venetian courtyard deep in the twisting alleyways of Antiparos.

→ **Soar** through the air from the lip of Fano Cave, before swimming back through its mouth into a guarded rock pool to do it all again.

→ **Steel** yourself and scramble down to Archilochos Cave to watch its walls glow like fire in the rays of the setting sun.

→ **Wallow** in the mud with locals at Kalogeros Beach and let it work its therapeutic magic.

→ **Bid** farewell to the day from Korakas Lighthouse on the island's northern tip, perhaps accompanied by a bottle of something local.

→ **Reflect** on time well spent at Sigi Ikthios, enjoying morning-fresh squid beneath the fairy lights of Nousa's buzzing, bewitching marina.

Paros is famed for the Parian marble extracted for centuries from beneath Mount St Pantes. This is the heart of the island, its peak descending on all sides down to maritime plains of quaint white-and-blue fishing settlements, punctuated by lazy swimming spots and sea caves. Antiparos, lying south-west over the narrow Antiparos Strait, is its more relaxed, undulating smaller cousin – irresistible given the proximity.

Mined since the 6th century BC, the famous marble made Paros an ancient cultural epicentre. Sculptors of antiquity championed its clarity and consistency, using it for masterpieces from the Venus (strictly Aphrodite) de Milo to the Acropolis of Athens. It's still possible to visit some of the shafts from which it came. At Marathi, in the so-called Cave of Nymphs, some even navigate the fence to descend into the blackness connecting its three entrances.

But Paros and Antiparos hold other geological wonders, too. The Parian poet Archilochus reportedly used to find solace in Archilochos Cave, which makes a perfect place to watch the sun setting over the Aegean. Roofless Fano Sea Cave, which connects a pool to the open sea, awaits at the bottom of a small jump. And in southern Antiparos, the curved mouth of Antiparos Sea Cave, casting the eastern side of a rocky bay into shadow, is a delight for daring swimmers and jumpers alike.

You might even feel somewhat subterranean inside Paros' warren-like alleyways, and those of Naousa are particularly beguiling. Whether you're perusing the local produce at Arsenis, ordering a mix-and-match box of takeaway delights at Lemon or enjoying an evening of fresh seafood and harbourside mirth at Sigi Ikthios, don't hesitate to get a little lost. Not too lost, though. Be sure to find your way to the delicacies of Kamarantho Farm in the rolling country to the south, or pleasant immersion of a different kind at luxury wellness retreat The Rooster.

No overview of a Greek island is complete without its beaches, of course, and Paros and Antiparos offer plenty. In northern Paros, Lageri's lazy dunes, hazy vibes and shallow waters make for an endless afternoon. Further south, the perches and swimming nooks at Sigi Rocks welcome knowing locals but scant tourists. On Antiparos, the waters of Faneromeni Beach, lapping into a deep, uniform cove, feel like a natural swimming pool. Monastiria Beach, on the other hand, feels particularly wild and solitary thanks to the rough road that deters those disinclined to a little hiking.

12

BEACHES

1 LAGERI BEACH

The sandy dunes of this long, peaceful, nudist-friendly beach are dotted with trees and bushes for shade. A place oozing serenity.

→ About 400m E from Lageri, by Santa Maria Beach, turn N. For the more secluded S end, park at the first L after 350m (37.1350, 25.2753), and follow the dirt track 400m, past an abandoned building complex and onto the dunes.

10 mins, 37.1358, 25.2700 🏊🏖🚫

2 KALAMIA BEACH

A small, unassuming but perfectly formed sandy beach. Popular with nudists.

→ Driving N from Kolimpithres, turn R off the road 350m after passing the windmill and tennis courts and pull over R (37.1395, 25.2223). Walk 50m to the beach.

2 mins, 37.1394, 25.2231 🏖🚫

3 TOURKOU AMMOS BEACH

Tucked away at the tip of the island, this secluded beach is still a quick trip from Naousa. Beware sea urchins, and be prepared for little shade.

→ Follow the coast road N from Kolimpithres to its end in the car park for Paros Park and Archilochos Theatre (see entry). Walk the coastal path clockwise for another 1km.

20 mins, 37.1440, 25.2327 🏊🏖👣🆅

4 THEOLOGOS BEACH, ANTIPAROS

A nudist-friendly beach with small dunes facing the tiny island of Fira across a shallow, swimmable channel.

→ Follow the road N from Antiparos, past the entrance to Camping Antiparos, and park in the dunes behind the beach just to the E.

2 mins, 37.0487, 25.0850 🏊🏖🚫

5 LIVADIA BEACH, ANTIPAROS

This wide, sandy and easily accessible beach is best visited on calm days, unless you bring your surfboard.

→ Drive W from Kampos, turning R at the T junction after 600m, then keeping L. Park in the shade of a couple of trees at the E end of the beach.

2 mins, 37.0205, 25.0464 🏖

6 MONASTIRIA BEACH, ANTIPAROS

A remote and dramatic beach with a smattering of trees set in a deep, narrow cove between tall green headlands.

→ After the rough but manageable approach 3.4km SW from Kampos, park on the bend where the road has zigzagged down to the riverbed (37.0028, 25.0332). Walk the final rough 700m.

20 mins, 37.0031, 25.0266 🏖🏊

7 FANEROMENI BEACH

A stunning cove so narrow and indented it feels like a swimming pool with a small sandy beach. Well worth the trip to this lumpy peninsula at the end of the island.

→ Follow the coastal road S from Soros for 5km and park in the first clearing at the end (36.9474, 25.0699). Walk the last 200m.

5 mins, 36.9445, 25.0696 🏊🏖⛺🏕

8 UBINI ROCKS

An outcrop of otherworldly rock formations shaped like coral, honeycombs and crashing waves. Bring appropriate footwear if you fancy a dip.

→ Park as for Faneromeni Beach (see entry) and walk NE.

3 mins, 36.9485, 25.0717 🏊🏖

9 MAKRA MITI BEACH

A lovely beach, frequented by locals but largely unknown by tourists.

14

13

16

→ Follow the main road S from Voutakos Agkerias for 1.3km, past the turning L to Alilki, and park at the R bend in the road with a sandy area and footpath on the L (36.9970, 25.1210). Walk S for 150m.

5 mins, 36.9951, 25.1204

10 SIGIS ROCK

A stretch of rocks punctuated by shallow pools and ladders for easy exits, popular with locals taking a quick dip.

→ Drive SE from Aliki for around 1.5km and turn R onto a track in the next settlement, where the stone wall on the R gives way to hedge (36.9881, 25.1526). Park at the end of the lane, right by the rocks.

2 mins, 36.9867, 25.1520

11 TRIPITI BEACH 2

A secluded beach sheltered by a long cove; include a trip to Fano Cave (see entry) for a great day out.

→ Turn S off the main road around 2km W of Agios Ioannis Tripitis at 36.9857, 25.1674. After 300m park at the two gates. Take the R gate and walk 200m to the beach.

5 mins, 36.9807, 25.1667

12 GLIFA COVE

Expect to be alone on this pretty pebble beach, surrounded by a horseshoe of squat cliffs. Not to be confused with the larger, sandy Glifa Beach to the west.

→ Driving E from Agios Ioannis Tripitis, turn R signed for 'Beach Glyfa' and 'Beach Trypita' and continue to the shore. Turn L and continue 1km, past the beaches and back inland. Turn R past the church, and R at the end, to park before the villa gates (36.9903, 25.2041). Follow a small path L downhill for 100m to the beach.

2 mins, 36.9897, 25.2053

13 KALOGEROS BEACH

This sandy beach is renowned for the mud scraped from its cliffs, said to have therapeutic healing properties for skin conditions. You will find it busy with locals covered in the stuff. Don't hesitate to join them!

→ Follow the lane S from Molos and park in the clearing at the end, behind the dunes.

2 mins, 37.0475, 25.2695 B

SEA CAVES

14 FANO SEA CAVE

A grand natural pool connected to the open sea by a swimmable cave. Jump straight into

the open sea before floating into the shallow waters of the cave.

→ Park as for Tripit Beach 2 (see entry). Take the L gate and follow the coastal path for 700m to a field. Go through an opening in the fence at the SE edge, leading to the pool.
30 mins, 36.9774, 25.1740 🍴🏖🚶🏊🐚

15 ANTIPAROS SEA CAVE

Antiparos has a famous land cave with organised tours, but also lesser-known sea caves. Magnificent caverns, shallow waters and cliff jumping make this headland a perfect stop on any boat trip around the island.

→ Boat access only; rent at Pounta Port. Sea Kings come highly recommended (+30 69 5527 9615).
1 min, 36.9573, 25.0524 🍴🐚🏊

CAVES

16 ARCHILOCHOS CAVE

A coastal cave looking directly out to the sunset. The great poet Archilochus, who gives the cave its name, reportedly used to seek solitude here. He must have been a confident scrambler, because it's a steep, loose route. Take care!

→ Follow the roads W from Krotiri to the coastal road just W of Marcelo Beach. Bend

R to cross the headland, keeping R, and park before the gates (37.0967, 25.13490) where the path roughens. Walk NE to the coast and scramble down from the end of the cliff N of the cave (37.0997, 25.1372).
15 mins, 37.0987, 25.1357 📷🏔🚶🌄📷

17 ANCIENT MARBLE QUARRIES

The renowned marble of Paros was one of the most desirable materials for ancient sculptures and architecture. Access to these abandoned shafts is technically blocked, though adventurous folk have been known to skirt the fence and head underground for 190m between three connected entrances (with a head torch, solid shoes and some gumption). The site is worth a visit either way, especially if you encounter the charming man selling marble crafts.

→ Head E from Paros for about 3km and park R at the signed bend (37.0852, 25.2001). Follow signs to the first entrance.
5 mins, 37.0825, 25.2004 🚴🌄❓📷

VIEWPOINTS & RUINS

18 KORAKAS LIGHTHOUSE

Perched at the very tip of the island, this is a discerning choice of location for a panoramic

sunset across the Aegean, especially when the spring flowers of Paros Park are in bloom.

→ Park at the end of the road N from Kolimpithres, as for Tourkou Ammos Beach (see entry). Follow a well-marked footpath N for 1km up and over the headland.
20 mins, 37.1543, 25.2248 📷🏔🚶

19 NAOUSA CASTLE

This small but sturdy Venetian ruin stands proudly on a protrusion in quaint Naousa harbour, a remnant of the larger fort once arrayed here, mostly to protect against pirates. It remains a worthy diversion during a pre-dinner stroll.

→ A prominent feature on the harbour breakwaters. Walk to the R side of the harbour to reach it.
10 mins, 37.1257, 25.2373 🚴B

20 ALL SAINTS CHAPEL

The highest point on Paros is marked by a chapel (usually closed) affording magnificent views across to Anitparos and the Cyclades beyond. Don't be put off by the looming antennas on the approach.

→ Ascend SW, W, and then NW from Lefkes for about 7km, and park just before the chapel.
2 mins, 37.0463, 25.1796 📷🏔✝

ACTIVITIES

21 ARCHILOCHOS THEATRE

If you've ever thought it would be fun to watch Greek drama or even listen to jazz in an ancient Greek amphitheatre, this one, built into the rocks surveying Naousa, is for you. It hosts an eclectic events programme each summer during the Paros Park Festival, and there are open-air film screenings on site.
➔ Park as if for Korakas Lighthouse and Tourkou Ammos beach (see entries). +30 22840 53573, parospark.com.
1 min, 37.1471, 25.2248

22 THANASIS FARM RIDING CENTRE

A unique way to experience the bucolic beauty of the island, with lessons and a variety of trail rides on offer for all abilities.
➔ Turn S off the road from Naousa to Ampelas about 850m after leaving the main road heading S (37.1107, 25.2532). Continue 750m to the headquarters (+30 69 9841 3813).
1 min, 37.1051, 25.2503

23 KAMARANTHO FARM

Take a half-hour or hour guided tour and sample the local delicacies at this organic farm, from olives and pomegranates to the local speciality *souma*, a twice-distilled spirit made from figs.
➔ Kamari 844 00, +30 69 8834 1929
1 min, 37.0125, 25.1492

LOCAL FOOD & DRINK

24 SIPAROS

Sunsets and seafood, both spectacular at this stunningly located seashore restaurant not far from Naousa.
➔ Naousa 844 01, +30 2284 052785
37.1264, 25.2666

25 SIGI IKTHIOS

Situated in the absurdly picturesque, buzzing heart of Naousa harbour, this fantastic seafood restaurant may cater largely to tourists, but is a quintessential and beautiful Greek dining experience.
➔ Naousa 844 01, +30 2284 052639
37.1249, 25.2376

26 SOSO

Soso whips up old Greek classics that feel new in a romantic alleyway accented with pink bougainvillea. The moussaka is a highlight and the local wine list is extensive.

➔ Naousa 844 01, +30 69 7487 8281
37.1236, 25.2391

27 ARSENIS

A small grocery store stocking products from all over Greece, as well as produce local to Paros. The fruit and veg come from the owners' own gardens.
➔ Paros 844 00, +30 2284 026477
37.0865, 25.1522

28 LEMON...E

The invariably scrumptious dishes here are cheap, authentic, unpretentious and served buffet style by the wonderfully warm owner, so you can build your own banquet and get it to take away to the water. It may well be the tastiest, best-value meal of your trip.
➔ Paros 844 00, +30 2284 024852
37.0849, 25.1546

29 STRATIS BAKERY

The best bakery on the island. Traditional techniques have been passed down the generations here since 1904.
➔ Lefkes 844 00, +30 2284 044090
37.0564, 25.2065

30 BYZANTINO

This brilliant taverna in a picturesque little village makes a great stop at the end of the Byzantine walking trail. It's family-run, and you can tell.
➔ Prodromos 844 00, +30 2284 045273
37.0513, 25.2389

STAY

31 SANTA MARIA SURFING BEACH

Beach huts, bungalows and camping are all options at this fun beachside location. The team specialises in organising water-based activities at adjacent Santa Maria Beach.
➔ Santa Maria 844 01, +30 2284 052491
37.1298, 25.2754

32 ACRON VILLAS

A collection of villas characterised by minimalist Cycladic architecture inside and out, all with private pools and superb views over the picturesque fishing village of Naousa. The villas sleep up to ten people.
➔ Kolymbithres 844 01, +30 2108 993790
37.1253, 25.2044

33 PAROCKS

This enchantingly simple luxury hotel and spa sits in a lofty position overlooking the Aegean. Get your adventuring done before checking in, because you won't leave before you have to.

→ Ampelas 844 01, +30 2284 440500
37.0947, 25.264 €

34 MAGAYA BEACH HOUSE

A smart and cosy Cycladic house with two charming private courtyards, just a few steps away from a secluded beach, and also within walking distance of town. Sleeps five.

→ Parasporos 844 00, airbnb.com/rooms/7469423
37.0790, 25.1425

35 SEESOO

Beautifully designed beach-boho rooms of wood and wicker with organic breakfasts and sea and sunset views. Rooms sleep two to five.

→ Pounta 844 00, +30 69 7339 3100
37.0420, 25.1082

36 FEEL LIKE HOME, ANTIPAROS

Three beautifully lit, design-led villas sleeping up to eight within walking distance of Antiparos town, all with wonderful Aegean vistas.

→ Antiparos 840 07, feellikehome.net
37.0452, 25.0811

37 HOUSE IN THE KASTRO

A charming 15th-century Venetian home with wonky whitewashed walls, minimalist decor and a wooden balcony overlooking an internal courtyard and old castle tower. Basic kitchen facilities, but very friendly neighbourhood cats. Sleeps two plus a tot.

→ Antiparos 840 07, airbnb.com/rooms/3005605
37.0407, 25.0794

38 THE ROOSTER, ANTIPAROS

A luxury wellness retreat with private villas overlooking unspoiled Livadia Beach (see entry) with private pools, yoga sessions and a spa across 30 acres of hills, sand dunes, rock features and old abodes.

→ Antiparos 840 07, +30 2284 440900
37.0188, 25.0480

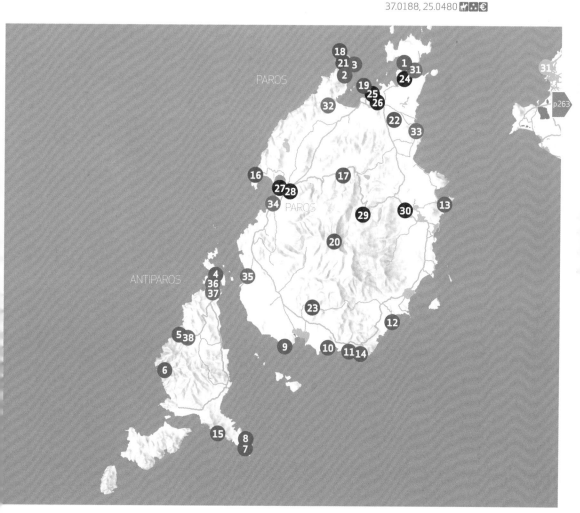

NAXOS &
ISLANDS

Our perfect weekend

→ **Emerge** into cinematic, omega-shaped Itonas Bay for an afternoon of splendid isolation.

→ **Greet** the day with a delicious breakfast freshly harvested from the farm at Philoxenia Cottages.

→ **Explore** the fascinating formations in Zas Cave, legendary hiding place of the infant Zeus.

→ **While** away the morning among the dunes of sleepy Psili Ammos Beach, hidden deep in southeastern Naxos.

→ **Steel** yourself and swim slowly into the blackness of remote Rina Sea Cave. How far dare you go?

→ **Lose** track of time in a sandy pocket of Alyko Cedar Forest with a picnic blanket and book.

→ **Pick** between Matina and Stavros Taverna and Dalas Taverna, both serving hearty Greek food with homegrown ingredients in delightful Koronos courtyards.

→ **Leap** courageously from a cliff above Ksylompatis Caves, before exploring this astonishing stretch of coast by snorkel and foot.

Dedicated to Dionysus - the Greek God of wine, insanity and festivity - Naxos is the largest Cycladic island and was once the centre of Bronze Age Cycladic culture. Its deep peacefulness today is therefore somewhat surprising. The promenades and snaking back alleys of Naxos town give way to a green hillscape of ruined castles, abandoned settlements and, in particular abundance, sacred sites. Each stretch of coastline here feels distinct, especially in the Lesser Cyclades to the south, which harbour some of Greece's most distinctive swim spots.

Mount Zeus reigns and rains over Naxos' hilly heartlands, surveying foothill strongholds and settlements and summoning the clouds that help explain the island's plentiful vegetation. The peak trail passes Zas Cave, where myth holds that Zeus was raised in hiding and empowered with lightning. Nearby Apano Castle was Naxos' strongest in the Middle Ages, built on a rocky plateau with an imperious defensive vantage point. And Apaliros Castle, more remote and rugged, anchored Byzantine Naxos until the Venetians invaded in the 13th century. Pretty Filoti is well worth exploring in this area, but for food head to Koronos, where Dalas and neighbouring Matina and Stavros tavernas both serve delectable home-grown cooking in charming nooks.

Naxos is especially replete with religious outposts. St George Church overlooks a cute cove in the north-east, flanked by jumping rocks and cave-pocked headlands. Pair a visit with fresh fish, garden vegetables and homemade wine at Definaki, a little to the south. St Sozon Church also sits by the water, along a hiking or quad-bike trail skirting the arid southern coast. The 17th-century Jesuit Kalamitsia Monastery, cocooned in an oasis of cacti, olives and palms, is the pick of the inland churches and monasteries, and it lies just south of Villa Galante, a renovated croft house in a sea of vineyards.

Fine swim spots circle Naxos. The remarkable omega-shaped Itonas Bay, protected from the choppier northern tides, makes a brilliant beach day from Naxos town. The gentle dunes and rock pools of Psili Ammos Beach epitomise the island's southeastern tranquillity. And labyrinthine Alyko Cedar Forest is dappled with sandy hideaways as it stretches beyond the mural-covered Alyko Hotel Ruins – a spooky night adventure, perhaps followed by a skinny dip. Thrillseekers will also love Pyrgaki Cliff Jumping, an azure inlet lined with increasingly high platforms.

The choicest dips await across the water, however, on Iraklia and Koufonisia of the Lesser Cyclades archipelago. The sunken German aeroplane at Iraklia's Alimias Beach, in a picturesque cove beneath St Ioannis Cave, is a memorable snorkel. Even more memorable though is Koufonisia's northeastern corner, where you can walk between the dramatic Ksylompatis Sea Caves, enclosed Gala Beach with its underwater passage access, a plunge pool known as the Eye of the Devil and the swimming and jumping inlets that make up Alejandra Bays.

10

BEACHES

1 ITONAS BAY

This omega-shaped bay is almost fully circular, creating exquisite views from the hills above and placid, lagoon-like water.

→ Take a 1km dirt track starting from the W coastal road about 3.5km from its most N point (37.1829, 25.5153). Go R past the buildings then L. Continue 600m, dogleg L, keep R and then keep L for 1km to the beach.
1 min, 37.1935, 25.5114 🏊🏻‍♂️🏖️⛺🦪🚣

2 ALYKO CEDAR FOREST

A coastal labyrinth of sandy, nook-riddled cedar forest and dunes. An enchanting place to get lost with a picnic.

→ Head S along Naxos' W coastal road and fork R just before the road bends E to Pyrgaki beach (36.9804, 25.3915). Park along the road and delve R (N) into the forest. There are paths aplenty for nearly 1km.
1 min, 36.9838, 25.3881 🏊🏻‍♂️⚑🏖️🌲⛺🚶

3 ALYKO BEACH

Relaxed beach hidden behind an abandoned hotel complex (see Alyko Hotel Ruins) and surrounded by gorse and cedars. A fine campervan spot, sometimes with pricey food truck.

→ Turn off the coastal road as for Alyko Cedar Forest (see entry) and take the first L down to the S shore.
1 min, 36.9787, 25.3899 🏖️🚣

4 ROOS BEACH

A miniature sandy bay tucked around a large headland from the nearest village.

→ Head N from the E end of Pyrgaki Beach on the track with a hydrant (36.9760, 25.4035). Take the first major R at 700m, then follow the main track 1.3km to a R leading to the beach.
1 min, 36.9713, 25.4117 🏊🏻‍♂️🏖️⛺🚣🦪

5 ALIMIAS BEACH, IRAKLIA

Snorkel above the sunken Second World War German reconnaissance plane, marked by a buoy 50m from shore. It's 10m down but crystal clear in the divine water of this deep, protected cove with a small sandy beach.

→ Easiest access is by boat (many day trips leave from Agios Georgios marina). For challenging and shadeless foot access, walk a 2.5km trail W from Irakleia to St Ioannis Cave (see entry), then 45 mins further, following Trail 5 E before scrambling the final stretch.
90 mins, 36.8285, 25.4237 🏊🏻‍♂️🏖️🏊🦪

6 KALANTOS BEACH

Hidden miles from any bustle at the end of a long and rough valley road, and surveyed by a tiny lighthouse sitting on a breakwater, this vast sandy beach is scattered with long grass.

→ Navigate to the hamlet of Kalantos, a 24km mountain-pass drive S of Filoti. Do not attempt to drive around from the W coast; the route is a path more than a track in places.
1 min, 36.9369, 25.4712 🏖️⛺

7 PSILI AMMOS BEACH

A gem of a beach in Naxos' languid southeastern corner. Shallow dunes, rock pools and sandy pockets hidden between trees await at the southern end.

→ Park by the road 1km S of Kanaki hamlet (37.0121, 25.5655). Walk a track 100m E to the beach.
3 mins, 37.0138, 25.5684 🏊🏻‍♂️🏖️⛺🚣

ADVENTUROUS SWIMS

8 ROUTSOUNA WATERFALL

Misty waters spilling 20m into a cold pool until mid-summer. A refreshing plunge, alongside the odd turtle and crab, after the climb from Keramoti via the old bridge.

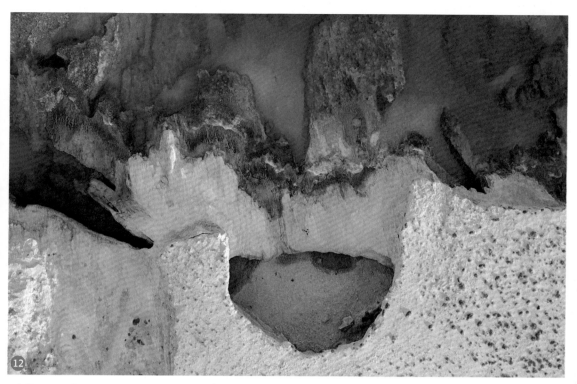

→ A 2km track offering uniquely beautiful scenery begins at the NW end of Keramoti.
45 mins, 37.1164, 25.4994 ⛰🚶

9 PYRGAKI CLIFF JUMPING

A narrow sea gorge flanked by jumping perches (with a rope to clamber out again). A thrilling place to spend an afternoon, probably accompanied by a smattering of young folk. Take care traversing the rocky lip.

→ Park at the taverna at Pyrgaki Beach's E end. Follow the track E, bending R with houses on L, to a R fork leading 200m to the spot.
10 mins, 36.9710, 25.4063 🍴🏖🏊⚓🚶

10 RINA SEA CAVE

This wonderful, swimmable sea cave extends deep into the flank of a remote bay, frequented only by boats and bushwackers. How far dare you swim?

→ Boat access is easiest by far (many day trips leave from Agios Georgios marina). But you can also follow a network of farm tracks S from the road at 36.9752, 25.4928 to a wall at 36.9564, 25.4916, hop over and make an arid 1km descent, trending R.
20 mins, 36.9474, 25.4915 🍴🏖🏊⚓❓🚶🦎

11 KSYLOMPATIS SEA CAVES, ANO KOUFONISI

A barren, plateaued peninsula of overhanging cliffs and swimmable sea caves, making an aquamarine playground for adventurous swimmers, jumpers and boaters.

→ Drive or walk around 2.7km NE from Koufonisia village, or take the cheap all-day boat taxi from Koufonisia marina. Park near Wave restaurant and walk 200m N.
2 mins, 36.9479, 25.6211 🍴🏖🏊⚓🏖🦎

12 GALA BEACH, ANO KOUFONISI

Surrounded on all sides by cliffs, this unique pebble beach in a collapsed sea cave is connected to the open sea by an underwater channel. Climb down with care, or enter via an exhilarating swim, in the right conditions.

→ Park as for Ksylompatis Sea Caves (see entry) and follow a faint track 600m E from the N end of Pori Beach. Fork R then L, and follow the coast L when the trail fades.
10 mins, 36.9468, 25.6269 🏖⚓🚶🏊🦎

13 THE EYE OF THE DEVIL, ANO KOUFONISI

A natural and jumpable plunge pool connected to the sea by a swimmable underwater tunnel.

→ Walk the tracks 1.4km from Fanos via Italida Beach and Alejandra Bays (see entry) from the S, or 1km from Ksylompatis Sea Caves (see entry) via Pori Beach from the N.
5 mins, 36.9396, 25.6246 🍴🏖🏊⚓🚶

14 ALEJANDRA BAYS, ANO KOUFONISI

A string of alluring narrow inlets lined with jumping ledges E of Alejandro Beach. Follow your nose and enjoy.

→ Park at Fanos Beach and walk L round the coast towards Italida Beach, where a 100m path cuts across to the first bay, just under 1km in all. You can also walk 1.5km from Ksylompatis Sea Caves (see entry) via Pori Beach to the N. Either way, you can't go wrong.
10 mins, 36.9365, 25.6238 🍴🏖🏊⚓🦎

CASTLES & RUINS

15 SKEPONI

Cradled in a northern Naxos valley, this ghost settlement, including its church and mansion tower, were abandoned to the undergrowth in the mid-20th century.

→ Drive the coastal road S from Chilia Vrisi 2.8km and turn sharp L after crossing the bridge below the dam at 37.1403, 25.4622. Continue 3km, passing the reservoir and forking L just after a building, and park by the ruins.

2 mins, 37.1429, 25.4943 ⚡✝🚶

16 APANO CASTLE

This castle was the strongest on Naxos in the Middle Ages; the inner fort is mostly Venetian. From its rock-slab perch it provides a sweeping panorama of the central island, well worth the sharp trail up.

→ On the road S of Ano Potamia, take the steep, paved track up at 37.0682, 25.4486 (best approached from the E to avoid an awkward turn). Park after 500m on a L bend and take a rough track E, with a low wall on your R, passing a church and ascending R to the castle.

10 mins, 37.0669, 25.4598 🏞️⛰️⚡🚶🏖️⚓

17 APALIROS CASTLE

The centre of Byzantine Naxos until the Venetians arrived in the 13th century, this ruined castle complex is named after the rare apaliries bushes surrounding it. It clings to a towering, rocky ridgeline overlooking southwestern Naxos and its interior mountains.

→ Fork L off the road about 3.5km SE from Ano Sagkri (37.0237, 25.4423) and follow the track 950m past St Ioannis Church to a clearing in the hamlet of Kastri. Turn L, curve R for 400m and park around 37.0173, 25.4496. A tough, pathless 1km scramble begins by climbing the ridge to the L (SE). Turn R along the ridge at the top, then bend L and up to the obvious peak.

30 mins, 37.0113, 25.4527 🏞️⛰️⚡🚶🏖️⚓🌊

18 ALYKO HOTEL RUINS

The carcass of an abandoned hotel project from the 1970s, now adorned with psychedelic art amidst the encroaching greenery. A vibrant if eerie presence among the cedars.

→ Park as if for Alyko Beach (see entry). You can't miss the hotel.

1 min, 36.9777, 25.3874 ⚡🏖️

24

CAVES

19 ZAS CAVE

Greek mythology holds that Zeus was raised in this cave, which overlooks the western foothills of Mount Zas to the plains beyond. There are calcite formations, and Neolithic and Roman remnants have been found. Whether you continue to the peak (where Zeus received his lightning bolt) or not, quench your thirst at the trailhead spring.

➜ Head S from Filoti and take the signed R on a hairpin bend 750m after the edge of town (37.0444, 25.4927), below St Irini Chrysovalanto Church. Continue 1.4km to a small parking area and follow the 550m trail, initially paved, up to the cave. The peak is an hour beyond.

20 mins, 37.0347, 25.4992 🏕🥾📷🏊🚲

20 ST IOANNIS CAVE, IRAKLIA

Crawl into this limestone cave to find a remarkable labyrinth of stalagmites and stalactites, explorable with a strong light. There is another cave opposite, so don't go to the wrong one.

➜ Walk a shadeless 2.5km trail W from Irakleia, starting just S of the church (36.8369,

25.4543). The cave is on the L, marked by a bell in a tree, just as the path climbs R towards a ridge.

45 mins, 36.8289, 25.4371 📷🏊🚲

WILD SACRED SITES

21 ST GEORGE BEACH

A secluded pebble cove with a small church, remnants of an old port and jumping rocks – an island and a world away from the beach of the same name in Naxos town. The surrounding headland contains small, explorable sea caves.

➜ Drive 1.5km N from Mesi and take a track E (37.1585, 25.5556). Continue 3km along the obvious track to the beach. The final stretch is bumpy.

1 min, 37.1679, 25.5713 🍴🏄🏊†🐚📷🚲

22 VIRGIN DROSIANI CHURCH

The oldest Christian church on Naxos, dating back to the 6th century, and considered one of the most important Byzantine churches in the region, tucked unassumingly off a bend in the road.

➜ Follow the road from Moni 1.5km as it snakes around and down the head of the valley to the W and park in a layby on the L, on a bend

below the church. Climb the short steps round the corner to the church.

2 mins, 37.0811, 25.4933 †🐚

23 KALAMITSIA MONASTERY

The remnants of a 17th-century Jesuit monastery resting in an oasis of cacti, olives and palms. You can carefully explore the unrestored kitchen, laundry rooms, stables and cells.

➜ Signed in Greek only S from the hairpin bend just S of Melanes (37.0873, 25.4371). Follow 1km, turning L at the first fork, R at the second and taking the middle road at the third.

1 min, 37.0785, 25.4375 †🐚🦋

24 ST MAMAS CHURCH

A striking 9th-century church sitting forlornly on a small grassy plateau in the central Naxos foothills; perhaps the perfect setting for the patron saint of shepherds.

➜ Take the road snaking W and N from the S end of Kato Potamia for 850m. Turn L (37.0706, 25.4292) then immediately L again and follow a 1km track S, taking the second fork L and then forking L again. Park 150m after this final fork, when you see the church.

1 min, 37.0604, 25.4283 †🐚

25 FOTODOTIS MONASTERY

This solid Byzantine monastery, founded in the 6th century and fortified in the 16th, is the oldest on Naxos. One side is shaded by a tall canopy; the other offers a valley-framed view of distant Donousa.

➔ Drive 3.8km SE from Filoti, forking R at 3km, and bear up L onto a signed dirt track (the lower one of two) opposite a church on a bend (37.0449, 25.5071). Continue 1.6km to the monastery.

1 min, 37.0504, 25.5214 🏔️🐾✝️

26 PROPHET ELIAS CHURCH

An accessible white church surveying Filoti and surrounding peaks from one of Naxos' many steep, angular hills.

➔ Drive 3km E from Filoti and fork R for Danakos. Park in the layby between two hairpins after 170m (37.0462, 25.5044) and climb the path 100m.

5 mins, 37.0461, 25.5029 🏔️✝️

27 ST SOZON CHURCH

Dedicated to the patron saint of sailors by a merchant who survived a shipwreck, this wonky white chapel clings to waterline rocks on a rugged stretch of Naxos coastline.

➔ From Agiassos Beach take a rough 6km coastal track S. In a 4x4 or quad, park 200m short and finish on foot. Alternatively, walk the whole wild way.

3-90 mins, 36.9244, 25.4340 🍴⚓️✝️🚶🏊

28 DELFINAKI

A lovable family cooking up delicious Naxian cuisine by the waters of a remote bay. Fish is caught daily, vegetables grow in their garden and the wine, raki and treats are homemade. Try the zucchini balls and octopus.

➔ Lionas 843 02, +30 2285 051290
37.1368, 25.5857 🍴⚓️🅱️

29 MATINA AND STAVROS TAVERNA

Eat twice in Koronos, here and at Dalas (see entry). Exceptional traditional dishes with home-produced ingredients, wine and pastries. The magnetic Matina warms a delightful courtyard befitting the charming village.

➔ Koronos 843 02, +30 2285 051243
37.1174, 25.5360 🍴⚓️

30 DALAS TAVERNA

A lovely family serving seasonal, homemade dishes with ingredients from their garden.

Excellent prices and portions. Simple Greek dining at its best, in a picturesque village far from the Naxos noise.

➜ Koronos 843 02, +30 2285 051219
37.1173, 25.5360 🍴🖼

31 DOUKATO

Superb Greek dining in an elegant, beautifully atmospheric Naxos Town garden. The ingredients are either home-grown or local, and the (swordfish) souvlaki will be the best of your trip. Be sure to reserve.

➜ Naxos 843 00, +30 2285 027013
37.1073, 25.3753 🍴🖼

32 GIORGIS

An excellent taverna specialising in meat dishes from the family farm. The rooster is the standout.

➜ Melanes 843 00, +30 2285 062180
37.0904, 25.4384 🍴🖼

33 M.G. VALLINDRAS DISTILLERY

A traditional distillery in pretty Chalkio specialising in *kitron*, a signature Naxian liquor produced with citron leaves. You can taste samples while browsing the mini museum to learn about the distillery's history and production techniques.

➜ Chalkio 843 02, +30 2285 031220
37.0631, 25.4822 🍴

34 TAVERNA AXIOTISSA

A homely taverna with an open terrace, leafy gardens and community of adorable cats. The menu creatively blends Naxian, Greek and southeastern European cuisine with a fantastic beer and wine selection.

➜ Kastraki 843 02, +30 2285 075107
37.0053, 25.3950 🅱

STAY

35 VILLA GALANTE

A renovated croft standing tasteful and alone among vineyards and orchards. The hosts offer fresh food from their farm, and the roof terrace and outdoor shower emphasise the solitude. Room for four.

➜ Akrotiri 843 02, airbnb.com/
rooms/24221802
37.1317, 25.4361 🖼

36 PHILOXENIA COTTAGES

An idyllic farmstay with simple rooms, studios and a pool among olive, fig and almond trees. A wonderful, freshly harvested breakfast each morning.

➜ Galini 843 00, +30 2285 062022
37.1260, 25.4272 🖼

37 GEORGILAS CAVE HOUSE

A sprawling pink farm cottage renovated into six funky, independent suites sleeping two to eight around a shared pool. The jacuzzi and farm-cooked breakfast are lovely touches.

➜ Galini 843 00, +30 69 3231 4049
37.1218, 25.4282 🖼

38 EYE OF NAXOS VILLA

Modern Cycladic home for six, spilling onto a luxurious terrace hewn into an open rockface with pergolas, beanbag sofas, a barbecue and a small plunge pool – all with dreamy views over Naxos Town and the Aegean.

➜ Agkidia 843 00, +30 69 4804 4204
37.1026, 25.3947 🖼

39 NIKOLAS' FARM HOUSE

Simple, sea-view cottage rooms on a small farm in Naxos' slow southeastern corner. Pick fruit and vegetables from the garden, learn about beekeeping and participate in farm activities.

➜ Kanaki 843 02, +30 69 7739 3239
37.0183, 25.5698 🖼🖼

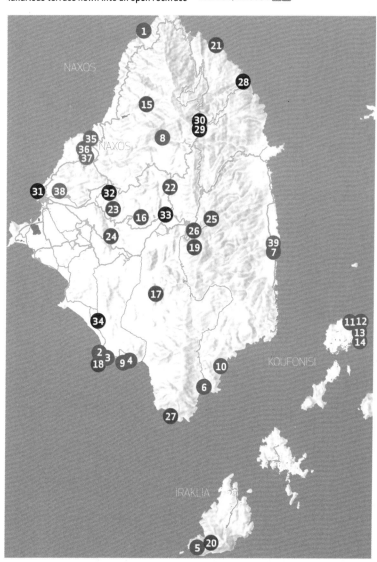

SANTORINI

Our perfect weekend

→ **Amble** the ridgeline alleyways of Ancient Thera, imagining the lives of the founding 8th-century Spartans.

→ **Savour** morning-fresh fish in the atmospheric Cave of Nikolas, waves lapping beside the dining terrace.

→ **Feel** the hot presence of volcanic history in the sulphurous springs and smouldering craters of Nea Kameni Volcanic Park.

→ **Visit** the hardy Church of the Seven Holy Children, tucked at the base of caldera cliffs, and jump into the waters from its jetty.

→ **Stroll** the remarkable Fira Oia trail, agog at the relentless sunset vista.

→ **Storm** Skaros Rock, a ruined 13th-century Venetian fort on a striking promontory protecting Imerovigli.

→ **Leap** from the famous ledge into the cooling waters of Ammoudi Bay, far below Oia's cutesy cobbles.

→ **Enjoy** local wines and dishes cooked with passion at charming Krinaki, hidden from the crowds but not Santorini's signature panorama.

Celebrated for its opulent cave homes and whitewashed clifftop chic, Santorini is not Greece's wildest island, but it is one of the most naturally striking. The main island and its smaller neighbours mark the breathtaking, sea-filled remains of a caldera created by repeated powerful volcanic activity – most notably the massive Minoan eruption of 1600 BC. The caldera is fringed with otherworldly beaches and layered cliffs of all colours, and dotted with unlikely ruins. Elsewhere, the continuing volcanic activity feels all too ominous.

From the moment your ferry floats into its embrace, Santorini's vertiginous crescent dominates everything. To trace it on foot from labyrinthine Fira to the cutesy cobbleways of Oia is to walk a well-trodden but thoroughly remarkable track. En route, scramble up the ruined Venetian fortress of Skaros extending from Imerovigli on a stark promontory. Once in Oia, descend to Ammoudi Bay for a rewarding plunge. Many buzzing seafood tavernas will tempt you, and the island is famous for its wines, but be sure to save an evening for the slow warmth of neighbourhood favourite Krinaki.

To really feel Santorini's volcanism, visit Nea Kameni Volcanic Park, an island in the active centre of the flooded caldera. Boat trips include the chance to swim in volcanic hot springs, muddy and sulphurous, and walk among smouldering, gaseous craters. You can learn about how volcanic activity has shaped the region – most recently in the powerful and destructive 1956 Amorgos earthquake – and how activity is monitored today.

For less frequented spots, head south. In the southeast, combine the sprawling ruins of Ancient Thera, founded by 8th-century BC Spartan colonists, with a short walk to the hidden Kamari Necropolis and Zoodochou Pigis Chapel, the latter built into a holy cave. At the end of the day, swing by family-run Metaxi Mas for delicious Cretan cuisine.

To the southwest lies Vlichada Beach, arguably Santorini's best stretch of coastline, with its mind-bending rock formations and expansive, heat-absorbing black sand. Or, for a quirkier, quieter swim, descend the curious Steps to Nowhere for a semi-private swimming platform. Afterwards watch the sunset from Akrotiri Lighthouse, followed by fresh, beachside fish in the atmospheric Cave of Nikolas.

6

BEACHES & BAYS

1 COLUMBO BEACH

This striking black beach is protected from the wind by a towering cape at its southeast end. There are no facilities, so it is an ideal quiet picnic retreat.

➔ Pull off the coast road at a bend about 2km E of Paradisos resort and park on the dunes (36.4753, 25.4164). Walk E 400m through the dunes to the beach.

5 mins, 36.4736, 25.4208 🏖️

2 KANTHAROS BEACH

The pebbles and steep descent deter many of Oia's comfort-seeking visitors from this rugged, rocky beach with black sand. Excellent for a wild, quiet sunset.

➔ Head N and W from Oia to where the road hairpins L down to Ammoudi Bay (see entry). Continue straight on to park at the restaurant at the end (36.4666, 25.3691). Good footwear recommended for the short, steep descent from here.

5 mins, 36.4673, 25.3685 🏖️🍴🏊

3 AMMOUDI BAY

A glistening swim spot a short, pretty walk from the busy seafood tavernas. Swim from

the rocky shore to the islet, which has a small church and a renowned ledge from which to leap back into the sea.

➔ Take the road to the tavernas N and W out of Oia then S along the coast, or walk down the broad cobbled steps from the town's SW edge. Follow the coastal path 300m S to headland.

5 mins, 36.4579, 25.372 🍴🏊⚓✝🅱️

4 STEPS TO NOWHERE

Steep, zigzagging steps lead to a red rock platform at the water's edge. A unique place for a dip, possibly with a fisherman or two for company.

➔ Park at Panorama taverna 1km NE of Akrotiri and follow a path from the parking area to the start of the steps.

4 mins, 36.3616, 25.4083 🏊🏖️🐚

5 CALDERA BEACH

A black-pebble beach lined with trees. Its deep reef is excellent for snorkelling, and fishing boats putter in and out beyond an inviting taverna at the W end.

➔ Follow the zigzag road down to the beach from the end of a roadside parking area on the E edge of Akrotiri opposite St George Church.

1 min, 36.3611, 25.4048 🏊🏖️

6 VLICHADA BEACH

The standout features of this long, volcanic beach are the mind-bending formations and coloured layers of the cliffs. Organised at either end but with lots of wilder space in between. Nudism welcome.

➔ Park at the end of the beach in Vlichada and walk to the quiet middle of the beach.

2 mins, 36.3421, 25.4292 🏖️🚫📷

SACRED SITES

7 CHURCH OF THE SEVEN HOLY CHILDREN

A tiny sailors' chapel with a jetty, hunkered at the foot of mighty red cliffs. A fine place to swim below the ancient volcano.

➔ Only accessible by boat. Rent A Boat Santorini SeaBreeze in Perissa is excellent (+30 69 8375 7660).

1 min, 36.4576, 25.3969 🏊🏖️⚓✝🏛️

8 ST NIKOLAOS CHURCH

An elegant church overlooking lunar rock formations. Perches aplenty, including a heart-shaped rock window, to watch the sunset in peace.

➔ Turn off the coastal road at the SW of Megalochori, to R of a church on the bend

(36.3746, 25.4263). Take the track R after 60m and park in the open area. The church is 100m towards the sea.

2 mins, 36.3757, 25.4243 📷⛰️✝️

9 ZOODOCHOU PIGIS CHAPEL

The name of this picturesque chapel, shaded by a sprawling carob canopy and built into a high gorge cave, refers to the 'life-giving spring' hidden in the cave that once provided drinking water for Ancient Thera (see entry). Bring your own today, it's a steep climb!

→ A path climbs 400m directly from Kamari; 270m from the last switchback bend on the road down into Kamari, turn L to a small parking area (36.3712, 25.4768). Another leads down 350m past Kamari Necropolis (see entry).

5 mins, 36.3714, 25.4748 ⛰️✝️🥾

10 KAMARI NECROPOLIS

A set of ancient tombs, small square and round cists, were carved into the rocks around 3,000 years ago. They are hidden just above the footpath leading from Ancient Thera to Zoodochou Pigis Chapel (see entries).

→ A footpath leads from the fifth switchback down on the road to Kamari, with parking (36.3688, 25.4745). Walk 100m N.

2 mins, 36.3699, 25.4746 🗿

RUINS & LIGHTHOUSES

11 SKAROS ROCK

This 13th-century Venetian fort was the medieval capital of Santorini. It was brought down by volcanic eruptions and has long been in ruins. Walking the isthmus and carefully scrambling up its striking promontory remains a wondrous experience.

→ The stepped, 250m trail leads W from the edge of Imerovigli (36.4325, 25.4215). If driving, park by the main road where it enters the village and bends L, by the bus stop (36.4328, 25.4240) and head W through the streets and winding paths.

10 mins, 36.4324, 25.4184 📷⛰️🥾🌊

12 ANCIENT THERA

An ancient city founded in the 8th century BC by Spartan colonists and populated until an eruption covered it in a layer of pumice in 726 AD. The extensive excavations, arrayed for over 800m along a striking ridgeline of Mesa Vouno, more than merit the €6 ticket price. The nearby Kamari Necropolis (see entry) is believed to have held its dead.

→ Park off the roundabout above the switchback road to Kamari and walk up the entrance road.

1 min, 36.3637, 25.4782 ⛰️🥾ℹ️

11

13 AKROTIRI LIGHTHOUSE

A whitewashed 19th-century lighthouse, one of the oldest in Greece, sits high on Santorini's craggy and quiet southwest tip. An excellent place to watch the sunset, but do not expect to be alone to enjoy it.

→ Drive the paved road to the SW tip of Santorini. Park at the lighthouse or, if full, 100m short at 36.3579, 25.3593.

1 min, 36.3577, 25.3571 🗺🏔B

VOLCANIC WONDERS

14 FIRA OIA TRAIL

This famed 10km trail skirts Santorini caldera's most precipitous stretch, connecting the quaint alleyways of Fira and Oia. Bring supplies and savour this geographical wonder.

→ The footpath starts in Fira at the Candlemas Holy Orthodox Cathedral (36.4166, 25.4316) and in Oia at the castle viewpoint (36.4601, 25.3730), though you can start where you like and walk as much as you please.

4 hrs, 36.4546, 25.4222 🗺🏔👟🏊

15 NEA KAMENI VOLCANIC PARK

Take a boat trip to the volcanic island of Nea Kameni to swim in sulphurous hot springs and walk the barren, gently smouldering

craters of the active volcanic heart of Santorini's caldera. It's a fascinating, otherworldly place with a more recent history than you might imagine.

→ Boat trips (around 20 minutes each way) leave from Fira harbour, at the bottom of the famous Karvolades stairs – allow an hour for the walk or take the cable car. Expect to pay €20 per person per ticket, plus €2.50 to enter the park.

20 mins, 36.4106, 25.4002 🏊🚣🤿

LOCAL FOOD & DRINK

16 KRINAKI

Enjoy delicious Greek food and house wine at this relaxed family taverna in a tiny converted winery. Local ingredients, traditional techniques and a passion for food shine. A sanctuary within walking distance of Oia's buzzing promenades.

→ Finikia 847 02, +30 2286 071993
36.4631, 25.3934 🏔🍽

17 METAXI MAS

Wonderful Cretan cuisine served by a family on a quiet village terrace far from the crowds. The baked asparagus is one of many highlights.

→ Exo Gonia 847 00, +30 2286 031323
36.388, 25.4575 B

14

15

18 SANTORINI BREWING

The first craft-beer brewery on Santorini, using locally grown wheat, hops and barley. Their fresh beers and donkey trademark have won a fine reputation, and you can buy them locally or visit the brewery for a tour.

➜ Mesa Gonia 847 00, +30 2286 030268 36.3841, 25.4645 B

19 CAVA ALTA

Excellent Mediterranean food prepared with traditional techniques in an old winery, all with fabulous views over pretty Pyrgos Kallistis. Booking is recommended, as are the oxtail doughnuts.

➜ Pirgos Kallistis 847 00, +30 2286 033932 36.3831, 25.4496 A B

20 GAVALAS WINERY

This excellent family winery is slower and quieter than others on the island, with the same superb tasting options.

➜ Megalochori 847 00, +30 2286 082552 36.3756, 25.4306 ⑪

21 GEROMANOLIS

An unassuming village taverna serving traditional Greek food at very reasonable prices, mostly to locals. Enjoy a humble alternative to the Santorini swank.

➜ Megalochori 847 00, +30 2286 082892 36.3739, 25.43 ⑫

22 THE CAVE OF NIKOLAS

This atmospheric taverna started life as a cave built by Uncle Nikolas to protect his fishing boat, but became a restaurant for workers at the Akrotiri ruins excavation. The fresh seafood still comes straight from the family boat, moored in the water lapping against the sheltered dining terrace. Park at the shore below the ruins and stroll in along the beach.

➜ Akrotiri 847 00, +30 2286 082303. 36.3494, 25.4 🏖️🌴 B 📷

STAY

23 WINDMILL VILLAS SANTORINI

Three luxury villas sporting pretty windmill sails, each sleeping five. All come with a private pool, flower garden, barbecue and breakfast delivered daily. Nikos can also set up an open-air cinema. The views and interior design are sumptuous.

➜ Pori Beach 847 00, +30 2286 025207 36.4527, 25.432 🏔️ 🌐

24 KAPARI NATURAL RESORT

Among Santorini's most breathtaking suites, with patios featuring sumptuous sea views and private jacuzzis or pools, some partly indoors.

→ Imerovigli 847 00, +30 2286 021120
36.4338, 25.4216 🖼️🏔️💶

25 EMPORIO CAVE HOUSE

An old winery restored with sustainable, traditional materials into a chic cave home with a splendid rooftop terrace. A retreat from the hubbub with room for four. The owners offer similar cave houses nearby.

→ Emporio 847 03, airbnb.com/
rooms/11050915
36.3627, 25.4476 🖼️🏔️🖼️

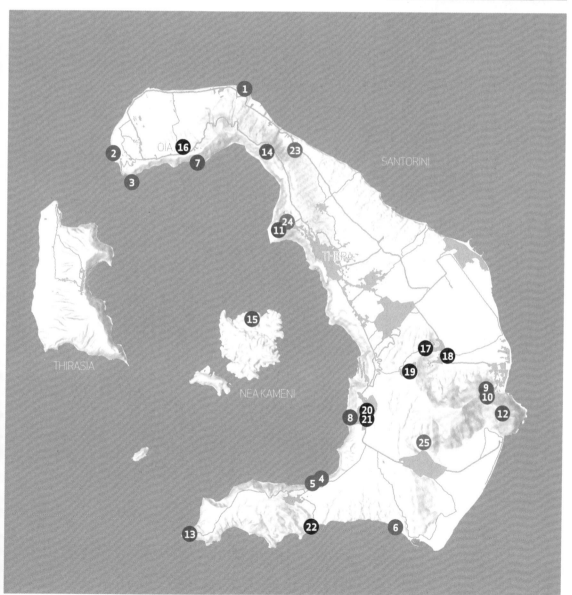

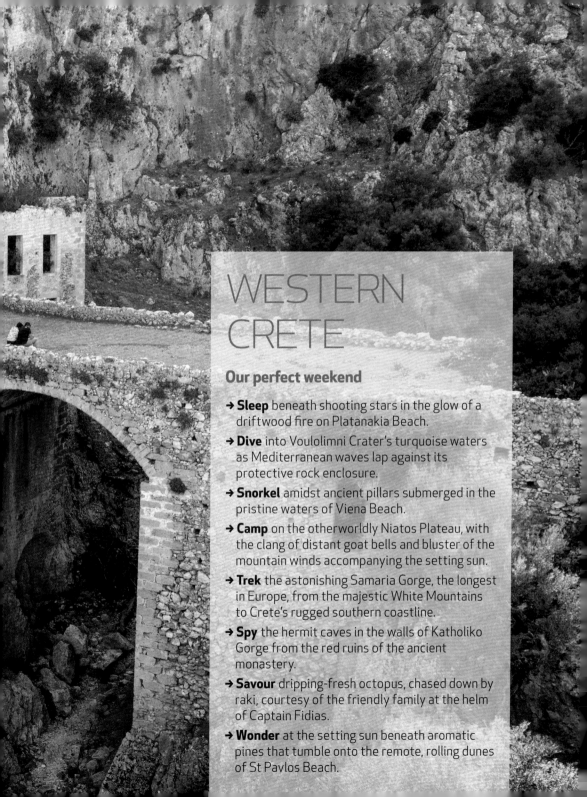

WESTERN CRETE

Our perfect weekend

→ **Sleep** beneath shooting stars in the glow of a driftwood fire on Platanakia Beach.

→ **Dive** into Voulolimni Crater's turquoise waters as Mediterranean waves lap against its protective rock enclosure.

→ **Snorkel** amidst ancient pillars submerged in the pristine waters of Viena Beach.

→ **Camp** on the otherworldly Niatos Plateau, with the clang of distant goat bells and bluster of the mountain winds accompanying the setting sun.

→ **Trek** the astonishing Samaria Gorge, the longest in Europe, from the majestic White Mountains to Crete's rugged southern coastline.

→ **Spy** the hermit caves in the walls of Katholiko Gorge from the red ruins of the ancient monastery.

→ **Savour** dripping-fresh octopus, chased down by raki, courtesy of the friendly family at the helm of Captain Fidias.

→ **Wonder** at the setting sun beneath aromatic pines that tumble onto the remote, rolling dunes of St Pavlos Beach.

Western Crete grows wild the moment you duck off the highway connecting Chania with its neighbouring towns. The northern and western coastlines harbour magical nooks aplenty, and the region crescendos where the White Mountains (Lefka Ori) cascade onto Crete's rugged southern coastline. Further south still, undeveloped Gavdos island, Europe's most southerly point, offers wonderfully remote beach adventures. Take a day trip from Sfakia or Paleochora or stay longer – legend says the goddess Calypso detained Odysseus here for seven years.

The Akrotiri Peninsula, home to Chania airport, extends a tantalising Cretan welcome or farewell. Katholiko Monastery is tentatively considered Crete's oldest, associated with St John the Hermit, and surrounded by hermit caves. Descending through its ruins and hermitage caves before leaping into the turquoise waters of Katholiko Beach makes clear the harmony between Crete's religious and natural histories.

Travelling south-east from Chania towards deep-blue Lake Kournas, Crete's only freshwater lake, you'll pass a string of fabulous tavernas. Menuless Maza Cafe is quintessential mountain-village dining, while the wood-fired clay ovens of farm-to-table taverna Ntounias are an island highlight. And Gordeli Taverna's foraged menu pairs excellently with a jump into the secluded bay below.

Crete's western coastline presents a smorgasbord of delights. Spectacular Elafonisi and Balos beaches are the famous jewels in the crown, for good reason. But Platanakia, Kedrodasos and Kokkino beaches offer wildness and solitude, each with their own unique character. Don't forget your sleeping bag and food for the fire, or to cool off at Voulolimni Crater or Aspri Limni Beach as you pass through.

Inland, orange and citrus fields give way to the olive-clad foothills of the majestic White Mountains. Riddled with limestone gorges snaking between 40 peaks above 2,000m, this is western Crete's most spectacular terrain. Samaria Gorge is a five-to-seven-hour hike through vertiginous, pine-blanketed cliffs via the ancient village of Samaria, making it Europe's longest. It's unmissable, if you can time it to avoid the crowds. But don't neglect nearby St Irini Gorge: quieter, more accessible and almost as spectacular.

The best way to bask in this remarkable landscape is to trace the coastline between Agia Roumeli and Loutro. You can by boat, but even better is the E4 hiking trail, which runs 500km along the island and links many of the beaches in the west. The popular Marmara Sea Caves offer a brilliant adventure swim, while Domata and St Pavlos beaches, where aromatic needles carpet soft, rolling dunes beneath the setting sun, are two of Crete's most enchanting places. Bring a companion and a bottle, and gaze south towards Gavdos, where more adventure awaits.

1

BEACHES

1 SEITAN LIMANIA BEACH

This protected turquoise inlet is popular with locals at weekends, but still fantastic for a last dip before heading to the nearby airport. Cliff jumpers can use the fixed rope 50m out on the right, and you can explore inland along Diplohahalo Gorge.

→ Follow the road SE from Chordaki through Rizoskloko, then after 350m fork R downhill and continue 2.3km to the car park below a set of switchbacks. A steep path leads to the beach.

10 mins, 35.5518, 24.1934 🍴♨️B

2 MENIES BEACH

The slow pilgrimage to one of Crete's most remote beaches is rewarded by a stunning, sweeping cove of sand and pebbles protected on each side by sheer rockfaces.

→ Follow the road N up the peninsula from Rodopos for 19km, forking R at 15km. Park on the beach. This will take nearly an hour; it is a rough road that requires careful attention.

1 min, 35.6645, 23.7678 🏊♨️🚻❓▽

3 BALOS BEACH

Turquoise waters, white sand, a rocky island and an expansive lagoon make Balos Crete's most famous beach, and possibly its most beautiful, on many 'world's best beaches' lists. This means it's busy. But if you can arrive early, late or in the shoulder seasons, it remains a spectacular trip.

→ There is a €1 fee per person to access the peninsula by car, and much of the 8km road from Kaliviani is unsurfaced and slow. Paid parking is at the end, but at times cars park along the road as much as 2km back. From the car park it's a steep downhill hike via a stonking viewpoint; the return climb may take an hour. You can also take a ferry with Gramvousa Balos Cruises (+30 2822 305200) from Kissamos. Tickets are €27 per adult and €13 per kid aged 3-12.

20 mins, 35.5834, 23.5882 🏊♨️⛰️🚻B

4 PLATANAKIA BEACH

This sweeping pebble beach, flanked by amphitheatrical headlands, feels fantastically remote all year round. The abundant driftwood confirms it as a supreme wild camping spot.

→ A short but tricky option is walking the sometimes steep and elusive trail from the S end of Sfinari Beach, through a campsite and over the headland. Alternatively, drive the 4.5km dirt track on the L 2.3km out of Kampos on the road to Sfinari (35.3973, 23.5742). Without a 4x4 you may need to park early and walk.

40 mins, 35.4134, 23.5547 🏊♨️⛰️🏕️

5 ASPRI LIMNI BEACH

A sprawling, otherworldly lagoon fed by the sea and overlooked by mountains. Plenty of shallow pools for exploration from a small beach with a handful of parasols.

→ Approach the monastery in Moni Chrisoskalitissis, take a L on final bend, then after 450m turn R. Continue 1km to parking behind the beach, taking a L bend at 400m.

1 min, 35.3099, 23.5251 ♨️⛰️〰️

6 ELAFONISI BEACH

Heavenly Elafonisi is a heaving hotspot, and for good reason. But its golden sands, with their famous shifting areas of pink, stretch onto a duned peninsula where wilder stretches and secluded nooks appear. Early morning is the most rewarding time to visit.

→ Clearly signposted 5km from Moni Chrisoskalitissis, at the end of the main road, with free parking.

2 mins, 35.271, 23.5408 🏊♨️B

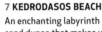

7 KEDRODASOS BEACH

An enchanting labyrinth of juniper trees and sand dunes that makes you feel lost even when it's busy. Best enjoyed with a picnic blanket, barbecue and tent. Two further bays lie to the SE.

→ Follow the road for Elafonisi beach (see entry) but near the end turn a hairpin L just after a restaurant with a car park and follow a dirt road 2km. Bear L at the first three forks and R at the fourth, then keep L at 1.6km and go R past greenhouses at the end. Park in the clearing and walk the final 100m down to the beach. It is also on the E4 hiking trail.

3 mins, 35.2693, 23.5605 🏊🚭⛺🅱

8 KOKKINO BEACH

This serene, secluded beach promises a magical sunset campfire. An easy scramble over large rocks at the northeast end leads to neighbouring Kambi Beach.

→ Follow a dirt road W along coast from the greenhouses at Agia Kiriaki, turning R uphill at 2km (35.2362, 23.5870) and keeping L at forks for another 1.8km to park by the church (35.2475, 23.5796). A faint footpath winds down to the beach.

5 mins, 35.25, 23.5778 🚭⛺🏊

9 VIENA BEACH

Ruins of the ancient city of Viena descend into the pristine water of this wild but protected beach. A sandy slither with a lone tamarisk tree is the best base. Bring your snorkel.

→ Follow the road for Kokkino Beach (see entry) but don't turn R. Park and look for a quick, well-marked trail – part of the E4 hiking route – down on the L (35.2371, 23.5858).

10 mins, 35.2386, 23.5782 🏊🚭🐚

10 DOMATA BEACH

A remote, rugged paradise surrounded by vertical, tree-lined cliffs. Stay the night if you can.

→ Follow the E4 hiking trail from Sougia to the W (5 hours) or Agia Roumeli to the E (2.5 hours). Alternatively, rent a boat from Hora Sfakion; Notos Mare (+30 2821 008536) is well reviewed.

3–5 hrs, 35.2273, 23.9134 🚭⛺🏊🏔🐚

11 ST PAVLOS BEACH

Aromatic pines cascade onto the gently sloping sands of this wild beach. Take a blanket or a bivvy and a bottle of Cretan red to its eastern end, beyond the small chapel, for a spectacular sunset.

→ Take a boat from Loutro or Hora Sfakion to Agia Roumeli and hike E along the E4 route. The sandy track is sometimes faint, but you can't get lost. Alternatively, take a longer hike from Loutro or through Samaria Gorge (see entry).
50 mins, 35.2209, 24.0016 ⬛🏊🏕️🧍🏊🐾

12 PERIVOLAKIA BEACHES

Two open, sunny beaches offering a wilder alternative to nearby Glyka Nera Beach (see entry).

→ On the E4 trail and easily reached from Loutro to the W or via Glyka Nera Beach to the E.
35 mins, 35.1988, 24.0995 🏊⬛🧍

13 GLYKA NERA BEACH

A long, shallow beach backed by almighty cliffs. Nudists lounge on sunbeds shaded by tamarisk trees, with easy access to a floating taverna. A quiet retreat from surrounding towns.

→ Follow the road from Kampia village towards Hora Sfakion for 7.5km as it switchbacks down to the coast and park near the last bend (35.2019, 24.1174). Hike the rugged E4 trail W for 1km. You can also hike or hop on a boat (multiple times daily) from Hora Sfakion or Loutro.
20 mins, 35.2019, 24.1076 🏊⬛🧍B🏊

14 PLAKAKI BEACH

Jutting rock formations creating a string of private beaches, each with nooks and crannies to explore by foot or sea.

→ About 1km E out of Hora Sfakion take a R signed for Vritomartis Hotel. Pass the hotel on the R, keeping L at any junctions, for about 1km. Finally, take the L fork just above Filaki Beach to park by a track. Scramble down to coves along the coast to the E.
5 mins, 35.1942, 24.1587 🍴🏊🏊

15 ST IOANNIS BEACH

A sprawling, golden dune beach on tiny Gavdos, populated by gnarled cedars and free-spirited summer campers. A taverna, convenience store and showers nearby allow for an extended stay.

→ Park at Theofilos Livykon taverna, at the end of the road along the N coast, and walk W through the dunes to find your spot. You can also get a bus from Karave to nearby Sarakiniko beach and walk 2.5km.
5 mins, 34.8678, 24.0847 🏊⬛🏕️

16 POTAMOS BEACH

Cliffs tumble down to deep orange sand studded with wizened pines, all kept free of crowds by the walk from Ampleos. A wondrous place with no facilities.

→ Walk 2km from the end of the S coast road in Ampelos, with a steep finish. If you don't have a car, you can take a bus to Gavdos Lighthouse, near Ampelos, and walk around two hours.
45 mins, 34.8591, 24.0622 🏊⬛🏕️🧍🏊

17 TRYPTI BEACH

This long pebble beach with a dried sandy lagoon behind it is named for the dramatic sea arches overlooking the Libyan Sea. Above them sits a giant chair sculpture marking the southernmost point of Europe.

→ The walk from Vatsiana is around 4km and hot. You can also take a boat tour through Gavdos Boat Trips on Sarakiniko beach (+30 2823 041106) or Gavdos Boat Cruises in Karaves (+30 69 7829 4043).
60 mins, 34.8043, 24.1236 🏊⬛🏕️🧍🏊

ROCKY INLETS

18 KATHOLIKO BAY

A creviced inlet perfect for a dip and snorkel at the end of a dramatic hike in; do bring plenty of water. Once a port for Katholiko

Monastery (see entry) above, it features a sizable cave for shade, a boat-shaped rock and a picturesque, crumbling arch.

→ From Katholiko Monastery continue down the gorge about 700m to the coast.
40 mins, 35.5921, 24.1500 🍴🏊‍♀️🚶‍♂️

19 GORDELI TAVERNA BAY

This sumptuously located taverna once served a five-dish menu with ingredients foraged from local hills, using an off-grid setup that meant dusk was closing time. But it's sadly been closed since the pandemic. The rocky bay, with high jumping rocks, remains a splendid swim spot though. Who knows, maybe the taverna will reopen one day.

→ 2km E of Drapanos, turn R and switchback steeply down to the old taverna. If you don't like steep driving, you may prefer to park at the turning and walk the 1.3km.
35.4359, 24.2562 T-1

20 OMPROGIALOS

A rocky north-facing cove featuring swimming platforms with handy steps into the sea. An unassuming, rarely visited Cretan corner, where the sun sets early behind the hills.

→ Head S from Drapanos for 1.8km and turn L, immediately passing a chapel on your L. Follow the road 4km to the coast, with a L switchback at 1.7km. Park just after the taverna.
2 mins, 35.4254, 24.2586 🏊‍♀️

LAKES & SEA CAVES

21 VOULOLIMNI CRATER

This breathtaking turquoise lagoon, connected to the sea by a thin channel and surrounded by rock ledges for jumping, seems designed for a serendipitous afternoon dip.

→ Approaching Moni Chrisoskalitissis from the E, turn R just before the mini market. Turn R after the hotel then keep L 300m to the end. Ample space to park next to the pool.
1 min, 35.3152, 23.5335 🏊‍♀️

22 MARMARA SEA CAVES

Exploring this row of sea caves, two of which are linked by a thin channel, makes for an enthralling adventure swim despite their popularity.

→ You can hold rocks while swimming to help access the first caves, but not those further away. The quickest hike to the beach is from Loutro; it's a longer half-day hike from Agia Roumeli. There

31

are also regular boats from Loutro.
50 mins, 35.1968, 24.0586 🚣🏊🅱️🚌

23 KOURNAS LAKE

The only large natural lake in Crete is brilliant blue and surrounded by olive groves and looming peaks. It's a popular spot, with nick-nack shops, eateries and a jetty with pedalos and kayaks to rent, but its size means it's rarely too crammed.

→ Well signposted from all directions and an easy 3km from just outside Georgioupoli on the road to Asproulianos. Free car parks on the NE shore.
2 mins, 35.3309, 24.2758 🏊🚣🅱️

GORGES

24 ST IRINI GORGE

Second only to Samaria (see entry), this lush, shady gorge is bursting with the aroma of sage and the clicking of cicadas. Keep an eye out for eagles, kestrels and vultures, and bring water.

→ Signed off the main road 2km S of Koulouridiana (35.3293, 23.8369). There is a car park by a café at the start; there may be a €2 charge. About 7km will take you to Oasis Taverna, a good turning point where you can

also call a taxi, or you can walk all the way to the coast (3 hours).
2 hrs, 35.3256, 23.8408 🚶🏃

25 SAMARIA GORGE

Crete's premier outdoor attraction is Europe's longest gorge. Pristine switchbacks descend pine-forested slopes with sensational views to a rugged gorge-bottom path. This passes ruined Samaria village and threads through an arresting ravine just 4m wide but 300m deep, known as the Iron Gates, to finish in Agia Roumeli (16km).

→ Most people walk downhill from N to S, then get a boat from Agia Roumeli to Sougia or Hora Sfakion and a taxi back to the start or public transport onwards. The reverse is possible though. Daily buses run from Chania to the starting point. Entry is €5. To walk in peace, start before 7am or after 11am.
4–7 hrs, 35.2916, 23.9582 🏔️🚶🅱️🚗🏃

PLATEAUS

26 NIATOS PLATEAU

A fantastic, surreal wild-camping spot at 1200m, amidst surrounding peaks. Only the distant goat bells will disturb you here.

→ With a 4x4 you can drive to the plateau

25

26

8.7km from Ammoudari village; the road is signed 'Tavri Tableland', a lower plateau on the way. Alternatively, park at 35.2938, 24.1694, before the road becomes a track, and hike the E4 route up through deciduous forest and goat meadows.
90 mins, 35.2922, 24.1464 🏔🔺🚶⛺

27 MANIKAS PLATEAU

A high mountain plateau with an abandoned village occupied only by shepherds. Carry water, and pick pears and figs from the trees outside the church to replenish your energy after the gruelling but stupendous hike in.
→ On the bend in the road just S of Kalikratis village, turn S and follow 1km, then turn L on a bend and park at the dead end by a church after 300m (35.2354, 24.2563). Follow the path S from here; the first half is marked by cairns, the second with blue rock paint.
60 mins, 35.2182, 24.27 🏔🚶⛺

RUINS & NATURAL WONDERS

28 KOMOLITHI

A curious assortment of conical white-clay hills, formed through natural erosion. Only a small area, but well worth an otherworldly stroll.
→ Turn E off the main road in the middle of Potamida village and continue about 600m, around a hairpin R. There is no organised parking. Pull off the road carefully and follow the trail to the R edge of the hills.
5 mins, 35.4718, 23.6987 🏔🚶

29 KOULES OF LOUTRO

Quieter, more intact and with better views than Loutro's older Venetian fort at the headland, this 19th-century Turkish castle ruin features two primary chambers, a staircase, a tower and upper windows.
→ A short, sharp hike up from Loutro's harbour starts with an alleyway L of Daskalogiannis Hotel, opposite the jetty (35.1984, 24.0792).
10 mins, 35.1979, 24.0772 🚴

30 LERA CAVE

This small hillside cave affords tremendous views back over Stavros and the coastline beyond and hides flowstone formations within. It was in use from the Neolithic to the Byzantine period, with an ancient shrine in the innermost chamber, and more recently featured in the Oscar-winning film Zorba the Greek, playing the part of a mine.

→ Park at the E edge of Stavros town and beach (35.5894, 24.0979). Follow the dirt path parallel to the shore 50m further, then turn R onto the trail straight up the hill to the cave.
20 mins, 35.5905, 24.1024 🏔🚶🚴

31 KATHOLIKO MONASTERY

Snooping through the 11th-century ruins of Crete's oldest monastery, huddled by an impressive bridge at the foot of steep and cave-pocked Avlaki Gorge, is a magical experience. Be sure to scramble up to the cave hermitage, perched 100m along the gorge on the left. As a bonus, on the way in you pass Gouverneto Monastery (built when Katholiko Monastery suffered pirate attacks) and church ruins at Arkoudospilio Cave, and you can continue for a dip at Katholiko Bay (see entry).
→ On the road from Chorafakia to Kalorrouma, continue straight at 3.4km for 500m to From Holy Trinity Church. Follow the road L here, then ignore any tracks L for 3.7km to park at Gouverneto Monastery (35.5825, 24.1400), where there may be a small entry charge. Follow the stone path downhill past the monastery and Arkoudospilio Cave to steps at the end. Wear proper shoes.
30 mins, 35.5903, 24.1462 ⛪🚴🏊🚶🎣🚴

LOCAL FOOD & DRINK

32 CAPTAIN FIDIAS

The sons return a daily haul, the mother recommends dishes and the father hosts with twinkling eyes at this delightful beachside seafood restaurant. Fresh octopus, dripping on the line, is the recommendation as you gaze across the ocean from beneath the pines.
→ Sfinari 730 12, +30 2822 041107
35.4161, 23.5622 🏖

33 ROTONTA CAFÉ

A small menu of humble, home-cooked recipes with fresh veggies grown on the family farm, all served with panoramic mountain views.
→ Kalathenes 734 00, +30 2822 051227
35.4347, 23.6717 🍴🏖

34 EMILIA'S TAVERNA

The original Cretan recipes in this friendly taverna use mostly home-produced vegetables, cheese, meat and grapes. The rest is sourced locally, from the mountains over which diners gaze. A wonderful place to eat.
→ Zourva 730 05, +30 2821 067060
35.3857, 23.9622 🍴🏖

35 NTOUNIAS TAVERNA

Sumptuous Cretan cuisine slow-cooked in wood-fired clay ovens with organic ingredients from the family farm. The spectacular approach and views cement its must-visit status. You will very often see this spelled Dounias – don't be fooled, it's the same place!

➜ Drakona 731 00, +30 2821 065083
35.409, 24.0149 🍴🏔

36 OXO NOU CAFÉ

A hidden Chania gem. Excellent coffee and pastries with seating spilling onto a secret sandy cove.

➜ Chania 731 33, +30 2821 045585
35.5215, 24.0443 🏖

37 MAZA CAFÉ

The heartbeat of Maza, a sleepy mountain village. Owner Costas patrols the square, inviting people in with a big smile. The menu is simply whatever local produce is available; embrace the surprise with some raki and enjoy rural life unfolding beneath the peaks beyond.

➜ Maza 730 07, +30 2825 051615
35.3581, 24.2132 🏵

38 GRAMMENO CAMPING

Tents, cabins and motorhomes on sandy pitches among peaceful beachside groves. There are hammocks, a restaurant, nightly barbecues, a shop and bicycle rental.

➜ Paleochora 730 01, +30 69 7922 8612
35.234, 23.6362 🏕

39 MILIA MOUNTAIN RETREAT

A eco-settlement of converted 16th-century shepherds' cottages nestled in the White Mountains' trail-threaded foothills. Most food is grown on site, and organic and renewable are guiding principles.

➜ Vlatos 730 12, +30 2821 046774
35.4127, 23.6637 🏡🏕

40 CABANON CONCRETE RETREAT

Contemporary concrete cabins created by Greek artist Antonis and Swedish art curator Sofia. Everything here is elegant, minimal and close to nature; you are even invited to pick your own seasonal veg from the garden every day.

➜ Kissamos 734 00, +30 69 7297 1174
35.4642, 23.7014 🏔🏕

41 VILLA ROKKA

A modern villa with a pool, jacuzzi, outdoor cinema and wood oven enjoying sensational garden views of Rokka Gorge. Sleeps five.

➜ Rokka 734 00, +30 69 7192 0477, airbnb.com/rooms/23675249
35.4737, 23.7334 🏔🏕

42 ZOURVA STONE HOUSE

An exquisite century-old stone house hidden in the heart of the White Mountains in the tiny village of Zourva, with room for five. A rustic terrace overlooks the cypress-lined gorge below.

➜ Zourva 730 05, airbnb.com/rooms/11691832
35.3852, 23.9628 🏔🏕

43 METOHI KINDELIS

Three apartments in an elegantly restored 16th-century Venetian farmhouse surrounded by organic orchards. Each has its own pool, patio and garden for al fresco dining.

➜ Chania 731 00, metohi-kindelis.gr
35.4944, 24.0043 🏔€

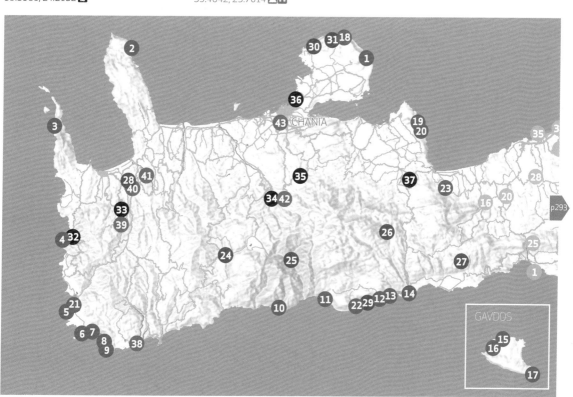

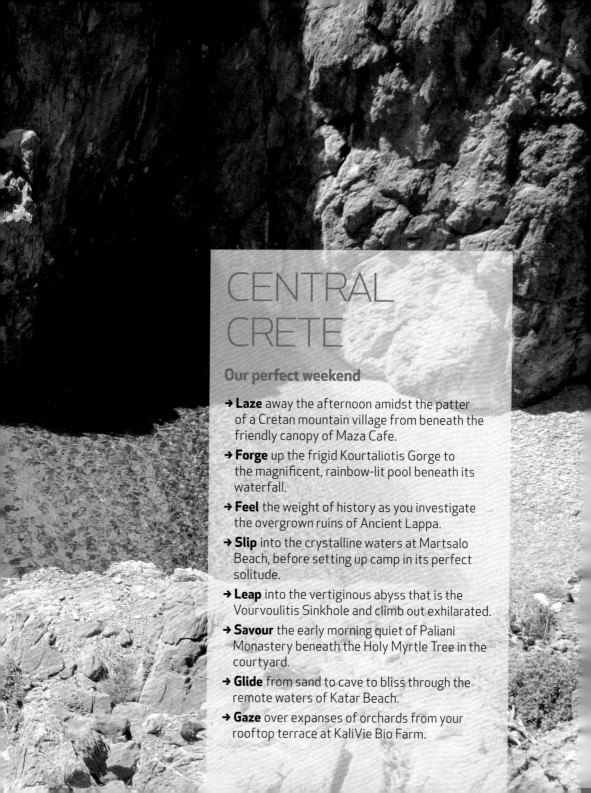

CENTRAL CRETE

Our perfect weekend

→ **Laze** away the afternoon amidst the patter of a Cretan mountain village from beneath the friendly canopy of Maza Cafe.

→ **Forge** up the frigid Kourtaliotis Gorge to the magnificent, rainbow-lit pool beneath its waterfall.

→ **Feel** the weight of history as you investigate the overgrown ruins of Ancient Lappa.

→ **Slip** into the crystalline waters at Martsalo Beach, before setting up camp in its perfect solitude.

→ **Leap** into the vertiginous abyss that is the Vourvoulitis Sinkhole and climb out exhilarated.

→ **Savour** the early morning quiet of Paliani Monastery beneath the Holy Myrtle Tree in the courtyard.

→ **Glide** from sand to cave to bliss through the remote waters of Katar Beach.

→ **Gaze** over expanses of orchards from your rooftop terrace at KaliVie Bio Farm.

Central Crete is dominated by the relentless mountain terrain of the Psiloritis massif. The highest peak and mythical nursery of Zeus, Mount Ida, is a serious hike, but there are plenty of more accessible ancient caves, seasonal waterfalls and deep gorges connected by a criss-cross of beguiling mountain lanes. Further south, breathtaking beaches and geological wonders mark where the Asterousia Mountains crash into the Libyan Sea. Throughout, scattered Neolithic, Minoan, Mycenaean and Roman relics whisper of a long human history.

Heraklion's archeological site of Knossos, populated since the Neolithic and epicentre of Minoan culture, is the region's most famous and popular historical monument. But wilder remnants await. The bewitching woodland relics of Ancient Lappa were once part of a powerful Mycenaean town. Matala's beach caves, carved as homes in the Neolithic period, have since sheltered Roman corpses and sixties hippies. Gria Mantra's eerie, ivy-clad tombs date back to Roman rule, while Paliani Monastery's Holy Myrtle Tree embodies both Crete's steadfast Orthodox heritage and ancient Minoan tree worship.

Enticing gorges carve the terrain west of Mount Ida. Mili Gorge, near Rethymno, takes its name from its many ivy-tangled mill ruins. Pastos Gorge's higgledy-piggledy via ferrata goes well with an evening by Amari Reservoir at its lower end. And Kourtaliotis Gorge offers an enchanting waterfall-swimming expedition, for those who dare.

Superb and disarmingly simple Cretan cuisine, often farm-to-table or foraged, is never far away here. Castello Taverna and Agreco Farm are highlights, while for full immersion, Enagron's luxurious but rustic reconstructed ecotourism village is a wonderful base.

Central Crete's otherworldly southern coastline holds abundant adventures. Agiofarago and Martsalo, two gorge-mouth beaches bookended by towering headlands within the protected park of Agiofarago Martsalo Kefali, are two of Crete's most sumptuous wild camps. Just a short scramble from Agiofarago Beach, the vertiginous Vourvoulitis Sinkhole is the island's most spectacular wild swim.

Further east, Virgin Vithanos Church and St Nikitas Beach capture the Cretan synergy between religious reflection and coastal seclusion. Nearby Katar Beach, Kaminaki Beach and the towering Aba Waterfall exemplify the oases hiding in this orange rockscape. The highlight though, awaiting the intrepid, is a swim through the glimmering passages of Sfakias Sea Caves.

BEACHES

1 KALYPSO BEACH

Not a beach as such, but a mini fjord with
excellent jumping, swimming and snorkelling
in its calm, crystal waters. It's organised,
with sunbeds to rent, but the unique setting
makes it a great day out.

→ Park on the street in the Kalypso village
resort just above the beach – you do not have
to be a resort guest.

2 mins, 35.1723, 24.4005 ⬛⬛Ⓑ⬛

2 PREVELI BEACH

This distinctive beach and old hippie haunt is
characterised by a palm grove extending up
Preveli Gorge; venture in for pools and mini
falls. The busy beach itself also features a
jetty, rock pools and a cafe.

→ From Lefkogeia head E 650m and turn
R (35.1808, 24.4526) signed for Preveli
Monastery. After 2km a L turn does lead to
beach access from the E, but for the best
views continue straight 2.2km, past the
monastery, then take a L fork down to a car
park (€2) perched on the cliff to the W of
the beach.

10 mins, 35.1524, 24.4742 ⬛⬛Ⓑ

3 VATHI BEACH

A relaxed beach at the end of a long, dusty
road. Its protected water is calm, with cliffs
for jumping and a small cave on the northern
edge, and a row of trees provides shade.

→ A 4x4 is advisable. Follow the road S from
Silvas towards Cape Lithinon for 14km, keeping
R passing the monastery at 6km, turning R on
a bend at 11km (34.9442, 24.7641) and then
again on a switchback shortly after. Park in the
shade behind the beach.

2 mins, 34.952, 24.7546 ⬛⬛⬛

4 MARTSALO BEACH

Cretan palms, pristine water and a narrow
jetty give the feel of a perfectly planned
hideaway. A stunning refuge.

→ 4x4 recommended. Follow the route for Vathi
Beach (see entry) but as the road descends at
about 11km (34.9445, 24.7672) take a track up
L and park by the church at the end. Walk 1km
directly down the gorge, passing the steps up to
Virgin Martsalos Church (see entry) at the start,
and through the trees to the beach.

60 mins, 34.93, 24.7705 ⬛⬛⬛⬛⬛⬛⬛

5 AGIOFARAGO BEACH

Wild camping spots abound throughout this
atmospheric gorge and at the sublime beach
cradled between imposing walls at its mouth.
After a morning dip, nearby St Antonios
Chapel in the gorge also warrants a visit.

→ About 3km N out of Kaloi Limenes on the
road to Sivas, turn L (34.9485, 24.7956) onto
a smaller dirt road that snakes SW along the
valley side to a parking area with Kuna Muta
food truck (see entry). From here walk on
through Agiofarago Gorge to the beach.

20 mins, 34.9256, 24.7782 ⬛⬛⬛

6 STENA BEACH

Stena, meaning strait, refers to the narrow
azure moat separating the sand and pebble
beach from the huge rock island dominating
the cove.

→ At the W end of Kaloi Limenes, take
a smaller L fork onto a coastal road and
continue 550m past the main beach on the L,
ignoring all L turns, and park on the side of the
road leading down to the cove.

2 mins, 34.927, 24.7984 ⬛⬛

7 KATAR BEACH

A small, remote beach nestled between the
walls of a small gorge. A cave offers shade,
and the sumptuous water leads to sea caves
on both sides, as well as rocks for jumping.
Well worth the sweaty hike.

5

11

12

→ A rough and poorly marked 2km coastal hike from Trypiti Beach to the W, which lies at the end of a twisty 9.5km road S from Vasliki. There is also car access from the E, forking L off the road to Trypiti after 7.5km and a set of switchbacks (34.9475, 24.9924), but a 4x4 is advisable for this.
60 mins, 34.9327, 25.0067

8 KAMINAKI BEACH

It doesn't get quieter than this sublime canyon-mouth beach, hidden in Crete's wildest stretch of coastline and only accessible by boat.

→ The nearest harbour is Tris Ekklisies to the W, itself a pretty village with a beach, where there are many small locally owned boats.
1 min, 34.9538, 25.1775

9 ST NIKITAS BEACH

A bright blue bay framed by severe orange cliffs, sitting in solitude beneath a monastery. Emblematic of the magic hidden deep in this untamed stretch of Cretan coastline.

→ Dusty dirt tracks wind for around 15km broadly clockwise from NE Achentrias (34.9948, 25.2264). Park by the monastery (still in use, and you can visit) and follow the steps down.
5 mins, 34.9642, 25.255

10 LISTIS BEACH

This pristine and easily accessible beach has many large rocks for jumping at its eastern end.

→ Head W for about 2km along the coast road from the marina in W Keratokampos. Park in a layby on the L on a bend and walk 50m down to the R of the rocky headland.
2 mins, 34.9902, 25.3554

WILD WATERS

11 KOURTALIOTIS WATERFALL

A short gorge expedition up to this waterfall plunge pool is a magical experience – rainbows shimmer through the mist, and the roar adds to the sense of secrecy. Retreat to the small beach below for secluded paddling beneath mossy falls.

→ Follow the road E from Asomatos 1.7km and park in the layby on the R (35.1944, 24.4638). Follow a paved path 100m N and head R through the arch. After another 100m take the lesser-trodden R fork down to paddle or swim at the plunge pool. The L fork leads to a chapel and stone bridge looking down on the falls. Secure footwear is advisable.
15 mins, 35.1969, 24.4663

12 AMARI RESERVOIR

Also called Potamon, this large, picturesque lake cradled in rolling hills was created by a dam in 2008. The shore is a haven for insects and amphibians, and visited by herons and coots. Patsos Gorge (see entry) descends to the southern tip of the lake.

→ Easy parking at either end of the dam at the N end. It's possible to drive around the whole lake, with several areas to pull off by the shore, but be careful with small cars on the dirt-track sections around the S edge.

2 mins, 35.2788, 24.5707 ⛰🏕🚶

13 VOURVOULITIS SINKHOLE

This spectacular, vertiginous sinkhole seems a black abyss before the sun kisses it. It is in fact a swimmable pool, connected to the sea by an underwater tunnel. The sides are a steep scramble, but for the sure-footed and intrepid, plunging from the surrounding rocks into its dark depths is utterly exhilarating.

→ The sinkhole is 50m above the E end of Agiofarago Beach (see entry). A path starts 300m up the gorge from the beach, or you can scramble right up and over from the beach. Proceed with caution; sound footwear is essential.

30 mins, 34.9255, 24.7801 🍴🐠🅻🆅

14 ABA WATERFALL

An epically tall cataract appears here in spring, hurtling from the edge of the gorge wall to the ground below. You will not be disappointed if your timing is right.

→ Follow the road SE from Paranimfi village 550m, past the cemetery, and turn R at the crossroads. Ignore smaller tracks immediately L and then R, and continue 750m to a viewpoint at the end, parking by the watermill ruins.

3 mins, 34.9646, 25.1320 🏞⛰🌲

15 SFAKIAS SEA CAVES

A sublime string of interlinked, swimmable sea caves, almost entirely unvisited due to their remoteness and tricky access. A rare gem awaiting the intrepid.

→ Easiest access by far is by boat; enquire about a rental or ride at Tsoutsouros marina. But land access is possible. Follow the road for St Nikita's Beach (see entry), but instead of taking the final turn to the monastery, continue 2km W and fork L (34.9607, 25.2370). Park at the end, by the buildings, and skirt round them to scramble down to the water's edge and swim to the caves.

1 min, 34.9577, 25.2335 🏊🏖⛰🅻❓🌅🐚

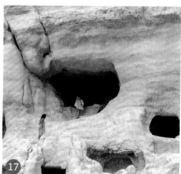

11

13

CAVES

16 ANCIENT LAPPA

Lappa was reputedly founded by Mycenaean King Agamemnon, flourished under Roman rule and is now the village of Argyroupolis. You can see foundations and a mosaic floor in the village, and the accessible chambers of the cemetery lie in quiet, shady woodland below.

→ There is some parking space by the road at the signed 100m footpath NE of Argiroupoli (35.2917, 24.3398). Alternatively park in the village by the church and preserved ruins (35.2857, 24.3352) and follow the road N 550m to a paved path that leads 300m down, crossing a road by a church, to the signed path. Mosaic at 35.2865, 24.3349.

3 mins, 35.2932, 24.3427 ⛵✝🏊🏃

17 MATALA CAVES

These Neolithic caves are a charming adventure despite being besieged by tourist infrastructure. Down the centuries they were inhabited by Romans and most recently hippies. A 10m cliff out to sea will also please daredevils.

→ There are several car parks in the village, some free. The caves are at the N end of the beach.

5 mins, 34.9952, 24.7491 ⛵🍴🅱🏃

18 GRIA MANTRA

A cluster of around 30 ivy-draped Roman tombs carved into the cliffs in the mountain village of Agios Thomas. One tomb doubles as a chapel.

→ There is free roadside parking as you enter the N end of the village from the W (35.1470, 25.0347), from where the tombs are signposted up the hill.

2 mins, 35.1466, 25.0337 ⛵✝🏊🏃

19 SKOTINO CAVE

Take good shoes and a torch to explore this huge, sleepy cave. It was an ancient Minoan place of worship, probably to a fertility goddess, and later became associated with St Paraskevi, with a church to her above.

→ Signed from the road on a hairpin bend 1.3km SW of Skotino village (35.2913, 25.3038). Follow the lane (which becomes a track towards the end) 2km and park by the church.

2 mins, 35.3048, 25.2976 🏃🏃

SACRED PLACES

20 ST ANTHONY CHURCH

One of Crete's numerous cave chapels dedicated to St Anthony, many of which are in this area. This one is wooden, built discreetly inside a cave in the heart of the cypress wood covering Roustika Gorge.

→ Park at the bridge on a sharp turn in the road about 1.5km out of Roustika towards Palelimnos (35.2923, 24.3838). A small footpath heads N from the E side of the bridge. Go through the gate and climb the steps to the entrance.

5 mins, 35.2932, 24.3839 ✝🏃

21 KERAMOTA PLANE TREE

Locals use the hollow trunk of this 2,000-year-old plane tree as a shrine. Although it is by the road, many miss it because you drive past the upper branches. A welcome pause if passing by, especially if the cute cafe next door is open.

→ The tree sits just off the road as it climbs into Keramota village from the E. Look for a small white block building tucked into the cliff; the tree is below this. Park where you can and walk down. There is a path down from the village, starting below the church.

2 mins, 35.3311, 24.7419 ✝🏃

22 VIRGIN MARTSALOS CHURCH

Built into a cave overlooking Martsalo Gorge, this early chapel was lost behind landslides

and rediscovered by shepherds in the 19th century. A bell and tree mark the entrance. Inside, frescos adorn the stone walls and a chandelier hangs from a domed roof 30m above.

→ Follow the directions for Martsalo Beach (see entry). For a longer hike, start at the parking for Agiofarago Beach (see entry) and go through a gap in the fence just S of Kuna Muta food truck (see entry). A footpath, poorly marked with red dots, starts here, heading W over the ridge.

10–50 mins, 34.9408, 24.7718 🐚🏖️🥾

23 VIRGIN VITHANOS CHURCH

This 1765 church affords panoramic views from its mountainous recess. Holy water drips from the ceiling – a gift, so the legend goes, from the Virgin Mary, after a shepherd found her icon here.

→ Follow the road S from Krotos village towards the port of Agios Faulos for 2.6km and park at the start of the 200m track to the church (34.9404, 24.9540). Walk the remainder.

5 mins, 34.9396, 24.952 ✝️⛰️

24 HOLY MYRTLE OF PALIANI

Paliani Monastery, built in the 5th century,

is one of Crete's oldest. An early morning stroll among its shrubbery is a delight, and this tree is the crowning glory. The branches are festooned with offerings, because an icon of the Virgin Mary purportedly rests within its trunk, and it is celebrated on 23rd September.

→ The monastery lies about 1.5km from Venerato village, on twisting roads to the SE. There is a car park. Enter the gates and head R to find the tree at the back.

2 mins, 35.1906, 25.0428 ✝️

GORGES & PEAKS

25 KYRIMIANOU PEAK

An accessible 805m peak giving spectacular views of Crete's southern coastline. Three small plateaus at the top, scattered with the remains of ancient buildings, will appeal to hardy wild campers or twitchers seeking the birds of prey circling beneath.

→ Take the dirt road SE from Kanevos and park in the layby on the L just outside the village. Walk the dirt path 2.4km to the end, passing a church on the R, a farm building on the L and one gate. When the path ends, it's a Grade 1 scramble up the NE side.

45 mins, 35.2145, 24.411 ⛰️🏕️🥾📷

26 MILI GORGE

A secretive tangle of crumbling, vine-ensnared mills and chapels abandoned in the 1970s. Stream and waterfall with plunge pool at the northern end all year round. Bring swimming gear and a picnic.

➔ Follow the road from Rethymno S towards Chromonastiri 4.2km and park carefully on the hard shoulder on the R, opposite a signed path down into the gorge (35.3375, 24.5038). A longer path with a small parking space starts at 35.3344, 24.5060.

5 mins, 35.3385, 24.5055 🏊🚶

27 PATSOS GORGE

This moody gorge and its water features are fun to explore, with ropes and ladders for help. There is plenty to explore, including a cave chapel to visit. It's fairly short, at just 2km, but can get rugged and wet after rain, so wear sound footwear. A popular taverna opposite the entrance offers replenishment – reserving in advance advisable at busy times.

➔ Signed from the road from Pantanassa to Prasies 1.4km W of the turning for Patsos village (35.2516, 24.5663). Follow 550m to the S end of the gorge and park just N of the taverna.

2 hrs, 35.2594, 24.5707 ✝🚶🏊

LOCAL FOOD & DRINK

28 CASTELLO TAVERNA

This quintessential taverna, led by charismatic host Vassilis, oozes hospitality and local produce. Ingredients are mostly grown on the family farm or foraged locally. Guests can join foraging tours and support the September wine-making process, all before a delicious Cretan lunch.

➔ Kastellos 741 00, +30 697 2801688 35.3088, 24.4484 🍴

29 AGIA FOTIA TAVERNA

Diners can literally jump into the azure sea from this excellent taverna. Ask for the catch of the day and enjoy the views. There are rooms too.

➔ Agia Fotini 740 53, +30 697 4621286 35.1447, 24.513 🏊🏠

30 AGRECO FARM

A traditional farm estate in the Rethymno foothills with an olive press, watermill, wine cellar and cacophony of animals. Take a tour or play farmer for a day, learning skills from wood-oven bread baking to sheep shearing. Or simply dine at the taverna serving organic

recipes made with farm flour, vegetables, fruits and herbs. Reservations required.

→ Adele 741 00, +30 283 1072129
35.3484, 24.5681 🍴🔺

31 ARAVANES TAVERNA

This wonderful mountain taverna and inn has its own fresh fruit and vegetable gardens and views across the lush Amari Valley. Pick any number of the dishes and finish with mountain tea.

→ Thronos 740 61, +30 283 3022760
35.2572, 24.6431 🔺

32 KUNA MUTA

A friendly man offering cold and hot drinks and simple Greek snacks from his truck. Perfect shady refreshment before and after forging on to the wonderful beaches of this Cretan corner (especially if you bag the hammock swinging outside).

→ Festos 704 00
34.9371, 24.7813 🐚

33 PESKESI

This sustainable, farm-to-table restaurant earns rave reviews for its fascinating blend of Cretan and Minoan-inspired recipes. Try the zucchini flowers and smoked pork, indulge in some olive oil tasting and digest a wonderful experience with their renowned raki.

→ Heraklion 712 02, +30 281 0288887
35.3403, 25.1325 🍴🔺💶

34 STILIANOU WINERY

A boutique family winery producing organic wines and olive oil. The fourth-generation owner leads tours and tastings with classic Cretan warmth.

→ Kounavi 701 00, +30 693 6430368
35.2359, 25.1914 🍴🔺

STAY

35 SUTOR CHIC MANOR

A luxurious hotel in a converted manor in the bustling heart of Rethymno's Old Town, under the walls of Fortezza fortress, with a beautifully crafted courtyard pool. A splendid option if you're after a city base.

→ Rethymno 741 00, +30 698 7190740
35.3704, 24.4734 🖲

36 ELIZABETH CAMPING

Clean beachfront camping, glamping and bungalows with a taverna, nearby shops and watersports. On the fringes of Rethymno, this is a good option for balancing city and camping life.

→ Rethymno 741 00, +30 283 1028694
35.3691, 24.5152 ▣

37 ALTERA CAVE VILLAS

A handful of stylish, secluded modern hideaways built into the hillside overlooking the sea. Take a dip in your private pool or at your (almost) private beach 200m down the hill.

→ Lampi 740 53, +30 697 3328972
35.1056, 24.5781 ▣

38 KAPSALIANA VILLAGE HOTEL

This elegant, pared-back haven set amidst Crete's largest olive groves was restored from the ruins of a historic settlement. The gastronomic delights on offer from award-winning chef Nikos Thomas alone make it worth staying here.

→ Kapsaliana 741 00, +30 283 1083400
35.3394, 24.6199 🖲

39 MERONAS ECO HOUSE

A traditional, higgledy-piggledy abode centred around a canopied stone courtyard and teeming with rustic paraphernalia, with space for five. Manolis, the owner, produces and sells olive oil, honey and soap in the village.

→ Méronas 740 61, +30 698 5120285
35.2361, 24.6300 ▣

40 ENAGRON ECOTOURISM VILLAGE

This reconstructed Greek village produces its own olive oil, raki and other delicious produce using traditional methods. Take part in regular farm activities, visit the spa and enjoy the taverna, built around a large fire pit with fantastic views of vultures circling the gorge.

→ Rethymno 740 51, +30 283 4061611
35.3143, 24.838 ▣▣

41 KALIVIE BIO FARM

A humble, affordable farm stay for four. One studio room plus a bathroom, but with a wonderful roof terrace looking over the expanse of orange, pomegranate and pear orchards that envelop it to the distant hills.

→ Moíraí 704 00, +30 698 4472933
35.0263, 24.8814 ▣

42 KTIMA ORGONIS

Four rustic stone cottages with gardens and terraces, cradled by the owners' organic farm and the mountains beyond.

→ Apostoli 700 06, +30 697 4891750
35.2194, 25.2963 ▣

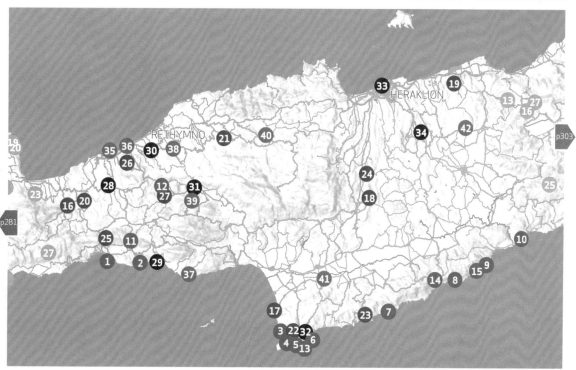

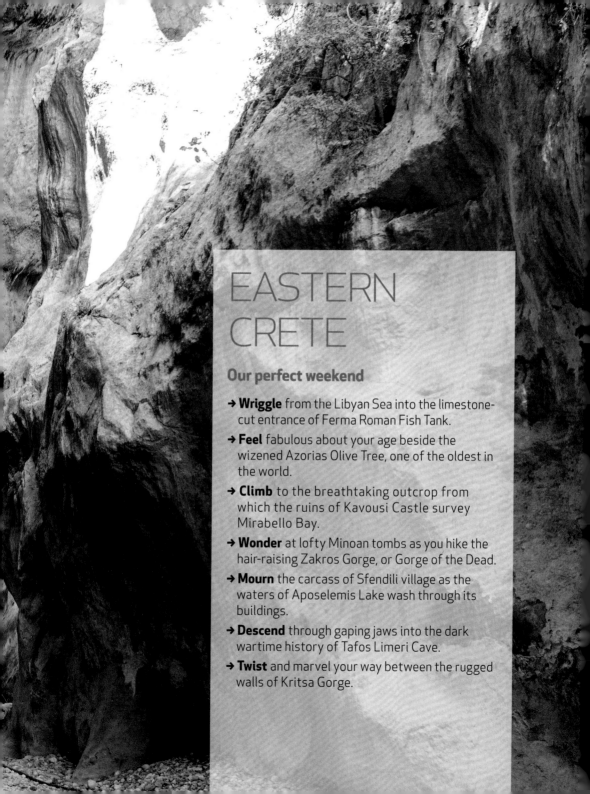

EASTERN CRETE

Our perfect weekend

→ **Wriggle** from the Libyan Sea into the limestone-cut entrance of Ferma Roman Fish Tank.

→ **Feel** fabulous about your age beside the wizened Azorias Olive Tree, one of the oldest in the world.

→ **Climb** to the breathtaking outcrop from which the ruins of Kavousi Castle survey Mirabello Bay.

→ **Wonder** at lofty Minoan tombs as you hike the hair-raising Zakros Gorge, or Gorge of the Dead.

→ **Mourn** the carcass of Sfendili village as the waters of Aposelemis Lake wash through its buildings.

→ **Descend** through gaping jaws into the dark wartime history of Tafos Limeri Cave.

→ **Twist** and marvel your way between the rugged walls of Kritsa Gorge.

Far from the island's major travel hubs, Crete's eastern reaches feel relatively remote, even forgotten. The landscape isn't quite as geologically dramatic here, but there are still intriguing ridgeline ruins and rugged gorge trails aplenty to entice you upwards, and spooky caves and strings of secluded beaches to tempt you back down.

Just west of chic and charming Agios Nikolaos, the narrow, twisting walls of Kritsa Gorge guide a shaded quest on a hot day, with plunge pools until early summer. For a darker outing, be swallowed by the gaping entrance of nearby Tafos Limeri Cave, site of the tragic betrayal of Greek guerrilla fighters during the Nazi occupation. The wild gorges and walks here demand proper footwear and plenty of water.

The entanglement of history and nature continues south-east. The almighty Azorias Olive Tree is among the world's oldest, and its branches were used for olive wreaths during the 2004 Athens Olympics. High above this majestic tree, at 710m, sit the atmospheric Dark Age ruins of Kavousi Castle, with breathtaking views across Mirabello Bay that amply reward the sharp ascent. Swing by Natural Taverna, entirely organic, on the way home.

Crete's eastern coastline boasts a multitude of remote beaches with calm waters, from Irini in the south to Psili Ammos in the north. Sandwiched between is the imposing Zakros Gorge, or 'Gorge of the Dead', named after the Minoan cave tombs in its walls. Pelekita Cave, a 90-minute coastal walk north, is another highlight, receding in pitch-black eeriness from its dramatic sea-view entrance, with treasures to reveal under torchlight. Keen hikers can continue to Karoumes Beach, arguably eastern Crete's most rugged.

Delightful and unusual escapades dot the rest of the region. To the west, the seasonally submerged ghost village of Sfendili stands as a melancholic memorial to places drowned by Greece's many reservoirs. In stark contrast, nearby Niki's Taverna exhibits Greek village life at its fullest. In the south, the Roman Fish Tank at Ferma is as curious a wild swim as any, while to the north-east, the year-round waterfall pool of temperate Richtis Gorge offers an oasis in a land of scorched beauty.

③

BEACHES

1 VRYONISI PATIO

This quirky spot feels like an abandoned private jetty, but is public. A permanent parasol provides shade on a tiled stone patio, with steps for sea access. Swim carefully amidst the breaking waves on the rocks.

➔ Follow EO90 from Istro 1.8km E and turn sharply L on a track just after the signed entrance to Mirabello Estate (35.1241, 25.7602). Follow the R fork 100m to a clearing and park. Walk back and follow the L fork 500m along cliffs to steps R down to the patio.

10 mins, 35.1281, 25.7613 🍴🏖🐚

2 AGRIOMANDRA BEACH

This sheltered beach was used as a Venetian port, as ruins of the old tax office attest. A tamarisk tree and wall caves provide shade.

➔ Follow signs for the beach for 2km along narrow lanes from W Kavousi (35.1219, 25.8552). Park just beyond the gate at the end, as the road deteriorates; it's an easy downhill walk from here through the gorge.

15 mins, 35.1304, 25.8322 🏊🏖🚶🏃

3 FERMA ROMAN FISH TANK

Also called Vothoni or Kakia Skala, this quirky historical relic makes an unusual dip, carved into soft sandstone complete with steps. Leap into the open sea and float carefully back into the shallow tank through the sluice openings. When the tank was built, sea levels were lower and only the highest waves would have washed through to refresh the water.

➔ Turn S off the main coastal road SE of Koutsounari, on the bend by Kakkos Bay Hotel, and continue to a large space for parking. It's then a 50m scramble over rocks to the S.

2 mins, 35.0114, 25.8418 🍴🏊🏖🐚

4 IRINI BEACH

High walls enclose this quiet, reflective cove. A tree for shade and a fishing hut provide the only company.

➔ The road here from Kalo Chorio Church and its tiny village is 8.5km and in bad condition, so unless you have a 4x4 avoid it. Better to hike in along the 2.5km coastal path from the S end of Amatos Beach (see entry).

45 mins, 35.0229, 26.1954 🏊🏖🚶🏕🐚

5 AMATOS BEACH

A small, open bay dotted with fishing boats and overlooked by a tall and rugged headland.

➔ S of Xerokampos village, take the fork signed (if coming from the W) 'Beach'. Follow it 2.3km along the coast as it becomes a dirt track and leads right down to the beach.

2 mins, 35.0282, 26.209 🏊🏖

6 ALONA BEACH

The dunes behind this large sandy beach are speckled with tufts of long grass, sea thistles and, in autumn, white sea daffodils that are magically scented when evening falls. Please don't be tempted to pick them, they are protected!

➔ Bear R off the coast road on the L bend just NE of Xerokampos (35.0526, 26.2364) and follow the track 1.1km, bending R then hairpinning back L, to a clearing at the end. Park here and walk 100m to the beach.

5 mins, 35.0581, 26.2427 🏊🏖🏕🌲🐚

7 KAROUMES BEACH

An expansive, exposed arc of shingle backed by windswept vegetation pocked with wells. Feels far from anywhere.

➔ Heading S through Chochlakies, take the signed L on a big bend (35.1465, 26.2464) and continue through the village to park by the church at the end (35.1464, 26.2498). Take the track heading E from just N of the

church through the olive grove and into pretty Chochlakie Gorge, which leads to the beach. From autumn to spring there will be water in the gorge.

60 mins, 35.1463, 26.2764

8 SKINIAS BEACH

Three pristine, secluded coves and a series of sea caves. Snorkel in the protected waters from the central beach, and head 200m right to investigate the caves.

→ Turn E off the tarmac road about 2km SW of Palekastro (35.1857, 26.2506). Follow the rough road R after 190m, keep L at two forks then R at one. About 1km beyond this it becomes rougher; park and walk the 1.5km to the beach.

20 mins, 35.1692, 26.2815

9 MARIDATI BEACH

Bookended by empty headlands and backed by tamarisk trees and reed fronds, this sweep of shingle is best enjoyed after fresh seafood and live music at Maridatis Taverna, just behind the trees (+30 2843 061055).

→ The taverna and beach are signed from the road just N of Viglia. Parking is available just behind the beach.

2 mins, 35.2216, 26.2734

10 KOKKINOS KAVOS BEACH

The name means 'red cape', and you can see why as you descend from the headland onto this deserted beach and into the embrace of a warm and calming hue.

→ Follow a steep, poorly marked path N over the headland from Maridati Beach (see entry).

45 mins, 35.2294, 26.2731

11 PSILI AMMOS BEACH

A long, sloping tongue of sand, lined with squat trees. Much quieter than neighbouring Vai Beach, though be aware there is a strong nudist presence.

→ Park at Vai Beach (€2.50) and follow the staircase up to the viewpoint from the S end and 250m over the headland.

10 mins, 35.2511, 26.2673

12 ITANOS BEACH

This lovely cove has large palms for shade and the ancient ruins of Itanos guarding at the northern end. A great alternative to packed Vai Beach down the road.

→ Follow the road N past the turning for Vai Beach for 1.5km to the end, at sandy parking for the ruins. Walk S for 250m along the coast, via the ruins (or 150m

N for equally beautiful, though busier, Erimoupolis Beach).

5 mins, 35.262, 26.2639 🏊🚣🚲

LAKES & WATERFALLS

13 ABANDONED SFENDILI

This reservoir is a product of the Aposelemi dam built here in 2012–14. Its victim, the village of Sfendili, dates back to the 16th century but now sits abandoned in its waters, emerging and submerging with the seasonal changes in level. Investigating its abandoned buildings, including a Byzantine church, is an eerie experience.

➜ The road from Avdou N up the E side of the reservoir leads directly to the sunken village.
2 mins, 35.245, 25.4104 🏔

14 MILONAS WATERFALL

A pleasant gorge walk incorporating an old aqueduct. The shaded falls are 40m high in spring and early summer, feeding a pool to cool off in.

➜ The falls are signed from a hairpin bend just W of Ferma. Follow 1.9km, keeping R at a fork after 1.3km and doubling back across the gorge to park in a small layby (35.0296, 25.8445). The trailhead is signposted from here.
10 mins, 35.0357, 25.8449 🏊🚶

15 RICHTIS WATERFALL

This temperate woodland walk over root and under bough starts by a beach and culminates in a plunge pool beneath a pretty 20m waterfall that flows down a mossy rock year round.

➜ Follow the road N from Exo Mouliana village to Richtis Beach, parking at the sharp L bend just before the final descent to the sand (35.1934, 25.9842). Follow the path S along the gorge.
30 mins, 35.1851, 25.9864 🏊🚶

GORGES

16 ROZA GORGE

A dramatic offshoot of Ambelos Gorge, with pink oleander bushes filling the bed. It offers a fine hike along the side wall (the bottom is too steep and uneven and frequently wet), with spectacular views from the start.

➜ For the lower entrance, take the signed road at the W edge of Gonies (35.2294, 25.4392) 700m to the car park, keeping L twice. For the upper entrance, about 450m S of Ano Kera village take a track forking R downhill off the road at a bend, and park at the R turn after 100m (35.2171, 25.4585). From

here it's a 10-min walk down switchbacks to the starting viewpoint.
3 hrs, 35.2172, 25.4544 🏔🚶

17 SARAKINA GORGE

An accessible gorge explorable in an hour via pools (in the spring), ropes and notched steps. Its sheer, water-sculpted walls are mostly less than 10m apart and up to 150m tall.

➜ Head NE from Mithi village and take the L turning after about 1km to parking at the S end.
60 mins, 35.0486, 25.5768 🚶

18 KRITSA GORGE

This beautiful gorge, 4km long and at points just 1.5m wide, offers a beguiling, shady wander on a hot day. Pools may punctuate the route in spring. The trail is very well marked, and via ferrata assists the exploration, as there are some boulders to clamber over. At the end you can return along the ridge above to the right.

➜ On the road NE from Kritsa, at the E end of a bridge on a bend about 500m out, a track leads N to a raised olive grove with a clearing where you can park (35.1641, 25.6481). A marked footpath leads NW from here into the gorge.
3 hrs, 35.165, 25.6465 🏊🚶

19 MESONAS GORGE

A marvellous, sometimes hair-raising walk tracing an old aqueduct along the gorge side. The riverbed below has many waterfalls, with sections requiring proper canyoning equipment.

➜ Azoria Archeological Site is signed from the main road just E of Kavousi. Follow the road 3km and turn R just after the Azoria entrance on the L. Park about 70m up the track at a bend (35.1157, 25.8668). A 3.5km walk leads SE along the aqueduct.

2 hrs, 35.1114, 25.8722

20 ZAKROS GORGE

Beautiful and accessible, the 'Gorge of the Dead' is so named because the Minoans interred their dead in the caves high up in its steep cliffs. A jaunt along its edge provides vertiginous views into this winding crack in the earth, while the easternmost end of the E4 hiking trail across the island runs below. Both lead to Kato Zakros, a seaside village with Minoan ruins and a shingle beach where you can hire a taxi back if you want.

➜ Find a car park and sign on the road 2.3km SE from the upper, inland village of Zakros (35.0968, 26.2354). From here two paths head E. Take the R track, and after 150m the path L off it, for the view from the top; take the L path at the other end of the parking to hike the gorge floor.

90 mins, 35.0997, 26.2501

CAVES

21 TAFOS LIMERI CAVE

Shimmying into the steep, sunken entrance of this cave feels like being swallowed, and its damp, single-chamber interior, complete with bats, holds a dark history. Members of the EAM, the Greek guerrilla army during German occupation through the Second World War, sheltered here before being betrayed and executed in the cave. Bring a torch and good footwear and don't disturb the bats.

➜ At the S end of Kroustas take the lane W down the R side of the school and follow the twisting road 4km to a sharp R turn. The cave is a short scramble up and N from this road.

5 mins, 35.1184, 25.6398

22 PELEKITA CAVE

Reaching this cave's splendid mouth, gaping over the sea, is only the beginning of the adventure. Just inside, a narrow section opens into a huge second chamber descending 300m into the pitch black, replete with all kinds of fantastical flowstone features and slippery rocks. Proceed with extra caution, an excellent head torch and nerves of steel.

→ The cave is a 2.5km walk from the N end of Zakros, along a rugged but well-maintained coastal path.

45 mins, 35.1198, 26.2779 🅅 ⚲

CASTLES

23 KAVOUSI CASTLE

These intriguing ruins, dating back over 2700 years to the Greek Dark Ages, sit at 710m with astonishing views across Mirabello Bay to Agios Nikolaos and beyond. The sharp hike up through terraced farming is invigorating, and richly rewarded.

→ Signed from the main road at the E end of Kavousi. Continue 4.3km – forking L at 230m, bearing R on a L hairpin at 1.8km and ignoring smaller turns – and park in the layby on the R (35.1100, 25.8629). It's a steep 1km hike up a

footpath, which climbs R and then arcs L.

45 mins, 35.1111, 25.868 ⚲ ⚲

24 MONTE FORTE CASTLE

This 14th-century Venetian castle was built on the site of an earlier one destroyed by a 1303 earthquake, itself probably built on an earlier Byzantine fort. It sits with St George Church atop a dramatic outcrop at 585m, and is also called Apano Castelli, or the Upper Fort. Superb views above the still-imposing fort wall.

→ A dirt track leads from the road just E of Kato Kria village 2km directly to the castle, turning R after 800m, keeping L at the fork and taking a R at end 250m from the outcrop.

5 mins, 35.1187, 26.0367 ⚲ ⚲

TREES & PLATEAUS

25 SMALL OMALOS PLATEAU

This expansive plateau is a springtime lake and river, a place of grazing goats in summer and a winterland of howling winds and snow. A rugged break from Crete's golden sands, where several mountain walks start.

→ Drive the dirt road for around 11km NW from Kato Symi. This is the best route, albeit quite long and winding.

2 mins, 35.0714, 25.4538 ⚲ ⚲ ⚲

26 AZORIA OLIVE TREE

The gargantuan, gnarly trunk of this olive tree stretches 5m across. It is estimated to be around 3000 years old, making it one of the oldest in the world, and possibly the oldest surviving grafted tree.

→ Azoria Archeological Site is signed from the main road just E of Kavousi, and the tree is on the R after 2km. There are multiple laybys for free parking and a café next door.

2 mins, 35.1152, 25.8608 🦮🐾Ⓑ

LOCAL FOOD & DRINK

27 NIKI'S TAVERNA

Run by a friendly family, cooking traditional Cretan recipes in a wood oven, overlooking the valley below. Try the pork or lamb, if you eat meat. Quintessential mountain-taverna dining.

→ Ano Kera 700 05, +30 2897 051204
35.2198, 25.4602 🏔

28 O PLATANOS TAVERNA

A classic village-square taverna nestled under a huge plane tree. See what the waiter recommends and let the raki, laughter and possibly music flow.

→ Fourni 724 00, +30 2841 090776
35.2592, 25.6625 Ⓑ

29 NATURAL TAVERNA

Tucked away behind a church is an entirely organic restaurant using ingredients grown in their own garden. Reasonable prices, big portions, delicious food and stunning views.

→ Lastros 723 00, +30 69 4978 4659
35.1579, 25.8943 🍴🏔

30 BOGAZI TAVERNA

The fish at this seafront taverna is renowned, even in a fishing village rife with competition; the little cove is lit up come evening. Following the waiter's recommendation is a good bet.

→ Mochlos 720 57, +30 2843 094200
35.1848, 25.905 🏔🍲

31 HIONA TAVERNA

This romantic fish taverna has been sitting quietly on the water here for over 50 years, and serves slightly more gourmet dishes. Seafood soups are one of the specialities.

→ Chiona 723 00, +30 2843 061228
35.1996, 26.2777 🏔

STAY

32 TRADITIONAL WINDMILL MILOS

Spend a few nights in this sensitively converted stone windmill overlooking Kroutas village. The shaded terrace offers sweeping panoramic views over the lush garden to the mountains and coastline beyond. Sleeps four.

→ Kroustas 721 00, windmillmilos.
tripcombined.com
35.1423, 25.6584 🏔

33 MINOS BEACH ART HOTEL

Beautifully located on Mirabello Bay in Agios Nikolaos, and remarkably idyllic given its city access. The luxury rooms and villas offer fantastic sea views and waterside patios.

→ Agios Nikolaos 721 00, +30 2841 022345
35.1997, 25.7153 ⓒ

34 THE WHITE HOUSES

Converted fishermen's houses sitting by the harbour of a sleepy village, sleeping between two and seven. The interiors present a carefully curated fusion of Greek and Scandinavian decor.

→ Makry Gialos 720 55, +30 2843 029183
35.0371, 25.973 🏘

35 NATURA COTTAGES

Artistic cottages of higgledy-piggledy whitewashed stone and carved wood, all set in aromatic gardens and carob glades overlooking the Mediterranean.

→ Potamos 720 55, +30 69 8432 7574
35.0470, 25.9866 🏔

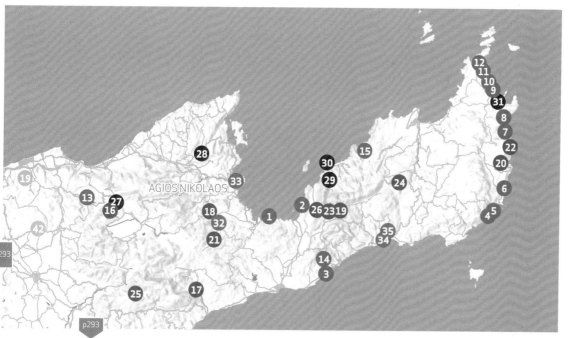

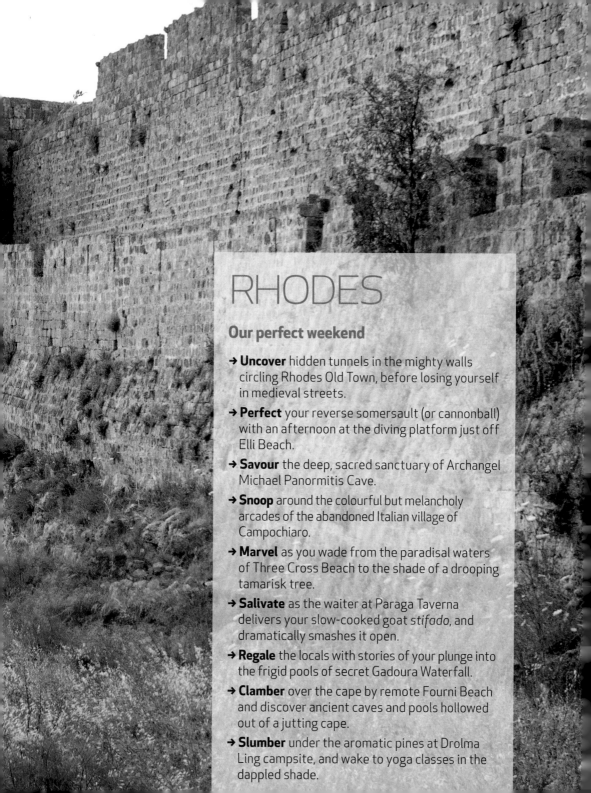

RHODES

Our perfect weekend

→ **Uncover** hidden tunnels in the mighty walls circling Rhodes Old Town, before losing yourself in medieval streets.

→ **Perfect** your reverse somersault (or cannonball) with an afternoon at the diving platform just off Elli Beach.

→ **Savour** the deep, sacred sanctuary of Archangel Michael Panormitis Cave.

→ **Snoop** around the colourful but melancholy arcades of the abandoned Italian village of Campochiaro.

→ **Marvel** as you wade from the paradisal waters of Three Cross Beach to the shade of a drooping tamarisk tree.

→ **Salivate** as the waiter at Paraga Taverna delivers your slow-cooked goat *stifado*, and dramatically smashes it open.

→ **Regale** the locals with stories of your plunge into the frigid pools of secret Gadoura Waterfall.

→ **Clamber** over the cape by remote Fourni Beach and discover ancient caves and pools hollowed out of a jutting cape.

→ **Slumber** under the aromatic pines at Drolma Ling campsite, and wake to yoga classes in the dappled shade.

Nicknamed the 'Island of Sun', after the sun god Helios, Rhodes is indeed one of Greece's hottest places. The island also harboured one of the seven wonders of the ancient world: the Colossus of Rhodes, a statue of the god that once dominated the port. Though that statue fell in an ancient earthquake, Rhodes remains replete with enticements both historical and, where its bustling eastern seaboard gives way to wilder land, intrepid.

Ferries to Rhodes dock in the Old Town, a UNESCO World Heritage Site sitting like a crown on the island's northern tip. Linger awhile, and walk the mighty, 12m-thick city walls, hunting for secret tunnels and marvelling at the moat now musical with birdsong. Another fine stroll follows the sunset-facing coastal path southwest via two remarkable cave churches – Archangel Michael Panormitis Cave and St Nikolaos Chapel – to the Acropolis of Rhodes and its imposing ancient Olympic Stadium.

When hunger strikes, make a beeline to Traditional Café Symi for fresh meze seafood at fantastic prices. Nearby Marco Polo is a little fancier, serving imaginative seafood, traditional dishes and desserts in an enchanting courtyard hushed by vibrant foliage. The finest meal on Rhodes, though, awaits in the foothills of Mount Profitis Ilias, at Paraga Taverna. Every dish here brims with local ingredients and tastes excellent, but the goat *stifado* – slow-cooked overnight in a bread-sealed clay pot and broken open at the table – will stay with you forever.

St Paul's Bay is one of the prettiest ports in Greece. Beneath the ancient gaze of the Lindos Acropolis, jump into azure waters almost entirely encircled by striking rock formations. For sandier and more secluded swims, either spectacular Three Cross Beach or the jumping ledges, ancient caves and hidden pools of Cape Fourni will comfortably fill a happy, hazy afternoon.

More energetic options await in Rhodes' rugged interior. The stratified rock formations and quirky pools of Jacob's Canyon provide a unique scrambling adventure, ascending the dry riverbed on the way out and descending as you return. Seven Springs is far more luscious, watered by seven year-round underground springs. There are trails aplenty here, but the highlight is the 186m-long tunnel through which spring water rushes to the lake. Walk it if you dare…

BEACHES

1 ELLI DIVING PLATFORM

At popular Elli Beach you will find a multi-tiered diving platform around 60m out at sea. A fun way to splash and bomb the hours away for kids and adults alike.

➜ Approach the beach from the old town and you can't miss the platform.

2 mins, 36.4540, 28.2247 🍴🏖️🐟️B

2 KATO PETRES BEACH

You won't feel like you're in town at this charming little spot. A small beach accessed via a lovely coastal path.

➜ Park behind Akti Kanari Beach on the NW edge of town and walk the coastal path 450m from the S end.

5 mins, 36.4436, 28.2083 🏖️🚶

3 TRAGANOU CAVES

The natural rock canopies of the caves at the tip of popular, pebbly Traganou Beach provide superb shady spots for a day by the clear water (and some seclusion from the sunbeds).

➜ Heading N on the EO95 turn R by the EKO garage, 1.9km past the junction at the N end of Afantou, and park behind the beach. Turn L; the caves are at the N end.

5 mins, 36.3104, 28.1948 🏖️🏖️🐟️B🏊

4 THREE CROSS BEACH

If you visit one beach on Rhodes, make it this one, with three crosses standing proudly on a rock at one end. A long curving beach, dotted with trees for welcome shade, frames a beautiful shallow bay. All this is backed by vertical layered cliffs, home to occasional intrepid goats. Bring supplies to last the day.

➜ Take the main track just under 3km S from E Archangelos, forking R twice. Park by the road at 36.1922, 28.1237 and take the path starting here down the hill. After 500m fork L and snake a further 500m to the beach, which appears dramatically.

15 mins, 36.1868, 28.1195 🏖️🏖️⛺🚶🐚

5 RED SAND BEACH

This gently sloping sandy beach develops a unique red hue where the waves meet land – a colour matched in the protective, sculpted cliffs close behind. A cracking and isolated beach.

➜ Scramble over the headland from the SW end of Three Cross Beach (see entry). The path is clear at first but soon disappears.

10 mins, 36.1842, 28.1167 🏖️🚶🐚

6 ST PAUL'S BAY

The Lindos Acropolis overlooks this developed but dramatic bay, which is almost entirely protected by natural breakwaters. Charming St Paul's Chapel sits on the southeastern side. Come before sunset for a swim and a drink, served to the beach by Tambakio (see entry).

➜ Just SE of Lindos; parking is free, the closest just to the S of the bay by the football pitch. Walk the 100m down to the beach from here.

5 mins, 36.0858, 28.0879 🍴🏖️🏖️⛰️🏖️B

7 NAVARONE BAY

A dramatic headland provides drama and evening shade at this unheralded beach just down the coast from Lindos. The water is perfect but rocky, so bring appropriate footwear.

➜ The turning off the coast road 1.6km S from Lindos has streetlamps and is signed St Nicolas Monastery. There are multiple parking areas thanks to the hotels at the N end of the beach. Take the footpath down to the beach and turn R towards the headland away from the sunbeds.

5 mins, 36.0753, 28.0757 🏖️

8 LIMNI BEACH

There is a natural shallow pool at this point along a majestic 5km stretch of beach – a perfect spot for the kids to paddle.

→ Follow Epar.Od. Ialisou Katavias 2.7km SW from Apolakkia and turn N onto the coast road. Follow it 2km and turn L to park in a clearing just behind the beach.

1 min, 36.0662, 27.7611 🏖️🚣

9 LACHANIA BEACH

A pair of wild, very quiet beaches separated by a jutting headland; walk to the top and take your pick.

→ Heading E from Plimmiri, turn R on the second obvious L bend (35.9321, 27.8565). Fork L onto a track at 200m, then L again at the next two junctions. Take the next R and continue 270m to park by a track leading R. Walk it 50m SE, where the path splits towards either beach.

5 mins, 35.9334, 27.8640 🏖️⛺

10 ST GEORGIOS BEACH

A sublime expanse of sandy beach guarded by gentle dunes. The most picturesque, secluded spot is a hidden cove at the southern end, over a small headland.

→ There are multiple access points from the dirt road that runs SW from Plimmiri. For parking, drive 3km to the end and turn L at the T junction. The hidden cove is at 35.9029, 27.8157.

2 mins, 35.9155, 27.8275 🏖️⛺🚣

11 PRASONISI BEACH

At the very southern tip of the island, this popular double-sided beach, dotted with windsurfers, almost stretches across to a small island you can wade to at low tide. For seclusion, cross to the coves on the island.

→ Follow the road from Kattavia S for 8km, passing the power plant on your R, to park on the beach. The best island beach is at 35.8812, 27.7644.

1 min, 35.888, 27.7717 🏖️🅱️

LAKES & WATERFALLS

12 GADOURA LAKE

The verdant hills of central Rhodes meet a tranquil lake here, with many a shady inlet to rest in. Relatively new, it is already a bird haven: look out for bee-eaters and crested grebe.

→ There is road access all around the lake, rough in places. The marked spot is 2km clockwise from the Gadoura dam.

2 mins, 36.1592, 27.9857 🔺🚶

13 GADOURA WATERFALL

An unexpected and serene waterfall in the heart of a forest. Best visited in spring as it usually runs dry in early summer.

→ Head 1.5km E from the Gadoura dam, turning away from the SE corner, and park where a rough trail leads L (36.1616, 28.0104). Take the path up a steep forested hill and follow it round to the R to an opening in the trees, where the path fades. Head straight for another 100m and, after a quick down and up, descend to the riverbed. The waterfall is 100m upstream.

20 mins, 36.1572, 28.0059 🚗🥾🧗🪜🐚

ANCIENT WONDERS

14 RHODES OLD TOWN

Designated a UNESCO World Heritage Site in 1988, this is the oldest inhabited medieval town in Europe. You can walk its full crescent perimeter, which is imposingly protected by gargantuan 12m-thick walls and an adjacent moat. The southern stretch is secluded, with secret tunnels.

→ Park outside the Old Town and enter via any of the ten fortified gates. The tunnel section is at 36.4403, 28.2264.

15 mins, 36.4403, 28.2264 🚲🚌🥾

15 OLYMPIC STADIUM

Built in the 2nd century BC, and situated on Rhodes Acropolis alongside an odeon, this stadium was excavated and restored by an Italian team during the early 20th century. Locals use it as a rousing workout spot.

→ Park opposite the entrance gates, just after Diagoridon bends L coming W from town (36.4399, 28.2095). You can also walk from town; it's under 2km from Rhodes Old Town (see entry).

5 mins, 36.4388, 28.212 🚲🚌 B

16 RODINI PARK

Probably the world's first landscaped park, today Rodini is a cool, tranquil haven for humans and peacocks, with picturesque paths weaving around a stream and Roman aqueduct.

→ Park at the main park entrance, forking R on the EO95 heading S out of Rhodes town (36.4266, 28.2212).

2 mins, 36.4262, 28.2182 🧍🚲🚌 B

17 MONOLITHOS CASTLE

Originally a Venetian watchtower, this ruined castle's cliff-top position affords stunning, far-reaching views over the forested coastline below.

19

17

18

→ Follow the road SW from Monolithos village and park after around 1.7km, on the first L hairpin by the taverna. Follow the track 50m. The best view of the castle itself is on the approach from Monolithos.

5 mins, 36.1244, 27.7262 🏖🛶🚲B

18 CAPE FOURNI

A series of ancient cave tombs and pools hollowed out of a jutting cape crowned with the stump of a 16th-century watchtower, in a quiet corner of the island. Over the cape from Fourni Beach is a tiny secluded beach, reachable on foot.

→ Continue SW 5km from Monolithos Castle (see entry); the road turns into a track and arrives at Fourni Beach. Park by the small food kiosk and walk to the L end of the beach and a short, winding path onto the cape. The caves are on the far side of the cape, towards its tip.

5 mins, 36.1041, 27.7371 🍴🏊🏖🚲🏊

SACRED PLACES

19 ARCHANGEL MICHAEL PANORMITIS CAVE

A tiny, tranquil and unique place of worship burrowed into the rock overlooking the sea, crammed with icons.

→ Follow the coastal path 350m N from Kato Petres Beach (see entry), or park in the adjacent layby on the coastal road.

1 min, 36.4457, 28.2112 🏔†🏃🏊

20 ST NIKOLAOS CHAPEL

A church carved into a rockface in a hidden corner of Rhodes. The serene entrance is bathed in dappled light, with a couple of benches strategically placed for quiet contemplation.

→ Heading W out of Rhodes on Diagoridon, turn R just before it bends L (36.4411, 28.2102) and park after 350m in a layby on the R, where steps descend to the hidden chapel.

2 mins, 36.4427, 28.2129 †

21 VIRGIN MARY TSAMBIKA MONASTERY

Three hundred steps lead to this tiny 18th-century monastery sitting atop a hill overlooking the sea. There is another monastery of the same name to the south-west.

→ Follow the EO95 S for 1.7km from the main crossroads at Kolymbia and take the first L after it bends R. Follow 1.2km and park by the taverna, where the steps start.

15 mins, 36.2358, 28.1495 🏔†🏰

GORGES

22 SEVEN SPRINGS

A stunning forested gorge fed by seven springs that run year-round. The most popular adventure is walking the narrow 200m underground tunnel that carries ankle-high spring water to a nearby lake (avoid if claustrophobic). Otherwise, take your pick from the many hiking trails.

→ Head 2.8km W from the Kolymbia crossroads on the EO95, along the S side of the river, and take the L signed Epta Piges Taverna. Park up the hill by the taverna.
5 mins, 36.2533, 28.1139 ⛅🚶B

23 XETRIPITIS GORGE

A deep, narrow gorge dissecting the heart of the island, with cool waters running along its bottom feeding aromatic shrubs.

→ Park by the bridge just over 1km S from Malonas (36.1891, 28.0698), and hike W up the riverbed. It is possible to drive a portion of this hike, but the road is poor in places.
90 mins, 36.2050, 28.0281 🚶🏞️📷

24 JACOB'S CANYON

An impressive canyon with strikingly layered rock formations to scramble up and then

back (remember: climbing down is harder!) Perfect if you fancy an alternative and adventurous hike.

→ Follow the road NE from Lakki to a T junction; turn R and after 1km park in a gravel layby on a R bend at the base of the canyon.
20 mins, 36.1932, 27.8050 ⛅🚶📷▽

ITALIAN OCCUPATION

25 CAMPOCHIARO

Italians built this village during the Second World War to harvest local timber and export it back to Italy. It now sits derelict and abandoned, the perfect urban-exploration ground for the adventurous.

→ Park in the tree-lined square at the centre of the abandoned section of town just S of Eleousa village.
1 min, 36.2737, 28.0269 🐚🏚️

26 EUCALYPTUS STREET

Created by the Italians who occupied the island for 30 years, this 2km stretch of road is lined end-to-end with over 500 majestic eucalyptus trees. Enjoy a run, drive or stroll and breathe in the soothing scents.

→ The street starts at the main crossroads in Kolymbia (36.2579, 28.1430), bends R then L and runs E to the coast.
1 min, 36.2554, 28.1540

LOCAL FOOD & DRINK

27 TRADITIONAL CAFÉ SYMI

Fresh, local seafood dishes served with a smile in a leafy, candlelit courtyard at excellent value.
→ Rodos 851 00, +30 2241 022881
36.4474, 28.2255

28 MARCO POLO

An enchanting restaurant in the courtyard garden of a small, stylish guesthouse in the heart of Rhodes Old Town. Oh, and possibly the best food in town. Book ahead.
→ Rodos 851 00, +30 2241 025562
36.4427, 28.2258

29 PARAGA TAVERNA

All ingredients in the Rhodian classics served here come from surrounding farmland. In traditional fashion, many dishes are slow-cooked in wood-fired ovens, including the show-stopping goat *stifado*

(stew), cooked overnight in a bread-sealed clay pot and smashed open at the table. A popular meeting place for locals.
→ Apollona 851 06, +30 2246 091247
36.2609, 27.9700

30 TAMBAKIO

A beach restaurant overlooking the ludicrously picturesque St Paul's Bay (see entry). Visit for dinner, when the beach path is aglow with lanterns, creating an intimate ambience.
→ Lindos 851 07, +30 2244 033000
36.0862, 28.0876

CAMPING

31 DROLMA LING

This charming campsite is situated on the edge of a small pine forest and offers yoga classes, massages and aromatherapy. There are also huts available for rent.
→ Theologos 851 06, +30 69 8697 0327
36.3737, 28.0428

32 VINSAN WELLNESS

A holistic wellness centre with a handful of beautifully curated luxury bell tents for glamping. Owners Egle and Gary run multi-day wellness festivals across the year focusing on fitness, yoga and mindfulness.

➜ Eleousa 851 06, +30 69 0966 3086 36.2781, 28.0194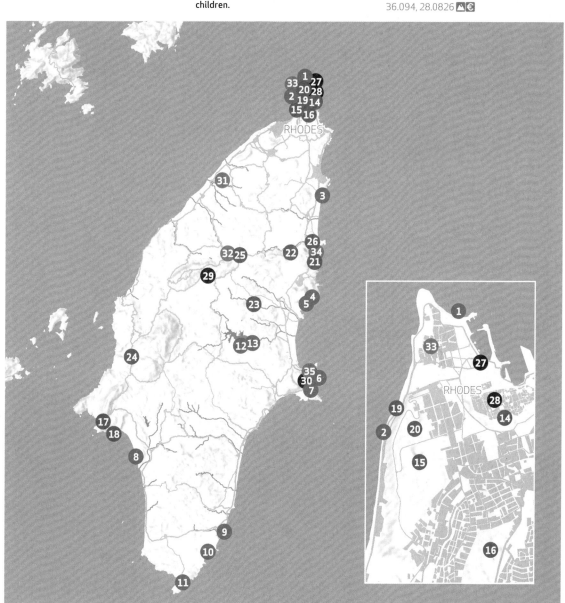

HOTELS & TOWNHOUSES

33 RHODES TOWNHOUSE

Hidden deep in Rhodes town, this neoclassical townhouse, built with an Italian influence, boasts a compact private courtyard with a private dipping pool. Sleeps four.

➜ Rodos 851 00, airbnb.com/rooms/46076371 36.4512, 28.2191

34 CASA COOK

A minimalist, modern, upmarket bohemian retreat cradled in the stunning rocky hills by Kalympia. Yoga classes available daily; no children.

➜ Kolymbia 851 02, +30 2241 056333 36.2421, 28.1552

35 CASITA LINDOS

Set on a hillside of olive groves on the outskirts of idyllic, car-free Lindos village, Casita Lindos is a chic, design-led retreat with pinch-yourself views of the village, the sea and the acropolis.

➜ Lindos 851 07, +30 2244 031865 36.094, 28.0826

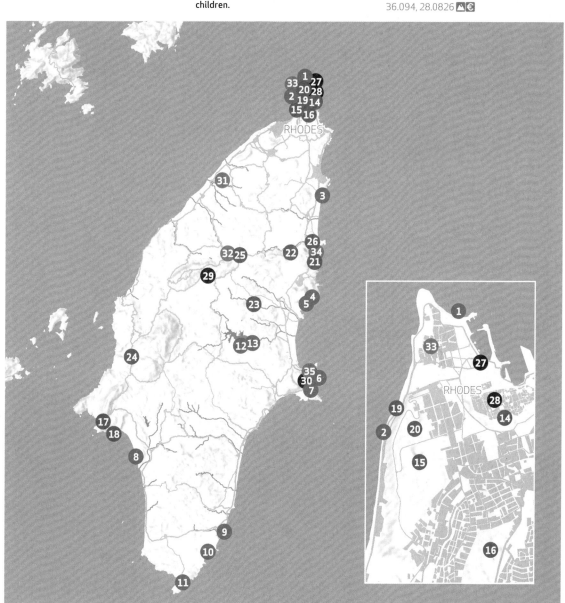

Chorgota Beach, Kefalonia & Ithaca p159

Wild Guide
Greece
Hidden Places, Great
Adventures and the
Good Life

Words:
Sam Firman & Nick Hooton

Photos:
Nick Hooton & Sam Firman
and those credited

Editing:
Candida Frith-Macdonald

Layout:
Rae Malenoir, Sam Firman
& Nick Hooton

Proofreading
Becky Hawkins

Distribution:
Central Books Ltd
50, Freshwater Road
Dagenham, RM8 1RX
020 8525 8800
orders@centralbooks.com

Published by:
Wild Things Publishing Ltd.
Freshford, Bath, BA2 7WG

Contact:
hello@
wildthingspublishing.com

WILD guide

the award-winning, best-
selling adventure travel
series, also available as
iPhone and Android apps.

Author acknowledgements:
A huge thank you to those who travelled with us: Marcus Comaschi, Jack Firman, Max Firman, Jill Firman, Will Bibby, Alex Botham and Issy Allistone. Nick would like to thank his fiancée Danielle van Rhijn for making every field trip the adventure of a lifetime, and his mum, dad and brother for their constant support. Sam would like to thank his partner Brianne Meikle for her love and support during the long months of writing. Also the many friendly Greeks who helped him out along the way, including the Peloponnese policeman who towed his rental car from the edge of what at the time felt like a fathomless ravine. Together we would like to thank Daniel and Tania for the amazing opportunity to write a Wild Guide, Candida for such thorough and thoughtful editing and Becky Hawkins for the careful proofreading.

Health, Safety and Responsibility:
The activities in this book have risks and can be dangerous. The locations may be on private land and permission may need to be sought. While the authors and publishers have gone to great lengths to ensure the accuracy of the information herein they will not be held legally or financially responsible for any accident, injury, loss or inconvenience sustained as a result of the information or advice contained in this book.

WILD THINGS PUBLISHING